Market Failure in Context

Market Failure in Context

Annual Supplement to Volume 47
History of Political Economy

Edited by Alain Marciano
and Steven G. Medema

Duke University Press
Durham and London 2015

Contents

Part 2. Market Failures: The Post–World War II Narrowing

Market Failure in Context: Introduction

Alain Marciano and Steven G. Medema

Market failure, conceived of as the failure of the market to bring about results that are in the best interests of society as a whole, has a long lineage in the history of writings on matters economic. As Steven G. Medema has shown in *The Hesitant Hand*, much of the history of economics can be read as a discussion of whether, and the extent to which, the self-interested actions of private agents, channeled through the market, will redound to the larger social interest. For much of this history, the answers given were negative, and it was assumed that the corrective hand of the state was needed as a constant and consistent regulating force. Thus we find Plato and Aristotle arguing for a wide range of legal restrictions to guard against macroeconomic (to use the modern term) instability; Aquinas making the case for rules that promote a measure of Christian justice in economic affairs; mercantilist writers lobbying for restrictions on various forms of trade (and support for others), as well as for regulations on

Correspondence may be addressed to Alain Marciano, University of Montpellier, Department of Economics, Rue Raymond Dugrand, CS 79606, F-34960 Montpellier, France (e-mail: alain .marciano@univ-montp1.fr); and to Steven G. Medema, Department of Economics, University of Colorado Denver, CB 181, PO Box 173364, Denver, CO 80217-3364 (e-mail: steven.medema @ucdenver.edu). The editors wish to thank Paul Dudenhefer for his diligent shepherding of this project from conference to published volume. His contributions, as always, go far beyond what a simple acknowledgment can capture. We are also grateful for the financial and other support provided by Duke University Press and Duke University's Center for the History of Political Economy.

History of Political Economy 47 (annual suppl.) DOI 10.1215/00182702-3130415

consumption activity; and physiocratic thinkers pleading for restrictions on manufacturers and support for agricultural interests[1]—all based on the view that the pursuit of individual self-interest through a relatively unfettered marketplace does *not* promote the best interests of society as a whole. It is indeed fair to say that the first two thousand years of Western economic writings were, as much as anything, a study in the analysis of market failure and, indeed, that this analysis was developed as a *response to* real-world economic concerns.

It was the genius of Adam Smith ([1776] 1976) to make the case for how, under certain conditions, the pursuit of self-interest *can* promote the general welfare, or at least one particular conception of it—national wealth. Viewed from this angle, Smith's message stood on its head the long tradition of market failure analysis and offered in its place a theory of market success. Here, the state was in important respects the enemy of the good; it was required to establish a framework within which markets could function effectively and to undertake certain functions that the market itself could not perform adequately or at all. But beyond this, said Smith, the state should not interfere with the natural flows of resources. The pursuit of self-interest within such a framework would, via "the invisible hand," grow the wealth of the nation and distribute that wealth in adequate measure to even "the lowest ranks of the people" (Smith [1776] 1976, I.1.10, IV.2.9).

The enormous influence of Smith's message needs no rehearsing here. But though this message was at the heart of a goodly amount of nineteenth-century literature that built on his work and led some to offer even more vociferous defenses of individual liberty and the market, the passage of time brought with it increasing recognition of inadequacies in Smith's system—that we do not live in the best of all possible worlds. The population and insufficiency of demand concerns raised by T. R. Malthus (against the claims of Jean-Baptiste Say), the industrial slums described so vividly by Jane Marcet in a political economy context and (later) by Charles Dickens outside it, and the discovery of certain chinks in the theoretical armor by the likes of David Ricardo, Nassau Senior, and John Stuart Mill brought issues of market failure back into play. Karl Marx's theory of exploitation, the rise of robber barons, concerns for limiting concentrated economic power and offering workers a measure of protection against their employers, and the impact of industrial fluctuations on national economic condi-

---

1. The notion that the physiocrats were promoters of laissez-faire is misguided, their rhetoric notwithstanding. See, e.g., Samuels 1962 and Medema 2009, chap. 1.

tions and individual livelihoods only added to the sense that political economy and its successor, economics, was incomplete in being sold as a theory of market success. But the operative word here is *incomplete*; Smith's vision of the market process as a foundation for economic growth remained central even as questions about the efficacy of a more or less unfettered system became more numerous and louder.

The modern analysis of market failure, then, has its roots in the inability of real-world market processes to measure up to the theory of those processes. Differently put, the origins of the theory lie in those contexts within which economic commentators lived and worked. The goal of the present volume, and of the conference that gave rise to it, is to explore the contexts within which "modern" (i.e., twentieth-century) notions of market failure were developed. The discussion here is by no means exhaustive, nor is it intended to be. Instead, our hope is that the case studies published here will serve as a stimulus to further analysis of how various notions and types of market failure made their way into economic analysis, the manner in which they have been treated, and the policy implications said to flow from them.

1. The Many Faces of "Market Failure"

The term *market failure* is of relatively recent lineage, even if the more general economic phenomena that it intends to capture are as old as economic thinking itself. The term owes itself to the MIT economist Francis Bator, who, in "The Anatomy of Market Failure" (1958), defined it as follows:

> What is it we mean by "market failure"? Typically, at least in allocation theory, we mean the failure of a more or less idealized system of price-market institutions to sustain "desirable" activities or to estop "undesirable" activities [among which he included both production and consumption activities]. The desirability of an activity, in turn, is evaluated relative to the solution values of some explicit or implied maximum-welfare problem. (351)[2]

In Bator's hands, the issue was the ability of the market to generate a Pareto-efficient outcome (352), and his analysis was derivative of a preoccupation among economists, particularly in the post–World War II period,

2. There were very few occurrences of the expression before Bator (King 1913; Wolf 1955), and the plural *market failures* was no more popular than the singular (Wolf and Mintz 1957). However, none of these uses of the term was within the economics literature.

with delineating the conditions under which a decentralized pricing system would do so. Market failure, so conceived, was at its heart an internalist theoretical construct, one that went to the definition of the properties of idealized systems. A market failure was a condition, rather than an economic phenomenon.

Even those things said to give rise to these so-called market failures were neatly tied to the theoretical properties of the activities and interactions taking place within the competitive model.[3] "The relevant literature," said Bator (1958, 356), "is rich but confusing. It abounds in mutually reinforcing and overlapping descriptions and explanations of market failure: external economies, indivisibility, nonappropriability, direct interaction, public goods, atmosphere, etc." His goal in "The Anatomy of Market Failure" was, as much as anything, "simply to sort out the relations among these"—to bring order to what was becoming a theoretical mess. This sorting, however, gave rise to a set of three classifications of market failure that revolved around the idea of externalities, a term also coined by Bator (1957). Thus Bator presents us with a typology of market failures including (1) "ownership externalities," where nonappropriability of resources gives rise to unpaid factors and attendant inefficient use; (2) "technical externalities," where increasing returns result in inefficiencies, including monopoly; and (3) "public good externalities," à la Paul Samuelson (1954, 1955), with their inefficiency-inducing nonrivalry and nonexcludability in consumption. Though Bator made occasional mention of real-world phenomena that reflect the theoretical properties with which he was concerned, the exercise was almost wholly along the lines of probing the world in the model. And if one looks to the literature with which Bator was dealing in this synthetic discussion, one finds that the illustrations, when they are given, are of the potted variety and not motive forces for the analysis.

So defined, the "context" in which the analysis of market failure developed was an insular theoretical one. There was no larger context that, for example, stimulated Samuelson to pursue his analysis of public goods. But if we adopt a less strict conception of market failure than did Bator—say, of the market's failure to generate outcomes that promote the best interests of society, however defined—a very different picture emerges. Consider, for example, the modern tripartition of the concept, which breaks down market failure into stability, distribution, and allocation variants.[4] The first

3. For an excellent recent analysis of the role of the modeling process in the history of economics, see Morgan 2012.

4. This conception of market failure has its roots in Richard Musgrave's (1959, chap. 1) demarcation of the essential roles of the state.

of these is concerned with macroeconomic stability and the potential inability of the market system to generate appropriate levels of aggregate prices, unemployment, and GDP. Distribution failure, meanwhile, goes to the question of whether the market system, left to its own devices, generates distributional outcomes that maximize social welfare (variously defined) or comport with society's vision of an appropriate distribution of income and/or wealth. Allocation failure goes to the efficiency concerns that occupied Bator and includes phenomena such as monopoly, externalities, and public goods. So conceived, market success and failure issues have been at the heart of economic thinking for two millennia.

But even this broad-based conception of our subject is not definitive, for the notion of "failure" is itself subjective. What is considered acceptable market performance on the price level or unemployment front, to say nothing of the distributional front, varies (and, over time, has varied) widely across economists, and the controversies that preoccupied welfare economics throughout much of the twentieth century point to the difficulties with hard-and-fast definitions. This matters theoretically, but also for policy, given that the perception of market failure is, for many, a siren song for state corrective action, while, for others, the perceived success of the market is a signal that such action is unwarranted at best and harmful at worst.

All of this makes just that much more interesting the history of economists' identifications of market failures, their attempts to bring the insights of economics to bear on those failures and, perhaps, develop new tools or modeling strategies to deal with them, and the development of policy prescriptions to remedy the failures. This volume, and the conference from which it emanated, presents case studies that contextualize the processes through which market failure analysis emerged in economics during the twentieth century. It does not pretend to be comprehensive, but exploratory—to present a set of snapshots with the goal of promoting additional work along these lines by historians of economics and others concerned with the development of economic ideas and understandings.

2. Contextualizing Market Failure
in the Twentieth Century

Our decision to focus on the history of "market failure(s)" in the twentieth century was grounded in factors both practical and conceptual. On the practical front, we needed an organizing principle for a conference and associated volume that would include, at most, a dozen papers that had a reasonable level of scholarly cohesion. But equally important, the twentieth century is the historical moment when the concept of market failure crystallized and thus where we have a particularly rich set of case studies to be probed. It also reveals a crucial distinction between the failure of *markets* as a system of economic and social organization, and the failure of a single market to perform according to the dictates of some objective function. This distinction is important, as it reveals a transformation in how economists view themselves and their discipline that was also operative during this century. Though making strict chronological demarcations is often dangerous, this transformation maps reasonably well around World War II (Morgan and Rutherford 1998) and so accounts for the chronological organization of the volume. This is a rough periodization, but it captures quite well the different approaches to the issues under consideration here.

2.1. Before "Market Failure(s)":
The Failure of the Market System

The absence of any precise definition of market failure in the pre–World War II period is, at least in part, an artifact of the lens through which economists viewed the problems of the market. With a handful of prominent exceptions—largely derivative of the writings of A. C. Pigou (Aslanbeigui and Oakes, this volume) and those who built on aspects of his analysis[5]—the dominant conception of market failure was a general one, relating to the functioning of the entire economic system. Thus, as Roger E. Backhouse (this volume) illustrates, we find references to "general market failure" and even the "failure of capitalism." The view was shared by opponents or critics of capitalism and the competitive market system—including the progressive reformers (Leonard, this volume) and the institutionalists (Rutherford, this volume)—and certain defenders of the system such as the University of Chicago economists Henry Simons (the author of the "failure of capitalism" reference) and Frank Knight, both of whom saw serious obstacles to the proper functioning of competitive markets (Backhouse, this volume). Despite the significant ideological gulf that existed between the progressives and the institutionalists, on the one hand, and Simons and Knight, on the other, there was a felt need in both camps to reform capitalism because of its perceived weaknesses and flaws.

---

5. Even here, however, we must be careful, for much of Pigou's concern was of this more general nature, despite the modern tendency to identify him with the problem of externalities—the analysis of which occupied only a small amount of his attention in *Wealth and Welfare* (1912) and *The Economics of Welfare* (1932).

There can be no doubt that the larger economic and social contexts played a nonnegligible role in shaping economists' attitudes toward capitalism and the market system at the time of the Great Depression. Economists were facing one of the major economic crises of all times, an event that could have shaken the confidence of the most convinced defenders of capitalism (Backhouse, this volume; Bateman, this volume), just as the 2007 crisis shook the confidence in capitalism of someone like Richard Posner (Bateman, this volume).[6] This is not to say that economists came to these positions solely because of the crisis, but it played a triggering role. The economic context for the work of the progressive reformers and of the institutionalists who wrote prior to the 1929 crisis played a different but no less important role. The institutionalist economists and the progressive reformers were interested in, and concerned with, the failure of a market-based free-enterprise system to spread the benefits appropriately—to effectively promote the general welfare of society—even in the best of times. Some of these concerns were a reflection of the mapping of economic outcomes onto particular ideologies and an attendant concern that the mechanics of the market system needed to be reformed to achieve a more acceptable level of well-being for groups, such as labor, not felt to be properly served by the existing system. Others, though, were derived from concerns that classical economics and the economics associated with the recent marginalist turn abstracted from important features of economic reality—features that were felt to be necessary for a proper understanding of the workings of a market system and for passing judgments on the outcomes to which it gave rise.

This larger frame of reference led the institutionalists to train a good deal of their attention beyond (or beneath) the market system proper, on the *legal-political institutions of capitalism*, to paraphrase John R. Commons. The institutionalists' approach was derivative of their perception that the focus of the analysis of a capitalist or any other economic system should be on the form of economic organization and the set of institutions that undergird it, as well as the implications of this for economic structure and performance. The legal and other institutions on which the economy was built could play a positive role and support its functioning, but they could also be the source of its failure. For example, Walton Hamilton considered the patent system flawed because firms used it to protect themselves and their

---

6. Of course, it is not simply a matter of "context." Knight, to name but one economist analyzed by Backhouse, and Keynes, of course, were genuinely political economists for whom economics was aimed at discussing the foundations and functioning of societies.

inventions rather than to promote invention. As a consequence, the prevailing market was guilty of underproviding what he termed "social goods" (Rutherford, this volume). Among those not identified with the institutional tradition, one could cite Henry Simons, for whom "the so-called failure of capitalism" was ascribed "primarily [to] a failure of the political state in the discharge of its minimum responsibilities under capitalism"— in particular, as respects ensuring the continued existence of highly competitive market environments (quoted in Backhouse, this volume). But Simons was an exception. As Backhouse's essay illustrates, economists tended to look inward, linking the failure of the economy to *economic* factors, blaming factors such as monopolies (e.g., Adolf Berle and Gardiner Means, Arthur E. Burns, Edward Chamberlain, J. M. Clark) or "the financial machine" (John Maynard Keynes). In other words, the failure of capitalism was seen, above all and fundamentally, as an economic failure, driven at least in part by the unrestrained actions of self-interest-seeking individuals and the inability of unfettered markets to successfully coordinate them in a wide range of circumstances.

These economic failures, however, were seen as genuinely problematic because their consequences went far beyond the boundaries of the economy. As Malcolm Rutherford writes in his contribution on the institutionalists—though it applies to all the economists dealt with in the first part of this volume—the failure of markets lay in their inability, in certain contexts at least, to guide "business activity in *socially* desirable directions" (emphasis added). Not surprisingly, a similar frame of reference pervaded economists' responses to the Great Depression. Unemployment was so massive that it was difficult to see it as simply a problem with the functioning of the labor market. Whether we look to the institutionalists, the progressive reformers, or even Pigou, the focus of discussion was not singular, specific issues but connections with other spheres or realms of social action. The concern, in short, was with the general social consequences of economic issues.

As a result, the institutionalists and reformers put the economic issues they discussed in a broad perspective. Thus, as shown by Nahid Aslanbeigui and Guy Oakes (this volume), the tariff reform controversy that took place at the beginning of the twentieth century was envisaged by the opponents of free trade—Joseph Chamberlain and William Hewins—as an "existential choice." Great Britain was, they claimed, at a historic crossroads. Pigou participated in this controversy—first as a defender and subsequently as an opponent of free trade—and what he wrote formed the basis for the later and much more general analysis found in *Wealth and*

Welfare (1912), the book from which evolved the very idea of "social cost" that informs significant elements of the modern approach to market failures. Though his analysis in *Wealth and Welfare* was grounded in the value of output produced in a society—the national dividend—it bears emphasizing that Pigou was not interested solely in prosperity, welfare, or in "economic" welfare somehow defined. The dividend was, in essence a theoretical convenience imposed by the Marshallian framework on which Pigou was building, a necessary compromise for erecting the scaffolding of economic science, as he conceived it, around important social issues. As Aslanbeigui and Oakes (this volume) point out, Pigou "saw no value in the study of the economy for its own sake," and his welfare analysis was thus at once an attempt to balance and integrate a response to pressing social problems, an extra-economic set of ethical norms, and the dictates of sound economic theorizing.

Though his technical economics was very different from that of the US progressives and institutionalists, Pigou was in important ways of like mind with both groups. For each of them, efficiency concerns were almost secondary; the failure(s) of the market system had social and ethical dimensions that, for them, were at the heart of how economic performance should be evaluated and how the analysis of the system should be conceptualized. The systemic social conflicts and the unjust distribution of resources that attended industrial capitalism were matters of grave concern (Rutherford, this volume; Leonard, this volume), and ethics constituted an important dimension of the reforms that they proposed. No wonder, then, that, as Thomas C. Leonard (this volume) tells us, the reformers were, tellingly, characterized as "the real philosopher[s] of social life" by Edwin Seligman. And what emerged from their analysis because of this were arguments for the introduction of new methods of *social*—and not simply economic—control. These controls were to be based on the recommendations of economic *experts*—"engineers" able to understand how to improve the economy and the society—and put into practice through the aegis of the state. The (ostensibly) competitive *system* was not able to channel forces of self-interest in directions that served the larger interests of society. More regulation was viewed as the answer—indeed, as the only answer.

2.2. Market Failures:
The Post–World War II Narrowing

After World War II, the social and economic contexts changed radically, and economic analysis changed with them. It was no longer the economic crisis of the 1930s that provided the background that legitimized and oriented economic analysis but rather postwar reconstruction and planning, and the tensions of the new—and cold—war that divided the world into two main blocks of nations. Predicting how the individuals of the other block would behave now seemed particularly vital, and this prediction was felt to require formal, axiomatized, mathematical models. The heyday of institutionalism was now past, its approach being criticized as too descriptive and unable to provide scientific guidance for understanding individual behavior and for making properly grounded public policy recommendations (Morgan and Rutherford 1998). Institutionalists largely disappeared from the intellectual landscape of economics, at least in terms of influence on the direction of research, and the dominant neoclassical economics that emerged during this period was typified by Samuelson's *Foundations of Economic Analysis* (1947) and by his undergraduate textbook, *Economics*, first published in 1948.[7] To see the influence of this turn on market failure analysis, one need look no farther than Samuelson's work in the area of public economics, which very much epitomized this transformation. As described by J. Daniel Hammond (this volume), Samuelson was convinced that mathematics was a valuable language for economic science, and one of the domains to which Samuelson applied his method was public goods–related market failures. The context here, though, was not the question of how best to provide certain types of goods demanded by society—goods that, as Adam Smith ([1776] 1976, IV.ix.51, V.i) had pointed out nearly two centuries earlier, the market could not provide in satisfactory amounts. Instead, "The Pure Theory of Public Expenditures" (Samuelson 1954) "was conceived as a demonstration of the usefulness of mathematics in economics" (Hammond, this volume).

Samuelson's article was by no means the first to formalize the analysis of a situation of market failure (Medema 2014), though its influence on the literature was far more extensive than that of previous efforts—see, for example, Meade 1952. But its importance was not limited to the *analysis* of market failures per se. It also captured and reinforced how economists increasingly envisaged market failure(s). At issue was the question of whether a particular market could achieve a Pareto-efficient allocation of resources in the presence of interdependencies of the type that we now

---

7. On the development and impact of Samuelson's *Foundations*, see Samuelson 1998 and Backhouse 2015. On *Economics*, see Giraud 2014.

label externalities or public goods.[8] This is exactly what Bator (1958, 351), Samuelson's MIT colleague, carefully stressed in the definition of market failure that he provided a few years after the publication of Samuelson's article: "Typically, *at least in allocation theory*, we mean the failure of a more or less idealized system of price-market institutions to sustain 'desirable' activities or to estop 'undesirable' activities" (emphasis added). Here, the distributional, ethical, and larger institutional dimensions of the problem posed by the failure of the market were set aside as the focus narrowed to the price mechanism, the allocation of resources, and the norm of efficiency. Samuelson's approach was emblematic of this transition. As Hammond writes, for Samuelson, "ethics trumps efficiency; yet ethics is not scientific, so a modern social scientist has little to say about its substance." We have moved from a discussion of the failures of competition or of capitalism, moral and otherwise, to a discussion of the impossibility for an "individual market [to reach] an efficient equilibrium," as Bateman (this volume) puts it. The perspective was obviously narrower, even as (and in part because) the tool kit was expanding.

If the nature of the problems being considered and the framework within which market analysis was undertaken were in many instances very different in the post–World War II period, the same cannot be said for the solutions envisaged to remove or otherwise deal with these issues. When markets were perceived to fail, even on a smaller scale, most economists seemed to contemplate no alternative other than an intervention of the state, whose coercive force would be guided by economic experts and expertise. This is the conclusion reached by Samuelson, even if, as Marianne Johnson notes, coercion was not really Samuelson's concern. His worry, rather, was the prospect that economic decisions could be "made by nonexperts" (Johnson, this volume). But coercion remains unavoidable: if individuals do not spontaneously and voluntarily internalize the external effects that their actions produce or if they do not pay for the public goods they consume, they have to be forced into "cooperation." This was a position that Richard Musgrave (1939) had defended some two decades prior to Samuelson's discussion.

While some strands of the early post–World War II literature were content to point to the prospects for market failure under certain assumed

8. Samuelson did not distinguish between public goods and externalities. He analyzed a situation in which there are (pure) public goods and these goods give birth to external effects or externalities because of the interdependence between consumers.

conditions and offered little or nothing in the way of policy remedy discussion (Medema 2014), Samuelson and Musgrave believed that government intervention was necessary to "solve" market failures because there is no other alternative. This theme was soon picked up more widely in the literature, slightly lagging but more or less along with the tide of Keynesian-informed stabilization policy prescriptions. The market process had done its work and had been found wanting, and there was no sense that the market itself or other private mechanisms could themselves be used to deal with these failings. In particular, no private arrangements based on direct bargaining between agents, that is, based on *voluntary exchange*, could reasonably and realistically be envisaged. Musgrave was clear about this in one of the first articles on voluntary exchange theories of the state in 1939, as shown by Johnson in her discussion of the initial Anglo-American forays into exchange-based approaches to public finance.[9] One reason for Musgrave's pessimism—a reason identical to that later put forward by Samuelson—was that individuals are too self-interested to engage in voluntary transactions that would facilitate collective action through the state. Because of this tendency to favor their own interests, individuals free ride. At the same time that Samuelson was formalizing the problematics of such arrangements, however, James Buchanan was taking issue with the pessimistic view. Though Buchanan admitted that individuals are self-interested and attempt to free ride,[10] and that markets may fail to allocate resources efficiently because of this, he rejected the claim that this implied the need for the intervention of the state. Drawing on work by Knut Wicksell (1896, [1896] 1958) a half-century earlier, Buchanan argued the case, both formally and informally, that private arrangements are, under certain conditions, both possible and desirable mechanisms for resolving the shortfalls of the market (Johnson, this volume).[11]

Between Samuelson and Musgrave, on the one hand, and Buchanan, on the other, we find Charles M. Tiebout, the subject of the essay by

9. Of course, the voluntary exchange approach to public finance has its roots in the work of Knut Wicksell (1896, [1896] 1958) and others writing in Continental Europe in the late nineteenth and early twentieth centuries. See, e.g., the discussions in Buchanan 1960, Wagner 1997, Medema 2005, Backhaus and Wagner 2005, and Eusepi and Wagner 2012, as well as the excerpts from Continental writings translated in Musgrave and Peacock 1958.

10. Buchanan came only reluctantly to the idea that individuals could free ride. His first real mention of such behaviors was in "What Should Economists Do?" (1964), and he treated this topic more explicitly, and more clearly, in "Ethical Rules, Expected Values, and Large Numbers" (1965). On free riding, see Fontaine 2014.

11. See also Marciano 2013 and forthcoming, as well as the brief discussion of Coase 1959 and 1960, below.

John D. Singleton. A student of Musgrave, Tiebout was interested in attempting to solve the problem that self-interest could represent for an optimal allocation of resources in the context of collective consumption. He demonstrated, in "A Pure Theory of Local Expenditures" (1956), that free riding is context-specific and that there are conditions under which coercion is not necessary to alleviate potential market failures induced by free riding. Individuals, he said, will reveal their demands accurately if they are able to select among communities that offer competing packages of goods and services and are free to move to the one that produces the bundle that satisfies their utility.[12] Though Tiebout's result did not have the immediate impact of Samuelson's, it gained increased traction with the development of a literature in state and local public finance over the next two decades (receiving a particular boost from the publication of Wallace Oates's 1969 article on the "Tiebout hypothesis") and is now one of the more well-known—both famous and infamous—results in economics.[13]

As Singleton shows, Tiebout's career is emblematic of the transition in economic analysis taking place during the Cold War period. Though he is identified exclusively in the professional mind with the Tiebout sorting of his 1956 article, an exercise in pure theory, Tiebout wrote much more extensively on "applied" problems of public finance, as exemplified by his work with Robert Warren and Vincent Ostrom on municipal governments. The quasi-institutional character of these writings likely played no small role in the lack of attention paid to Tiebout's work until comparatively recently, for his approach was going against the tide of an increasingly technical profession.

But Tiebout is far from being the only economist whose message or larger body of work was minimized or obscured by this technical turn. The same can be said for K. William Kapp, an economist often linked to the post–World War II institutionalist remnant (Rutherford, this volume; Berger, this volume) and who contributed both a particularly pointed critique of theory of the neoclassical theory social costs and an alternative approach to this arena of market failure during the 1950s. Influenced by both the socialist calculation debate and problems such as large-scale industrial pollution, Kapp attempted to move the debate over market

12. Tiebout's argument is frequently viewed as anticipating Buchanan's (1965) theory of clubs. This is not the case, at least, in the sense that Buchanan disagreed with Tiebout. See Boettke and Marciano 2014.

13. This result is usually viewed as a defense of "institutional" competition or pure federalism and a criticism of the intervention of the state.

failure away from the Pigovian-driven neoclassical framework and into the more broad-based frame of reference often associated with institutionalism. But, as Sebastian Berger shows, Kapp's impact was minimal at best, though the importance of his work was acknowledged by other important scholars such as Buchanan and Guido Calabresi.

A similar story could be told about Ronald Coase, who, though not treated to any great extent in the present volume (but see Colander, this volume), has been the subject of no small amount of discussion in the literature over the last two decades.[14] Coase's analysis of social costs—externality-related market failures—was not of the a-institutional variety that dominated the post–World War II market failure literature; instead, it was derived from the concrete context of how the US Federal Communications Commission should allocate broadcast frequencies, and, like Kapp's, it was written as a challenge to that literature's approach and conclusions. Coase was of the mind that the market deserved more consideration as a mechanism for frequency allocation than it had been given by economists, policymakers, and bureaucrats. The FCC paper (Coase 1959), and the more famous "The Problem of Social Cost" (1960) that emerged from it, argued that, in theory, market/exchange-based processes could efficiently resolve market failure problems—an insight that, in the hands of George Stigler (1966, 113), soon became known as the "Coase theorem." As Coase himself emphasized, however, the reality of the costs—often significant—associated with each of the various possible institutions that could be used to coordinate resource allocation necessitated a comparative institutional approach, including consideration of doing nothing at all about the ostensible market failures. Coase's overtly institutional-related message was largely lost on his audience, which was much more concerned—both positively and negatively—with the fictional world of the Coase theorem, an idea that lent itself to formalized modeling strategies in ways that comparative institutional analysis did not.

The evolution of environmental economics provides a further interesting illustration of the intersection of larger contextual concerns with the formalized post–World War II approach to market failures, but one that ran in a somewhat different direction in an episode that has yet to be extensively probed by historians of economics (including in the present volume). At issue was the question of whether economics had anything to add to the discussion of how to deal with the increasingly pressing prob-

---

14. See, e.g., Medema 1994, 2009; Campbell and Klaes 2005; and Bertrand 2010.

lems of air and water pollution, the social conversation over which became increasingly loud during the 1950s and 1960s. The economists provided an affirmative answer, albeit one that was rather slow in developing, and the path chosen was the grafting of the Pigovian-neoclassical theory of externalities onto environmental problems. In retrospect, this seems almost obvious; pollution is now a textbook case of an externality. But this decision to analyze environmental problems with Marshallian partial-equilibrium externality models set the course of environmental research and framed the way that economists came to view environmental problems and the policy prescriptions derived. By the late 1960s and early 1970s, however, leading scholars in the field were of the mind that this decision was an unfortunate one, in that it did not allow economists to capture within their models the broad-based effects of large-scale environmental pollution, something for which general equilibrium models—or, one could argue, some other alternative modeling strategy developed specifically to deal with environmental issues—might have been better suited (Kneese 1971).

While the analysis of externalities was perhaps *the* growth industry in market failure analysis in the last third of the twentieth century—the economic analysis of law and, in particular, property and contracts being another important illustration[15]—new avenues of analysis continued to emerge, or reemerge. Prominent among these was the analysis of information-related market failures (an issue that goes back at least to John Stuart Mill [1848]), perhaps most famously in George Akerlof's (1970) analysis of the market for lemons, but much more generally in environments within which strategic behavior (itself an artifact of incomplete information) was said to manifest itself and where the application of game theory revealed the plethora of suboptimal outcomes that can emerge in wide varieties of economic settings.[16] The range of inefficiencies suggested by the emerging work in behavioral economics has only compounded the sense that market failures are widespread and systemic, and, for those seeking empirical validation for their suspicions about the market, the economic crisis of the early twenty-first century provided ample ammunition for the argument that Smith's invisible hand was faltering at best.

15. See, e.g., the discussions in Marciano and Romaniuc 2014 and Marciano 2013.

16. In a 1998 survey, Stiglitz wrote, "In the last two decades, we have explored much more seriously the consequences of the informational assumptions implicit in the belief that markets are efficient" (3). J. O. Ledyard (2008) makes explicit the connection between asymmetric information and externalities/public goods as sources of market failure.

2.3. Public Policy and Market Failures/Failures of Markets

Though there have been moments in the history of economics when discussions of market failure were not accompanied by additional commentary on what might or should be done about it, the largest share of this literature has a significant policy-oriented component, whether that be ethically grounded arguments for or against laissez-faire, the derivation of optimal Pigovian taxes to correct situations of externality, or claims about the efficacy of fiscal/monetary stimulus. Throughout the twentieth century, the dominant view—what David Colander (this volume) calls the "market failure policy frame"—was, and continues to be, that market failures require correction via the intervention of the state. The revolution against this line of thinking, led by economists at Chicago and Virginia, took an opposing stance, asserting both that the extent of market failure was overstated in the literature[17] and that the view that the state could accomplish efficiency-enhancing corrections was misguided—the latter claims being grounded in emerging rational choice models of political/governmental decision-making processes.[18] On both market and macroeconomic levels, the great battle within economics during the last quarter of the twentieth century was over these contrasting gospels and whether the road to the heaven of efficiency ran directly through a relatively unfettered market system or required the mediation of the state.

As Colander points out, the contrast with the more broad-based and nuanced approach found in the "classical policy frame," as he labels it, of the late eighteenth and nineteenth centuries is stark. The concept of efficiency had not yet been invented, though issues of economic growth and development weighed heavily on the minds of economic thinkers. But the approach to policy here was broad-based and practical, not narrow and technical. The insights of economic theorizing were not sufficient for policy conclusions; ethics, too, featured prominently in the picture, as did the practical ability of the state to carry out meaningful reforms. Nirvana was largely absent from the discussion, either as a theoretical possibility or as a goal to strive for. The question, instead, was how to improve economic and social life for the citizenry, the answer to which lay in no singular institutional form or, for that matter, in the theory of the workings of the economic system.

---

17. See, e.g., Buchanan and Stubblebine 1962; Demsetz 1964, 1966; and Coase 1960.

18. The work of Buchanan and Gordon Tullock, together and separately, was instrumental here. See, e.g., Mitchell 1988 and Medema 2000.

3. Conclusion

The idea that markets could fail to perform in ways that best promoted the larger interests of society is as old as economics itself, and the question of the appropriate scope to be given to private action and to its collective alternative is one of the most crucial issues with which economic thinkers have had to grapple. It bears on the organization of the economy and brings into play the most fundamental, essential values undergirding the organization of our societies. Through two-plus millennia of economic commentary on failures of the market, the contexts—social, political, and intellectual—in which these discussions and debates have played out have loomed large, though our understanding of their roles remains limited and imperfect. It is our hope that the present volume goes some way toward addressing this lacuna, both directly and by stimulating additional scholarship exploring this important facet of the history of economics.

References

Akerlof, G. A. 1970. "The Market for 'Lemons': Quality Uncertainty and the Market Mechanism." *Quarterly Journal of Economics* 84:477–500.

Backhaus, J. G., and R. E. Wagner. 2005. "From Continental Public Finance to Public Choice: Mapping Continuity." In *The Role of Government in the History of Economic Thought*, edited by S. G. Medema and P. Boettke. *History of Political Economy* 37 (supplement): 314–32.

Backhouse, R. E. 2015. "Revisiting Samuelson's *Foundations of Economic Analysis*." *Journal of Economic Literature* 53:326–50.

Bator, F. M. 1957. "The Simple Analytics of Welfare Maximization." *American Economic Review* 47:22–59.

———. 1958. "The Anatomy of Market Failure." *Quarterly Journal of Economics* 72:351–79.

Bertrand, E. 2010. "The Three Roles of the Coase Theorem in Coase's Works." *European Journal of the History of Economic Thought* 17:975–1000.

Boettke, P. J., and A. Marciano. 2014. "Ethics, Self-Interest, and the Limits of Spatial Competition: Why Did Buchanan Criticize Tiebout?" Working paper, Université de Montpellier 1.

Buchanan, J. M. 1960. "*La Scienza delle finanze*: The Italian Tradition in Fiscal Theory." In *Fiscal Theory and Political Economy: Selected Essays*. Chapel Hill: University of North Carolina Press.

———. 1964. "What Should Economists Do?" *Southern Economic Journal* 30:213–22.

———. 1965. "Ethical Rules, Expected Values, and Large Numbers." *Ethics* 76:1–13.

Buchanan, J. M., and W. C. Stubblebine. 1962. "Externality." *Economica* 29:371–84.

Campbell, D., and M. Klaes. 2005. "The Principle of Institutional Direction: Coase's Regulatory Critique of Intervention." *Cambridge Journal of Economics* 29:263–88.

Coase, R. H. 1959. "The Federal Communications Commission." *Journal of Law and Economics* 2:1–40.

———. 1960. "The Problem of Social Cost." *Journal of Law and Economics* 3:1–44.

Demsetz, H. 1964. "The Exchange and Enforcement of Property Rights." *Journal of Law and Economics* 7:11–26.

———. 1966. "Some Aspects of Property Rights." *Journal of Law and Economics* 9:61–70.

Eusepi, G., and R. E. Wagner. 2012. "Tax Prices in a Democratic Polity: The Continuing Relevance of Antonio de Viti de Marco." *History of Political Economy* 45 (1): 99–121.

Fontaine, P. 2014. "Free Riding." *Journal of the History of Economic Thought* 36:359–76.

Giraud, Y. 2014. "Negotiating the 'Middle-of-the-Road' Position: Paul Samuelson, MIT, and the Politics of Textbook Writing, 1945–55." In *MIT and the Transformation of American Economics*, edited by E. Roy Weintraub. *History of Political Economy* 46 (supplement): 134–52.

King, C. L. 1913. "Municipal Markets." *Annals of the American Academy of Political and Social Science* 50:102–17.

Kneese, A. V. 1971. "Environmental Pollution: Economics and Policy." *American Economic Review* 61:153–66.

Ledyard, J. O. 2008. "Market Failure." In *The New Palgrave Dictionary of Economics*, edited by Steven N. Durlauf and Lawrence E. Blume, 2nd ed. London: Palgrave Macmillan. doi:10.1057/9780230226203.1029.

Marciano, A. 2013. "Why Market Failures Are Not a Problem: James Buchanan on Market Imperfections, Voluntary Cooperation, and Externalities." *History of Political Economy* 45 (2): 223–54.

———. Forthcoming. "Buchanan's Non-Coercive Economics for Self-Interested Individuals: Ethics, Small Groups, and the Social Contract." *Journal of the History of Economic Thought*.

Marciano, A., and R. Romaniuc. 2014. "Accident Costs, Resource Allocation, and Individual Rationality: Blum, Kalven, and Calabresi." Mimeo.

Meade, J. E. 1952. "External Economies and Diseconomies in a Competitive Situation." *Economic Journal* 62:54–67.

Medema, S. G. 1994. *Ronald H. Coase*. London: Macmillan.

———. 2000. "'Related Disciplines': The Professionalization of Public Choice Analysis." In *Toward a History of Applied Economics*, edited by R. E. Backhouse and J. E. Biddle. *History of Political Economy* 32 (supplement): 289–323.

———. 2005. "'Marginalizing' Government: From *la Scienza delle Finanze* to Wicksell." *History of Political Economy* 37 (1): 1–25.

———. 2009. *The Hesitant Hand: Taming Self-Interest in the History of Economic Ideas*. Princeton, N.J.: Princeton University Press.

———. 2014. "'Exceptional and Unimportant'? Externalities in Economic Analysis, 1940–1959." Working paper, University of Colorado Denver.

Mill, J. S. 1848. *Principles of Political Economy: With Some of Their Applications to Social Philosophy*. Vol. 2. London: John W. Parker.

Mitchell, W. C. 1988. "Virginia, Rochester, and Bloomington: Twenty-Five Years of Public Choice and Political Science." *Public Choice* 56:101–19.

Morgan, M. S. 2012. *The World in the Model*. Cambridge: Cambridge University Press.

Morgan, M. S., and M. Rutherford, eds. 1998. *From Interwar Pluralism to Postwar Neoclassicism*. Supplemental issue to vol. 30 of *History of Political Economy*. Durham, N.C.: Duke University Press.

Musgrave, R. A. 1939. "The Voluntary Exchange Theory of Public Economy." *Quarterly Journal of Economics* 53:213–37.

———. 1959. *The Theory of Public Finance*. New York: McGraw-Hill.

Musgrave, R. A., and A. T. Peacock, eds. 1958. *Classics in the Theory of Public Finance*. London: Macmillan.

Oates, W. E. 1969. "The Effects of Property Taxes and Local Public Spending on Property Values: An Empirical Study of Tax Capitalization and the Tiebout Hypothesis." *Journal of Political Economy* 77:957–71.

Pigou, A. C. 1912. *Wealth and Welfare*. London: Macmillan.

———. 1932. *The Economics of Welfare*. 3rd ed. London: Macmillan.

Samuels, W. J. 1962. "The Physiocratic Theory of Economic Policy." *Quarterly Journal of Economics* 76:145–62.

Samuelson, P. A. 1947. *Foundations of Economic Analysis*. Cambridge, Mass.: Harvard University Press.

———. 1954. "The Pure Theory of Public Expenditure." *Review of Economics and Statistics* 36:387–89.

———. 1955. "Diagrammatic Exposition of a Theory of Public Expenditure." *Review of Economics and Statistics* 37:350–56.

———. 1998. "How *Foundations* Came to Be." *Journal of Economic Literature* 36:1375–86.

Smith, A. (1776) 1976. *An Inquiry into the Nature and Causes of the Wealth of Nations*. General editors: R. H. Campbell and A. S. Skinner. Textual editor: W. B. Todd. Oxford: Oxford University Press.

Stigler, G. J. 1966. *The Theory of Price*. 3rd ed. New York: Macmillan.

Stiglitz, J. E. 1998. "The Private Uses of Public Interests: Incentives and Institutions." *Journal of Economic Perspectives* 12:3–22.

Tiebout, C. M. 1956. "A Pure Theory of Local Expenditures." *Journal of Political Economy* 64:416–24.

Wagner, R. E. 1997. "Choice, Exchange, and Public Finance." *American Economic Review Papers and Proceedings* 87:160–63.

Wicksell, K. 1896. *Finanztheoretische Untersuchungen*. Jena: Gustav Fischer.

———. (1896) 1958. "A New Principle of Just Taxation." In *Classics in the Theory of Public Finance*, edited by Richard A. Musgrave and Alan T. Peacock and translated by J. M. Buchanan, 72–118. London: Macmillan.

Wolf, E. R. 1955. "Types of Latin American Peasantry: A Preliminary Discussion." *American Anthropologist* 57:452–71.

Wolf, E. R., and S. W. Mintz. 1957. "Haciendas and Plantations in Middle America and the Antilles." *Social and Economic Studies* 6:380–412.

Part 1
Before "Market Failure(s)":
The Failure of the Market System

The British Tariff Reform Controversy and the Genesis of Pigou's *Wealth and Welfare*, 1903–12

Nahid Aslanbeigui and Guy Oakes

Conversation with the Colonial Secretary

On Friday afternoon, June 12, 1903, William Hewins met Joseph Chamberlain for the first time in the latter's private room in the British House of Commons to discuss the burning fiscal issue of the time: tariff reform. Chamberlain—committed imperialist, anti–Little Englander, and self-anointed leader of the reform movement—was colonial secretary in the Conservative cabinet of A. J. Balfour. Hewins was founding director of the London School of Economics, a conservative imperialist and critic of free trade, and a member of the international community of historical economists, with close ties to W. J. Ashley—professor of commerce at the University of Birmingham—as well as Gustav Schmoller, Berlin doyen of the German historical school. After this meeting, he would become Chamberlain's tariff reform consigliere. The controversy of 1903–6 was

Correspondence may be addressed to Nahid Aslanbeigui, Department of Economics, Finance, and Real Estate, Monmouth University, 400 Cedar Avenue, West Long Branch, NJ 07764-1898 (e-mail: naslanbe@monmouth.edu); and to Guy Oakes, Department of Management and Decision Sciences, Bey Hall, Room 253, Monmouth University, 400 Cedar Avenue, West Long Branch, NJ 07764-1898 (e-mail: goakes@monmouth.edu). Research on this essay was partly funded by Grants in Aid of Creativity and the Jack T. Kvernland Chair, Monmouth University. Our thanks to archivists at the Cadbury Research Library, University of Birmingham; the University Library, the University of Sheffield; the Modern Archives of King's College, the University of Cambridge; the British Library for generous assistance; and the participants of the 2014 *HOPE* conference, "Market Failure in Context."

History of Political Economy 47 (annual suppl.) DOI 10.1215/00182702-3130427

the most contentious domestic political dispute in Britain in the decade before the Great War. It split the Establishment, inflamed the public, created a disastrous rift in the Conservative Party, and ended in a landslide victory for the Liberals in the 1906 general election, beginning the long Liberal ascendancy that set the foundations of the British welfare state. *Wealth and Welfare* (1912), A. C. Pigou's early general formulation of his research program for economics, as well as the first systematic investigation of market failures, was linked to Chamberlain's conversation with Hewins. The present essay analyzes these conjunctions. It takes the form of a drama in three acts.

The action begins in May 1903, when Chamberlain challenged the principles of free trade and its benefits for the British Empire. In their various permutations, Chamberlain's proposed reforms included retaliatory and permanent protective tariffs as well as preferential duties. In an inspired move, he recruited Hewins as his chief publicist. Writing anonymously and ostensibly impartially, Hewins contributed some sixteen articles to the *Times* in 1903, extolling the virtues of Chamberlain's cause. Hewins proved to be a master of sophistry, deploying an array of seemingly impressive analyses, tables, graphs, and polemics calculated to persuade readers that without Chamberlain's tariffs, the economic structure of the empire was threatened by imminent collapse.

Act 2 begins with the notorious "Professors' Manifesto," a letter to the *Times* opposing tariff reform proposals and signed by thirteen eminent academic economists—including F. Y. Edgeworth and Alfred Marshall—as well as Pigou, then only twenty-six. The manifesto, an assortment of unsubstantiated claims, was a dismal public failure, pilloried in a deluge of letters and editorials, with many correspondents criticizing its authors for abusing their status as academic experts for political purposes.

In act 3, Pigou intervenes independently, reconfiguring the controversy as a debate over economic policy and how to analyze it. Developing logical strategies and modes of argument that he regarded as indispensable for understanding the problems at stake in the controversy and assessing solutions, he moved with apparent ease from academic and public lectures to journal articles, magazine pieces, and books. In this work, he explored the consequences of tariffs by examining their impact on the size, distribution, and stability of the national dividend—the analytical strategy he generalized in *Wealth and Welfare* shortly thereafter. In the course of his work on the tariff reform question, Pigou became a logician of policy analysis, in 1912 publishing the treatise that provided the analytical apparatus of welfare economics.

The Tariff Reform Movement and
the Chamberlain-Hewins Collaboration

The controversy over British fiscal policy, a mélange of inflammatory economic and political issues, erupted when Chamberlain delivered a fiery speech on his home ground of Birmingham on May 15, 1903. He argued that protective and preferential tariffs would redound to the benefit of British consumers, taxpayers, farmers, and industries. They would increase the revenue of the exchequer and achieve commercial consolidation of the British Empire, which was indispensable to its political unification as a United States of Albion. Otherwise, he saw impending doom for the "British race": collapse of the empire, the end of Britain as a world power, and its vulnerability to defeat in war. Chamberlain challenged the Cobdenite doctrine of the Manchester school, deeply ingrained in late Victorian political and economic thought and rhetoric, if not always implemented in practice. He mercilessly chastised Little Englanders for their myopic belief that political unification of the empire was futile—without it, the colonies would evolve into independent states, albeit sharing some sympathy for the mother country.[1] In Chamberlain's estimation, unification would increase the political and economic power of the empire under the aegis of London, neutralizing dangers posed by growing competition from the United States and Germany. An essential first step toward union was commercial alignment through tariff reform: Britain would impose protective and retaliatory tariffs on various agricultural and manufactured goods produced by "foreign" countries, defined as nations outside the imperial family. Bilateral negotiations within the empire would determine whether the same products would be exempt or receive imperial preference (speech of May 15, 1903; printed in Chamberlain 1914, 125–40).

Chamberlain was an astute politician motivated by both ideal and material interests. He understood that success of tariff reform depended on economic arguments that would gain wide popular appeal as well as endorsement of the political class in London. However, he lacked economic expertise. As he confessed to Hewins: "I once read Mill & tried to read Marshall," but the results were less than successful (recorded in Hewins's diary, January 17, 1904, Hewins/MS/74/178). To make a compelling case, he knew that it was necessary for him to convince diverse interest groups—business owners, workers, farmers, and political leaders—that pursuit

---

1. Chamberlain to Hewins, September 5, 1900, Hewins/45/35, Hewins Manuscripts, University of Sheffield Library. Hereafter cited as Hewins.

of free trade was detrimental to the welfare of Britain. However, he was sufficiently acute to see that he was not capable of producing the necessary arguments.

Although Chamberlain and Hewins had corresponded in summer 1900, they did not meet until some four weeks after Chamberlain's Birmingham speech.[2] The occasion was an invitation to Hewins from the *Times* to write a series of articles on imperial fiscal policy that would kindle controversy. Hewins presented the tariff reform–imperialist position and played his part admirably. In summer and fall 1903, he and Chamberlain conferred on various matters: the economic arguments Chamberlain should employ in his speeches as he stumped Britain speaking on tariff reform—early in Chamberlain's autumn campaign, Hewins sent him weekly summaries of economic objections that had been raised against him as well as counterarguments he could use against adversaries; the rhetorical style Hewins should adopt in his articles to enhance their persuasive force; and policy coordination between Chamberlain's speeches and Hewins's articles. Hewins feared that any sense of inconsistency between his journalistic efforts—in the *Times* as well as other publications—and Chamberlain's speeches would compromise the latter's objectives and thus the cause of imperial consolidation.

Hewins's articles were successful, stimulating considerable discussion and many letters to the editor of the *Times*. Writing under the pseudonym "An Economist," he worked confidentially and in tandem with Chamberlain. In Hewins's hands, tariff reform became a fiscal policy that would address market failure, secure the economy of Britain, increase its exports and rate of employment, unite the British Empire economically, and make the international system safe for the indefinite future under the hegemony of Britain. All this would be achieved at the middling cost of short-term and moderate increases in food prices produced by a tax on foreign corn (grain). Hewins expected this cost to be cheerfully borne by the British working class, which he celebrated for its phlegmatic patience, equanimity, and loyalty in supporting the greater national good (January 17–31, 1904, Hewins/MS/74/178).

2. Unless otherwise noted, our account of the association between Chamberlain and Hewins is based on Hewins's diary, written on January 17 and January 31, 1904. Passages from the diary were later included in Hewins's (1929) memoir. We employ the original text, housed at the University of Sheffield Library.

The Twilight of Laissez-Faire?
The Argument for Market Failure

Chamberlain and Hewins confronted the British public and its leaders with an existential choice.[3] The nation was at a historic crossroads with only two options: either free trade or imperialism—the union of the mother country with its dominions. In light of the circumstances under which they worked—Hewins claimed that his articles were first drafts composed under great pressure and generally not read in proof (January 17, 1904, Hewins/MS/74/178)—it is hardly surprising that the tariff reformers did not arrive at a cogent set of arguments that would satisfy academic economists, either then or now. That said, certain observations can be made about their conception of free trade and the conditions under which British national prosperity could be maximized.

In arguing their case, tariff reformers claimed that Little Englanders were motivated by two obsessions: minimizing consumer prices and maximizing the wealth of citizens of the United Kingdom. Hewins and Chamberlain had a more capacious objective: to achieve the "*maximum* prosperity possible in the circumstances of the time, both for the Empire as a whole and for its several parts" (An Economist [William Hewins], *Times*, August 21, 1903). They employed four desiderata for British welfare, happiness, or prosperity, terms they used interchangeably. First, intimate and affectionate unification of the British race across continents, which would enormously increase the political and economic power of the empire (speech of May 15, 1903; printed in Chamberlain 1914, 131). Second, political security: the ability of the empire to defend itself in war (137–38; An Economist, *Times*, August 7, 1903). Third, the psychological and physical health of the workforce, without which it would be impossible to maintain national industrial and military efficiency (An Economist, *Times*, August 14, 1903). The third consideration entailed two corollaries: secure supplies of food in both peace and war (An Economist, *Times*, July 3, 1903) and "continuous and remunerative employment" (speech of February 1, 1905; printed in Chamberlain 1914, 300), the basis of stable income and consumption. Finally, public education, which would improve knowledge of foreign conditions, production and communication technologies, and management techniques (An Economist, *Times*, August 14, 1903).

---

3. Neither Pigou nor tariff reformers used the term *market failure*, which seems to have been introduced in the 1950s (Bator 1958). Conceptually, however, it is not anachronistic to situate the idea in Victorian and Edwardian economic thought (Medema 2009, 26–53).

Tariff reformers were convinced that a flourishing international trade was indispensable to the prosperity of Britain and the empire (speech of October 6, 1903; printed in Chamberlain 1914, 148). However, competition from the United States and Germany had eroded the relative position of British trade. On this point, three considerations were paramount in their thinking. First, foreign countries, which were not wedded to Cobdenite notions of free trade, were quick to impose protective tariffs, establishing industries behind tariff walls and reducing British access to world markets (speech of October 6, 1903; printed in Chamberlain 1914, 149). Second, many countries were expanding industrially. Italy, Holland, Switzerland, Greece, Sweden, Spain, India, Japan, Korea, and China were all developing textiles, reducing their demand for British products. In addition, the raw cotton that Britain imported was no longer readily or cheaply available, increasing the cost of UK production. The United States was withholding much of its own raw cotton for domestic use, leading to crises in Lancashire textile mills. Hewins saw a relative decline in British exports under current trade policy. The result: laissez-faire would soon sink the United Kingdom to what he called "the rank of a fifth-rate Power" (An Economist, *Times*, July 10, 1903). Iron and steel were obviously indispensable industries, because, as Hewins put it, on "their efficiency depends the success of every other industry and the defensive power of the Empire." The per-capita production of British pig iron was dropping, as were its net exports. With Germany and the United States forging ahead, the United Kingdom would shortly be left in third place. Sweden, a producer of ore, could be expected to develop its own industry. Hewins refused to believe that high freight costs or wages damaged British competitiveness. Laissez-faire was the main cause: unlike its competitors, the British government had refused to employ financial and institutional instruments to manage its commercial policy intelligently (An Economist, *Times*, July 31, 1903). Third, the United Kingdom was expanding its imports at a much higher rate than its exports. Moreover, reliance on one country—the United States—was increasing. Hewins predicted that dependence on American wheat would expose Britain to permanently high costs of living. On the one hand, the United States was approaching diminishing returns in agriculture, which meant it could no longer meet both internal and external demands for food. He anticipated that in fewer than twenty-five years, most of the American food supply would be consumed domestically. On the other hand, as foreign nations industrialized, their populations would increase, putting further pressure on wheat prices (An Economist, *Times*, July 3, 1903).

Tariff reformers also held that the British policy of laissez-faire had failed the working class. Workers in free trade countries, including the United Kingdom, were relatively impoverished compared with their counterparts in protectionist economies. Several factors came into play here. Chamberlain claimed that British wages did not rise as rapidly as wages in protectionist countries. This was due to an unreasonably permissive immigration policy and unstable employment caused by unrestricted imports. He darkly warned workers of the consequences of unrestricted immigration. If millions of hopeful foreigners immigrated to the United Kingdom, British workers could expect increased crime, disease, and "hopeless poverty." No other nation spent as much as the United Kingdom on pauperism (speeches of October 28, 1903 and December 15, 1904; printed in Chamberlain 1914, 219–20, 263). Hewins's forecasts were also unremittingly bleak. Free trade would cause the contraction of "every branch of our trade and manufactures, a fall in profits, a fall in wages, constant disputes between masters and men," and an expansion of the "submerged class"—the bottom third of the British populace that was threatened by starvation. If Hewins was correct, his predication of permanently higher food prices would create a "national disaster" (An Economist, *Times*, July 3, 1903).

Chamberlain repeatedly claimed that laissez-faire had failed to ensure stable employment and income for British workers, without which discussions of high wages or cheap food were pointless (speech of October 27, 1903; printed in Chamberlain 1914, 201). British manufacturers jumped over tariff walls by moving operations to protectionist countries. Although these initiatives increased their wealth, it reduced British employment (speech of December 15, 1904; printed in Chamberlain 1914, 268). In depressions, protectionist countries managed employment by dumping surplus goods into free British markets below production costs (speeches of October 27, 1903, and October 28, 1903; printed in Chamberlain 1914, 199–200, 222). Free trade also exacerbated the damage produced by business cycles. "The trade of this country," Chamberlain claimed in a speech on October 28, 1903, "always runs in cycles." He predicted that in the next depression, "the evils which I dread and fear will be accentuated in their influence upon the working classes of this country" (Chamberlain 1914, 225). How would this happen? Under laissez-faire, many British industries—Hewins and Chamberlain mentioned watchmaking, plate glass, milling (flour), wire, iron and steel, cotton, shipping, and agriculture— had either curtailed their business or were threatened by collapse. In later economic parlance, the result was significant structural unemployment.

Proponents of laissez-faire assumed that displaced factors of production would be reabsorbed by expanding industries. Tariff reformers questioned this assumption. In reality, lucky workers would find employment in low-grade jobs such as sweeping or dock work. The less fortunate would move to casual employment and live on the edge of hunger. The truly wretched would either be forced into workhouses or sink into destitution (speech of October 28, 1903; printed in Chamberlain 1914, 221–22).

Addressing Market Failure

Chamberlain and Hewins believed that national prosperity depended on the growth rate of net exports. Because they were convinced that a rate sufficient to sustain prosperity could no longer be achieved under laissez-faire, they concentrated on the British capacity to extract resources from the colonies and sell them finished goods. Such an arrangement would require comprehensive management of production and trade, both within the empire and with foreign countries. Chamberlain maintained that if his protective and preferential tariffs were adopted, the commercial union of the empire would become "self-sustaining and self-sufficient, able to maintain itself against the competition of all its rivals" (speech of May 15, 1903; printed in Chamberlain 1914, 140). Imperial commerce would be regulated by a systematic and carefully calibrated set of regulations that would discriminate in favor of the dominions and retaliate against foreign nations that adopted protective measures. What would the package of tariff reform policies include?

In its current state, the empire resembled "the separate parts of the great machine, some highly finished, others scarcely begun, lying about amongst the *debris* of the workshop." Fiscal reform would construct the "perfect instrument which will do good service to mankind for many generations." "Mankind" was a euphemism for the subjects of the empire, who would not oppose dictates from London. Neither Chamberlain nor Hewins considered the possibility that another member of the empire, such as Canada or Australia, might replace the United Kingdom as the economically dominant imperial power. It was the "natural tendency of things" for Britain to be the "home of highly specialized industries." Fortuitously, the mother country and the colonies were at different stages of development, one of the happy "safeguards of an Imperial Scheme." British traders would retain their "natural position" (An Economist, *Times*, August 7, 1903). Canada would have an obvious advantage in food production and natural resources. Competition in manufacturing between Canada and the United Kingdom would diminish. Britain would, of course, produce goods for Canadian consumption, the demand for which would increase rapidly under a preferential regime (An Economist, *Times*, September 11, 1903). Australia, less industrialized than Canada, would specialize in primary industries—wool, meat, fruit, and wine—for which British industries and citizens had a demand (An Economist, *Times*, September 18, 1903).

A wide range of tariffs would be imposed, including a "modest" tax on foreign corn, the most controversial of Chamberlain's proposals.[4] A corresponding tax would be imposed on flour, protecting the dying British industry of milling. Foreign meat (excluding bacon), dairy, wine, and fruit would also be taxed. In return, Chamberlain proposed to reduce duties on tea, sugar, cocoa, and coffee. The colonies would receive preference on the taxed items, the extent of which would be determined in bilateral negotiations (speech of October 6, 1903; printed in Chamberlain 1914, 158–59). Chamberlain argued that the fall in some food taxes would more than offset the increase in others, leaving British consumers better off. Hewins took a different view, admitting that the cost of living could increase somewhat, albeit temporarily. Higher foreign food prices would increase the demand for Canadian corn. Increased production in Canada, which benefited from increasing returns, would lower food costs in short order (An Economist, *Times*, June 26, 1903). In the interim, British workers and manufacturers knew how to contend with the increase in food prices: "We save a little here and there, take cheaper holidays, do without this or that luxury for a time, and no great harm is done" (An Economist, *Times*, July 3, 1903).

Fiscal reform included a set of escalating tariffs on manufactured products that would protect various industries, averaging 10 percent but changing directly with the amount of labor embodied in the product (speech of October 6, 1903; printed in Chamberlain 1914, 162). Although textiles were high on the agenda, protection of iron and steel was much more critical. A case could be made that the United Kingdom would not be seriously harmed if the textile industry were "annihilated," assuming that another vibrant industry replaced it and redeployed the unemployed workforce. A comparable case could not be made for the decimation of British

---

4. Maize—consumed by the destitute and used by farmers as feed for stock—would be exempted.

iron or steel, which had no suitable substitutes: "If war is the ultimate test of national efficiency, success in war depends upon these trades." Recalling Adam Smith's dictum that "defence is more important than opulence," Hewins claimed that it would be preferable to maintain these industries at an economic loss rather than "suffer any considerable decline in their extent and efficiency" (An Economist, *Times*, July 31, 1903). Protection of domestic industry would stabilize employment for common workers and prevent the drain of displaced "young men of brains and ambition." Hewins extrapolated that without protection of key home industries, the British population would dwindle and the efficiency of its workforce would diminish. "Foreign nations, jealous of the power of England, would be foolish to go to war with us. They have a much surer method of attaining their ends ready to hand if they care to use it"—economic rather than military power (An Economist, *Times*, August 7, 1903).

Hewins argued that unlike the Corn Laws of the early nineteenth century, Chamberlain's food taxes would have numerous benefits. British manufacturing was beset by child mortality and disease. Protection of agriculture would support a higher proportion of the population in the more salubrious countryside, strengthening industrial and military efficiency. It would increase wealth, improve the fertility of land, and preserve "all the machinery of administration and management, which also is the creation of centuries of civilized effort." Hewins identified several weaknesses of British agriculture. The educational opportunities provided by ill-equipped facilities were seriously deficient. As a result, British farmers learned their trade in an informal and fortuitous fashion. Hewins proposed an ambitious program of educational reform for the agricultural sector, including not only primary, secondary, and vocational schools but university curricula designed for scientific farming. British farmers had no access to scientific literature, rarely studied foreign methods of farming, and seldom used the telegraph or telephone to stay current. An imperial agricultural policy could eliminate these deficits. In the main, British farms were remote from transportation centers. Private-sector railway construction in the countryside was not an attractive investment because of low population density and the irregular character of farming. The solution was state subsidies for the construction of cheap transportation that would link farming counties and cities. Hewins realized that the large short-term investment required for agricultural reform was inconsistent with laissez-faire. However, he was convinced that his agricultural program would make Britain "the home of a flourishing country life, which will maintain unimpaired the vigour of the race" (An Economist, *Times*, August 19, 1903).

Unlike the German *Zollverein* states, British colonies were noncontiguous entities, scattered across several continents. Tariff reformers did not find this obstacle formidable. The control of sea lanes was the key to British world domination. "If we retain command of the sea, the British Empire is invulnerable" (An Economist, *Times*, July 17, 1903). Foreign nations heavily subsidized their shipping, pricing the British merchant marine out of the market in other countries. The United Kingdom imposed differential regulations on the size and weight of ships, penalizing its own vessels. Preferential agreements between foreign nations and their colonies substantially reduced demand for British shipping. Several countries had excluded British ships from their "coasting trade"—for example, they could not navigate along American or Russian coast lines. However, British laissez-faire doctrine prohibited retaliation (speech of October 27, 1903; printed in Chamberlain 1914, 212–17).

Did Chamberlain and Hewins see the implications of their proposals for the expansion of the British state? If so, they did not acknowledge them. Fiscal reform, as they conceived it, entailed an unprecedented increase in the scope and responsibilities of the state. New regulations and bureaucracies as well as personnel to interpret and enforce rules and punish violators would be necessary. Preference schemes with the dominions would require continual renegotiation. The same would hold for trade agreements with foreign nations. The result: massive increases in the costs of fiscal policy both within and without the empire and expansion of public finance on a scale that had never been envisioned in peacetime. Would projected revenues from the proposed tariffs cover the costs of fiscal reform? Although Chamberlain and Hewins addressed this question, their calculations did not include the costs of instituting and enforcing policies. Moreover, they did not consider the possibility that the costs of waging commercial warfare against an indefinite number of foreign nations might outweigh the burden of prosecuting a conventional war—such as the recent Boer War, the expenses of which had imposed unanticipated demands on the exchequer.

The Manifesto

On August 15, 1903, roughly midpoint in Hewins's series of articles, the *Times* published a letter in opposition to tariff reform signed by fourteen academic economists, including a young fellow of King's College, Cambridge: Pigou (Bastable et al. 1903). Although firmly committed to amicable relations among members of the empire, the signatories were convinced that preferential duties would defeat this purpose, requiring instead an "immense and permanent sacrifice not only of material but also of higher goods." Chamberlain and his supporters had committed various sins of economic fact and logic. Their claim that higher imports raised the level of unemployment was refuted by evidence. Higher taxes on food would probably reduce real wages by increasing prices. In the long run, only a small share of the burden of duties would be passed on to foreign suppliers. It would be impossible to increase production in the colonies and protect agriculture in Britain without punishing British consumers. Moreover, the public would not be fully compensated, as tariff reformers confidently predicted, if proceeds of taxes on grain were redistributed as old-age pensions. Although consumers would pay higher prices on both foreign and domestic wheat, the state would collect tariffs only on foreign wheat. Finally, the professors intimated that other, more ominous, consequences could be expected: "loss of purity in politics, the unfair advantage given to those who wield the power of jobbery and corruption, unjust distribution of wealth, and the growth of 'sinister interests'" (Bastable et al. 1903).

In attempting to mobilize the public against tariff reform, the "Professors' Manifesto," as it was immediately christened, failed miserably. A deluge of hostile letters and editorials in the *Times* followed its appearance. L. L. Price, fellow and treasurer of Oriel College, Oxford, published his letter to Edgeworth, in which he had refused to sign the manifesto. His colleagues had made a serious error in condemning tariff reform proposals that had not yet been circulated to the public (*Times*, August 15, 1903). Under the pseudonym "Tariff Reformer," Leo Amery, a prominent *Times* journalist and opponent of free trade, ridiculed the document and its "platitudes" as "perhaps the most egregious production that has ever owned such distinguished parentage" (*Times*, August 18, 1903). Sir Vincent Caillard (1903), later chairman of the anti–free trade Tariff Commission, found the professors innocent of knowledge of affairs. In business, practical knowledge, which the professors seemed to lack, was much more important than theory. Herbert Foxwell thundered that as long as he was a member of the economics department at University College, London, he and his colleagues would never "pronounce or appear to pronounce, upon any economic proposal coming from responsible persons until the details of that proposal are before us" (*Times*, August 20, 1903). An editorial in the *Times* of August 18, 1903, was devastating.

> When fourteen professors say "we think" such and such things, and when among these things are propositions absolutely unsustainable by facts, they must not be surprised if the result is to shake their authority all round, and to suggest suspicions of their competence even in their own sphere, which our respect for established institutions causes us to contemplate with pain.

Most correspondents sided with Chamberlain, accusing the fourteen economists of abusing their status as academic experts (Coats 1964). Week after week, Hewins, an accomplished and lucid stylist, had pummeled free traders, arguing that the well-being of the British people had been neglected under laissez-faire. Compared with his articles, the manifesto had the appearance of a pretentious list of allegations, notable chiefly for their assertive tone, contorted syntax, academic diction, and deficiency in argument and evidence. Five days after its publication, Hewins, using his own name, challenged the signatories to prove that tariff reform proposals were "inconsistent with sound economics" (*Times*, August 20, 1903, Hewins). The following day, employing his pseudonym, he maintained that "no scientific case for economic Little Englandism has ever been stated" (An Economist, *Times*, August 21, 1903). And on September 4: "I am not aware that any great economist, in England or any other country, has ever even tried to make out a case for a general policy of free importation for a country situated as the United Kingdom is at the present time" (An Economist). Hewins had thrown down the gauntlet. Pigou was quick to pick it up.

Pigou's Engagement

Refutation

Pigou's efforts to advance the cause of free trade began in July and August 1903, when he published a series of articles for the *Pilot*, a weekly political and literary review, and the *Westminster Gazette*, a Liberal publication regarded as essential reading for politicians across the aisle.[5] The main

---

5. The prehistory of tariff reform began in the 1880s with the fair trade movement (Zebel 1940). There is no evidence that Pigou was influenced by this prehistory. On the various dimensions of the tariff reform controversy, see Coats 1968, Sykes 1979, Cain 1996, and Thompson 1997.

arguments of these pieces were reproduced in a small pamphlet (Pigou 1903a) and a short book, *The Riddle of the Tariff* (1903b), the latter completed immediately before Chamberlain began his autumn campaign in October 1903. In November, Leopold Maxse, a former president of the Cambridge Union and the Conservative editor of the *National Review*, was the target of the "fiery intensity and bitter sarcasm" displayed in a speech by Pigou.[6] A few weeks later, Pigou, J. E. McTaggart—Trinity College lecturer in philosophy—and H. O. Meredith, fellow of King's, announced a series of lectures in support of free trade. They followed lectures delivered by the economic historian William Cunningham, a Chamberlain supporter.[7] On January 27, 1904, Pigou spoke again at Cambridge in a small room at Guildhall, "overflowing" with enthusiasts.[8] On December 4, 1905, he lectured under the auspices of the Cambridge University Free Trade Association, of which he was a founding member. Speaking on "protection and the unemployed," he dwelt "at considerable length on Mr Chamberlain's arguments," giving "an admirably lucid account of the consequences which Protection, in its several senses, would naturally entail."[9]

In articles, pamphlets, books, and lectures between 1903 and 1906, Pigou fought tariff reformers on their own ground. His case against tariff reform was elaborate, addressing claims made by Chamberlain, An Economist (Hewins), and occasionally Ashley. His method was the technique of the aggressive pugilist, engaging adversaries toe-to-toe in an effort to hammer them into submission. He confounded tariff reformers with counterarguments, convicted them of facile and fallacious reasoning, and charged them with ignoring or obscuring crucial facts, deftly employing the logical and rhetorical skills of the Cambridge Union debater he had been as an undergraduate only a few years earlier.

The protection of infant industries, the only type of tariff Pigou was prepared to countenance, was of little practical importance for the mature

6. *Cambridge Review*, November 5, 1903, 55–56.

7. *Cambridge Review*, November 26, 1903, 98.

8. *Cambridge Review*, January 25, 1904, 131; February 4, 1904, 163.

9. *Cambridge Review*, December 7, 1905, 140. There is no indication that Marshall collaborated with Pigou as he developed his positions on tariff reform. However, there is evidence that Marshall followed Pigou's work on the controversy and approved of it. In a letter to an unknown recipient, written on June 6, 1907, Marshall lamented that there was no systematic analysis of free trade policies. However, he suggested that his correspondent would "find good answers" to some tariff reform criticisms in Pigou's *Protective and Preferential Import Duties and the Riddle of the Tariff* (Marshall 1996, 160–61).

British economy. Chamberlain's protective tariffs would not achieve greater economies of scale; they would increase prices, reduce the incentive to innovate, and increase inefficiency by reallocating resources from unprotected to sheltered industries (Pigou 1903b, 6, 11, 32; see also Pigou 1904c, 455). Pigou also rejected the analysis of dumping employed by tariff reformers. In some cases, what appeared to be dumping was merely price discrimination (Pigou 1903b, 38–39). Pigou was not impressed by real cases of intermittent dumping, designed to rid trusts of surplus goods. He saw no evidence that trusts had a significant impact on "the normal instability of industry."[10] Ashley's 1902 case of German companies dumping steel in the United Kingdom, for example, was inconsequential. Steel imports from Germany were a small fraction of total supply. Much of British industry operated on the basis of long-term contracts that remained unaffected by dumping. Large firms comfortably weathered lean years. Employment data in the iron and steel industries indicated no abnormal fluctuations for 1902, although the number of shifts worked per person had actually increased compared with previous years (Pigou 1903b, 41–42). Pigou acknowledged that predatory dumping was more pernicious but discounted its relevance. If they faced international competition, in which case they could not charge monopoly prices, predators would have no incentive to drive British businesses into bankruptcy. Global trusts were a rarity. Thus the conditions that would call for protective tariffs on this assumption were seldom realized (42–43).

Pigou had a similarly skeptical view of imperial preference, which benefited neither the United Kingdom nor its dominions. Preference would require protection of agriculture, an unwise policy, since reallocation of resources in its favor would promote an industry suffering from diminishing returns—increased production could be achieved only at higher costs and prices. The result would reduce the nation's real annual income and redistribute it to the advantage of affluent landowners (69–70). He considered the possibility that agricultural protection might reduce rural-urban migration and the number of town dwellers. However, it seemed implausible that urban conditions would improve as a result. Instead of fewer overcrowded towns, he anticipated more small overcrowded towns, the population of which would have to contend with higher food prices (72). He also contested the claim that food taxes were necessary to expand corn production in Canada. Expansion had already

10. Pigou 1903b, 41; see also Pigou 1904c, 451; *Cambridge Review*, December 7, 1905, 140.

begun "under the operation of purely natural causes" (75). As a result of increasing population density in New England, New York, and Pennsylvania and the extension of railway service west and north, tens of thousands of Americans had crossed the Canadian border in search of arable land. Pigou reminded his readers that British consumers were heavily dependent on foreign grain—80 percent of imported wheat was grown in countries outside the empire. Increases in wheat production in the United Kingdom and Canada would not be sufficient to reduce domestic and international prices. On the contrary, he expected higher food prices. The demand for wheat was inelastic, which meant that a corn tax would be punitive for British consumers. He criticized the cost-benefit analysis of tariff reformers on the ground that it failed to consider transportation; the success of imperial preference depended on whether colonial railway systems could be built to transport a higher wheat output to the United Kingdom (80–82).[11]

The imperial conference of 1902 demonstrated the weakness of tariff reform. Movements in the colonies for self-government made the vision of imperial union an illusion (Pigou 1904a, 267). The dominions were developing their own infant industries, which would require protection from even British goods. Moreover, they had no realistic alternative for public finance except indirect taxation or revenue tariffs. Thus any preference that favored Britain could be achieved only by increasing tariffs on foreign goods, not reducing taxes on British products. Reprisals from foreign trade partners were a probable consequence of such measures. Germany had already threatened that any large-scale imperial preference awarded to the United Kingdom could cost the British their most-favored-nation status, entangling the country in "continued tariff discussions, occasional tariff wars, and, in view of the present temper of the nation, in the permanent upkeep of a clumsy and expensive 'big revolver'" (Pigou 1903b, 88). Finally, the volume of trade that would be shifted from foreign countries to the United Kingdom would be insignificant. Sir Robert Giffen had shown that a large portion of colonial imports consisted of food and raw material that Britain lacked the capacity to produce (83–93). As to the argument favoring preference and food security in the event of a European war, Pigou countered that British food imports from the United States—which would most likely declare neutrality—would be less vul-

11. Tariff reform proposals were based on several theoretical propositions. Pigou (1904d) analyzed them algebraically and published the results in March 1904.

nerable to enemy attacks than imports from the colonies, which would engage in the war on the side of Britain (95).

Would imperial preference justify its costs if it strengthened consolidation of the empire? Pigou's answer was a "decisive and clear-cut negative" (96). Colonial preference would most likely be achieved by increased duties on foreign goods in the United Kingdom and the dominions. Both sides would pay more for food and manufactures. "Each party to the bargain is to inflict a considerable injury upon himself, in order to confer a small benefit upon the other. Both parties taken together are deliberately to cut themselves off from some of the advantages of international trade, and the imperial unit is to become more protective against the rest of the world, without the compensating advantage, obtained in a true *Zollverein*, of becoming more free-trading within its own borders" (97–98). Pigou anticipated inevitable occasions for "irritation and friction," both intercolonial and between each colony and London (99–100). His unsurprising conclusion: if adopted, imperial preference would harm the United Kingdom, the colonies, and the empire.

The institutional and administrative costs of intervening in markets did not escape Pigou. Several considerations were important. Because of ingrained sentiments in favor of free trade, any change in British fiscal policy would take the form of a compromise. He anticipated a complex and imponderable scheme of compromises, with more damaging consequences for commerce than any single policy component. A mix of general protective tariffs and preferential duties, for example, would be more pernicious than either a single policy of general protection or imperial preference.

> For every bargain with a foreign country, and every resort to retaliation, would mean a modification in the amount of the protection which some or all of them received. The result would be an unstable and incalculable situation, bad for enterprise, conducive to crises, and proffering great inducements to dishonest political wire-pulling. (105)

In addition, the costs of countering dumping by tariffs would be enormously high. In the case of intermittent dumping, it would be necessary to implement a sliding scale: tariffs would increase when products were dumped and decrease when there was no evidence of dumping. The result: "An extremely elaborate, mobile and inquisitorial tariff system would be required" (42). In the unlikely event that the United Kingdom became a victim of predatory dumping, the argument for tariff manipulation was fraught with difficulties.

For we should still have to consider the grave disadvantages which are bound to arise when ordinary human beings endeavour in practice to select the proper cases for intervention, the right time for beginning it, and, above all, the moment at which the temporary duty ought to be removed. Can we seriously suppose that a democratic Government, pressed upon all hands by interested suitors, bewildered by conflicting evidence, nervous of offending political adherents, would prove itself equal to that Herculean task? (44)

The question was, of course, rhetorical. Even if a protective tariff were introduced as a temporary measure, the obstacles in the path of repeal would be enormous. Businesses that benefited would be reluctant to sacrifice their profits. "While the theory is that Protection is needed for the weak, in practice it is those who can shout loudest, lobby best, and pull wires most effectively to whom that boon is prolonged" (45). It would also be difficult for the state to restrict protection to the industries intended; other producer groups would vie for preferential treatment. And if a protected industry produced inputs for other industries, downstream firms could be expected to demand protection (45–46).

Pigou noted that in the previous twenty-five years, the tariff policy of the British government was anchored in two principles: it did not engage in retaliation or concession, regardless of the policies of other countries; and it raised revenue not through protective tariffs but through taxes on products not produced domestically. Although he admitted that retaliation might occasionally be necessary, he questioned its wisdom. These principles had generally secured the country most-favored-nation status. A foreign tariff imposed on textiles would punish all countries in that industry, not only the United Kingdom. When foreign countries had discriminated against British colonies, their actions had been motivated by preference issued by a colony to the home country. The colonies were better advised to abstain from preferential treatment of the United Kingdom: the privilege was insignificant and the ensuing disputes expensive (50–58). In Pigou's assessment, tariff wars were the most likely outcome of retaliation. Foreign ministers did not possess "superhuman genius" (59). As a polity, the United Kingdom was in an especially weak negotiating position, since the government was subject to parliamentary interference. He concluded that the net gain of retaliatory tariffs would be quite modest even if negotiations were conducted by "a Cabinet of Solomons." They would be nonexistent when "the coefficients of human ignorance and frailty are introduced" (61).

Innovation

Neither Pigou, who wrote *The Riddle of the Tariff*, nor Edgeworth (1904), who reviewed it, believed that the book made theoretical breakthroughs. Its objective was modest: to assess the proposals of tariff reformers for the general public (Pigou 1903b, v). Nonetheless, it sketched the fundamentals of Pigou's later framework for analyzing economic policy. Tariff reformers argued that free trade was an obstacle to national prosperity because it failed to maximize British net exports. Pigou countered that this exclusive focus on trade as an index of British well-being—his unit of analysis—was deeply flawed. Following a natural disaster, both exports and imports could increase, hardly evidence of prosperity. Moreover, as Britain became more prosperous, trade would decline as a proportion of total income, because the public would increase its consumption of domestically produced services such as education, sanitation, sports, and holidays (2–5). Pigou presented no criteria for assessing the "advance of national well-being" (5). However, the national income and its size, distribution, and stability were embedded in his critique of tariff reform. Between 1861 and 1901, British national well-being had improved because real per-capita income had increased without damage to the distribution of income or increases in the rate of unemployment (6–9).

The Riddle was an exercise in unsparing criticism. However, in his article "The Known and the Unknown in Mr. Chamberlain's Policy" (1904b), he began to distance himself from the minutiae and ephemera of the controversy, his stance as a proponent of free trade, and his status as signatory of the manifesto. Instead of continuing his polemics against tariff reform, he posed a problem: what was the appropriate method for evaluating Chamberlain's tariff proposals systematically? Pigou suggested a "balance-sheet" representing both gains and losses likely to be produced if Chamberlain's program were implemented. As a first step, it would be useful to specify the several headings—some obvious, others not—under which estimates could be distinguished (Pigou 1904b, 36–37). This was the method he used to analyze policies for the rest of his life: disposing of red herrings, identifying issues of true significance for the problem at hand, and assessing their costs and benefits. He repeatedly warned that perplexities and uncertainties because of defective statistical methods, inadequate data, and unpredictable contingencies represented significant challenges to cost-benefit calculations (41–42, 44). It followed that the economist's conclusions were inevitably probabilistic, not definitive. This warning became a leitmotif of his work.

As the tariff reform campaign continued undiminished, Chamberlain and his supporters increasingly emphasized the importance of stable employment for British workers. Without it, discussions of high wages or cheap food were futile (speech of October 27, 1903; printed in Chamberlain 1914, 201). In late 1904, Ashley published *The Progress of the German Working Classes in the Last Quarter of a Century*, arguing that German protectionist policies had improved the condition of workers. In February 1905, Chamberlain spoke on the consequences of tariff reform for employment. Canada's preferential treatment of British manufacturing had created 32,000 jobs, supporting 160,000 people. This figure did not include secondary employment. "The shopkeeper benefits if the working man has more to spend. The man who supplies him with clothes, or with food, or anything else—all are benefited when the working man gets employment" (speech of February 1, 1905; printed in Chamberlain 1914, 305). Warming to this theme and ratcheting up his rhetoric in May 1905, he spoke to the organized labor branch of the Tariff Reform League, claiming that the "question of employment, believe me, has now become the most important question of our time. It never was so important before. It underlies everything; it underlies the position of the working man as a class; it underlies all trade unionism" (speech of May 17, 1905; printed in Chamberlain 1914, 317).

Pigou's article "Protection and the Working Classes" (1906a), written partly to counter arguments by Ashley and Chamberlain on the putative benefits of tariff reform for workers, is a critical artifact in tracing the genesis of *Wealth and Welfare*. He found their statistical arguments fallacious and their popular economic analysis spurious. In performing welfare calculations, a sound analysis would employ the Marshallian concept of the national dividend, which Pigou had previously called material wealth. The national dividend represented both the totality of the goods and services a nation produced as well as the aggregate pool of resources available for distribution among factors of production. From this "general principle," Pigou (1906a, 12) claimed, "it is easy to deduce the correct method of estimating the effect of Protection upon Labour." The correct method required three steps. First, the economist determines the impact of tariff reform on the size of the national dividend. Pigou suggested that there is a prima facie case for the view that any policy that enlarges the size of the national dividend is likely to improve the well-being of all factors of production, including labor. Second, the effect of protection on the distribution of the national dividend is established. An increase in the size of the national dividend does not qualify as improvement if it reduces the labor share of the total product. Third, the change in the "manner in which Labour receives its share" is assessed. Because the character and morale of the workforce are at stake, it is necessary to examine the consequences of protection for the following variables: the stability of employment; working conditions—the question of whether a higher proportion of workers is engaged in the "sweated industries"—and hours of work and leisure (12–13, 27; see also Pigou 1904c, 451–54). In *Wealth and Welfare*, Pigou used this same method in analyzing both economic and noneconomic welfare.

In late August 1906, Pigou notified his publisher that he was writing *Protective and Preferential Import Duties*, a "scientific" work that considered "popular arguments" only incidentally.[12] In this book, he generalized his new method of analysis to assess the impact of tariff reform on the entire British economy, not simply its workers. In addition, he made an explicit distinction between economic and noneconomic welfare: "To determine the goodness or the badness of a legislative proposal we need to balance the whole of its effects. Some of these will probably be economic; others will not. Of the others, the economist, as such, has no peculiar knowledge" (Pigou 1906b, 1–3). The implications of a policy for economic well-being were determined by the changes it produced in the size, distribution, and stability of the national dividend (36–79).

While on Christmas vacation in December 1907, Pigou drafted his "Memorandum for the Royal Commission on the Poor Laws and Relief of Distress."[13] In assessing the welfare impact of various modes of administering relief, he stressed the importance of a careful utilitarian analysis of all policy options—their effects on the well-being of the British public (Pigou 1907, 981). The memorandum was based on his new framework, which now included the concept of the good. Examining not tariff reform but the welfare implications of the Poor Laws, he distinguished three chief elements on which national well-being depended: people conceived as moral beings; social and other relations and the satisfactions that are derived from them; and the satisfactions produced by economic conditions

---

12. Pigou to Macmillan, August 25, 1908, Macmillan Archive, 1904–1938, Add55 199, vol. CDXIV 1904–38, British Library.

13. Pigou to Browning, ca. Christmas 1907, OB/1/A, Papers of Oscar Browning (OB), King's College Archive Center, University of Cambridge, Cambridge, England.

(981). All of them could be affected by Poor Law policy. Because the two noneconomic components of national well-being could not be quantified, he limited his account to the third element. Here, perhaps for the first time, he called it economic welfare, making the assumption that policies that were proved superior in delivering economic benefits were likely to be superior in improving welfare generally (982, 990). An assessment of the impact of Poor Law relief on economic welfare depended on two considerations: the magnitude of the national dividend and its distribution (987).[14]

In 1910, representatives from eighteen nations participated in the second international conference on unemployment. Before the conference, held at the Sorbonne in Paris, each country had formed a committee to select qualified representatives. These national committees also commissioned reports on "(a) the general conditions of unemployment, (b) statistics of unemployment, (c) labour exchanges, and (d) insurance against unemployment" (Royal Statistical Society 1910, 67). Seebohm Rowntree—the Liberal social reformer and industrialist—chaired the committee for the United Kingdom. It is reasonable to suppose that he nominated Pigou to write a report for the conference. Although Pigou did not attend, he wrote an essay, "The Problem of Involuntary Idleness," that examined its causes and distribution. Apologizing for his "scattered and incomplete remarks on a large subject," he confided to his readers that some years before, he had begun an ambitious study of unemployment, the result of which left him dissatisfied: "In pursuing that study I have found the subject so intertwined with many widely separated parts of economic science that any adequate discussion of it in a monograph devoted to it alone,—to say nothing of a brief paper—has seemed utterly impracticable" (Pigou 1910). *Wealth and Welfare* represented the "gradual growth and more extended scope" of that study (Pigou 1912, vii).

In the early pages of *Wealth and Welfare,* Pigou assembled a conceptual apparatus for analyzing the economic conditions that could be expected to improve human welfare. It was based on two fundamental components. First, he introduced a conception of welfare equivalent to the ethical concept of the good—which, following G. E. Moore, he claimed could neither be defined nor be analyzed, although he held that its elements could be specified by moral philosophy. Pigou conceived welfare as

---

14. Pigou did not consider the effects of Poor Law relief on industrial fluctuations and the stability of the national dividend, perhaps because he thought there were none.

states of consciousness that qualify as satisfactions because they are pleasurable.[15] Economic welfare comprises satisfactions the desire or demand for which can be monetized—subjected to what he called "the measuring rod of money." Although economic welfare should not be conflated with human welfare generally—there is no one-to-one correspondence between changes in economic welfare and total welfare—he regarded the relationship between the two as tight: unless there is evidence to the contrary, economic and total welfare probably vary in the same direction, even if not invariably in the same quantity. Second, Pigou also introduced three hypotheses for improving economic welfare that he proposed to substantiate in the book—even at its best, the Smithian system of natural liberty could fail to maximize satisfaction. In the literature of the past eighty years, they are commonly but erroneously called the Pigouvian "axioms" of welfare. All other conditions remaining the same, economic welfare is likely to increase if (1) the size of the national income increases; (2) it is distributed more equally, increasing the share allocated to "the poor," which, in the era of *Wealth and Welfare* was published, may be understood as "the working class"; and (3) fluctuations in the magnitude of aggregate output are reduced. This, reduced to its simplest terms, is the foundation of Pigou's conception of economics as an analysis of the causes of economic welfare. As we have shown, its outlines can be traced to his participation in the tariff reform controversy.

Concluding Remarks

The year 1906 marked a sea change in Pigou's engagement in the tariff reform controversy. The critical text was his January essay in the *Edinburgh Review*, "Protection and the Working Classes" (1906a), in which he abandoned his earlier polemical stance against tariff reformers and his defense of free trade. Thereafter, he withdrew from partisanship. Instead of adding yet another chapter to the tariff reform controversy, he raised a question that, at the time, qualified as innovative: what mode of economic analysis was required, on theoretical grounds, to address the principal issue in the controversy? In considering this problem, he developed an

15. Before his election to the chair of political economy at Cambridge, Pigou published several articles on moral philosophy. In "The Problem of the Good," he arrived at an eclectic and derivative concept of moral goodness drawn chiefly from Henry Sidgwick's utilitarian treatise *Methods of Ethics* as well as G. E. Moore's antiutilitarian *Principia Ethica* (Pigou 1908b, 80–92).

analytical apparatus, the main desiderata of which were drawn from the armory of his enemies of 1903. There is, of course, a delicious irony in this historical conjunction. Pigou's reconceptualization of economics as an analysis of market failure and a theory of the conditions under which economic policy could advance economic welfare had its birth in a controversy in which he took the position of a relatively full-throated advocate of laissez-faire.

What resources did he find in the speeches and writings of the tariff reformers? Their arguments were informal, occasionally tacit, and often labile—changing, especially in Chamberlain's speeches, in substance as well as rhetoric. However, in their attacks on laissez-faire, four key premises can be identified without difficulty. First, purely material wealth should not be confused with genuine welfare, prosperity, or happiness. The object of economic policy was to achieve the latter for the "British race." Second, the welfare of the British people depended on the productivity of the British economy. This is why tariff reformers were troubled by the relative decline they saw in British exports and an increasing dependence on imports. Unless this process were reversed, prosperity was impossible. Third, welfare also depended on an economy that achieved relative prosperity for the working class, protecting workers from pauperism by responsible economic policy. Finally, welfare required economic stability. Sound economic policy reduced fluctuations in the demand for labor, ensuring regular and predictable sources of employment and income.

By 1906, Pigou was no longer a policy advocate. He was committed to achieving conceptual clarity, methodological rigor, consistency, empirical validity, and pragmatic effectiveness in economic analysis—a position he spelled out in his inaugural address as Marshall's successor in the Cambridge chair of political economy in 1908. In *Protective and Preferential Import Duties*, he appropriated and recast the four principles of the tariff reformers after subjecting them to detailed analysis. The idea of British prosperity was reconceptualized as economic welfare. The three conditions for prosperity, implicit in their arguments, were made explicit and reconfigured as the fundamental causes of economic welfare—in essence a Pigouvian welfare function: economic welfare varied with the size, distribution, and stability of the national dividend.

Thus Pigou abstracted the ideas of the tariff reformers from the controversy, transposing them into an analytical framework. He translated their vocabulary from a politicized language designed to defeat opponents and convince skeptics into a theoretical discourse in which he elucidated the main problem at stake in the controversy and investigated the conditions under which it could become a legitimate object of economic policy. In 1906, he applied his framework to the consequences of tariff reform for the British economy. In his 1907 memorandum, he used the same framework to explore the economic impact of the Poor Laws. And in *Wealth and Welfare*, he generalized the framework, constructing a systematic analysis of market failures and the conditions under which they might be repaired.

The result: the early Pigouvian inquiry into the causes of unemployment was translated into an analysis of market failure in which economics was conceived as an investigation of the conditions that improve economic welfare. "By their fruit ye shall know them." This was the ultimate maxim of Pigouvian economics, a dismal science in a sense more fundamental than Thomas Carlyle supposed. Pigou saw no value in the study of the economy for its own sake. An inquiry into "mankind in the ordinary business of life" was not only dispiriting but inherently uninteresting, in large measure because the springs of action that govern human life are generally "mean and dismal and ignoble." If economics achieved no more than the discovery of facts or theoretical knowledge about the operations of the economy, substantiating no results that could be expected to elevate the human condition, its pursuit would be a crushing waste of time. Borrowing Francis Bacon's metaphor of experiments of light and experiments of fruit, Pigou (1908a, 11–13) maintained that if economics has any value, it must lie in the fruits it bears, its contribution to human well-being. In an ideal Newtonian economy in which there are no intractable market failures—breakdowns that cannot be repaired within the limits of markets and through market mechanisms—economics would not exist, beyond the limited public-intellectual function of exposing the misguided or malicious views of economic charlatans.

References

Ashley, W. J. 1904. *The Progress of the German Working Classes in the Last Quarter of a Century.* London: Longman, Green.

Bastable, C. F., et al. 1903. Letter to the editor of the *Times. Times,* August 15.

Bator, Francis M. 1958. "The Anatomy of Market Failure." *Quarterly Journal of Economics* 72:351–79.

Caillard, Vincent. 1903. Letter to the editor of the *Times. Times,* August 18.

Cain, P. 1996. "The Economic Philosophy of Constructive Imperialism." In *British Politics and the Spirit of the Age,* edited by C. Navari, 41–65. Bodmin, Cornwall: Keele University Press.

Chamberlain, Joseph. 1914. *Mr. Chamberlain's Speeches.* Vol. 2. Edited by Charles W. Boyd. Boston: Houghton Mifflin.

Coats. A. W. "Bob." 1964. "The Role of Authority in the Development of British Economics." *Journal of Law and Economics* 7:85–106.

———. 1968. "Political Economy and the Tariff Reform Campaign of 1903." *Journal of Law and Economics* 11:181–229.

Edgeworth, F. Y. 1904. Review of *The Riddle of the Tariff*, by A. C. Pigou. *Economic Journal* 14:65–67.

Foxwell, Herbert S. 1903. Letter to the editor. *Times*, August 20.

Hewins, William A. S. 1903. Letter to the editor. *Times*, August 20.

———. 1929. *The Apologia of an Imperialist: Forty Years of Empire Policy.* London: Constable.

Marshall, Alfred. 1996. *Towards the Close, 1903–1924.* Vol. 3 of *The Correspondence of Alfred Marshall, Economist.* Edited by John K. Whitaker. Cambridge: Cambridge University Press.

Medema, Steven G. 2009. *The Hesitant Hand: Taming Self-Interest in the History of Economic Ideas.* Princeton, N.J.: Princeton University Press.

Pigou, Arthur Cecil. 1903a. *The Great Inquest: An Examination of Mr. Chamberlain's Fiscal Proposals.* London: Southwood, Smith.

———. 1903b. *The Riddle of the Tariff.* London: R. Brimley Johnson.

———. 1904a. Review of *Free Trade and the Empire*, by William Graham. *Economic Journal* 14:267–68.

———. 1904b. "The Known and the Unknown in Mr. Chamberlain's Policy." *Fortnightly Review* 75:36–48.

———. 1904c. "Mr. Chamberlain's Proposals." *Edinburgh Review* 200:449–77.

———. 1904d. "Pure Theory and the Fiscal Controversy." *Economic Journal* 14:29–33.

———. 1906a. "Protection and the Working Classes." *Edinburgh Review* 203:1–32.

———. 1906b. *Protective and Preferential Import Duties.* London: Macmillan.

———. 1907. "Memorandum on Some Economic Aspects and Effects of Poor Law Relief." In *Royal Commission on the Poor Laws and Relief of Distressed.* Appendix Volume, Minutes of Evidence with Appendix, cd. 5068, 1910, 981–1000. London.

———. 1908a. *Economic Science in Relation to Practice. An Inaugural Lecture Given at Cambridge.* London: Macmillan.

———. 1908b. *The Problem of Theism and Other Essays.* London: Macmillan.

———. 1910. "The Problem of Involuntary Idleness." Paper presented at the Conférence Internationale du Chômage, Paris, September 18–21. Marshall Library of Economics.

———. 1912. *Wealth and Welfare.* London: Macmillan.

Price, L. L. 1903. Letter to Edgeworth. *Times*, August 15.

Royal Statistical Society. 1910. "The International Conference on Unemployment." *Journal of the Royal Statistical Society* 74:67–70.

Sykes, A. 1979. *Tariff Reform in British Politics, 1903–1913.* Oxford: Clarendon Press.

Thompson, A. S. 1997. "Tariff Reform: An Imperial Strategy." *Historical Journal* 40:1033–54.

Zebel, S. H. 1940. "Fair Trade: An English Reaction to the Breakdown of the Cobden Treaty System." *Journal of Modern History* 12:161–85.

Progressive Era Origins of the Regulatory State and the Economist as Expert

Thomas C. Leonard

1. Economics Ascending

American economics established its scientific and political authority during the turbulent economic times of the long Progressive Era, 1885 to 1918. The rise of American economics is a tale with three acts. In the first act, a small band of progressive economists, many of them Protestant evangelicals on a self-appointed mission to redeem America, transformed the nature and practice of their own enterprise. From 1880 to 1900, both fostering and benefiting from a transformation of American higher education, the progressive economists established economics as a university discipline, transforming American political economy from a species of amateur, public-intellectual discourse into a professional, expert, scientific discipline—economics.

In the second act, the upstart economists, writing with the scientific authority of their new professorial chairs, helped convince Americans and their political leaders that laissez-faire was doubly wrong, both economically outmoded and ethically stunted. Industrial capitalism, progressive economists said, created profound social conflicts, operated wastefully, and distributed its copious fruits unjustly. Moreover, the new economy

Correspondence may be addressed to Thomas C. Leonard, Department of Economics, 418 Robertson Hall, Princeton University, Princeton, NJ 08544; e-mail: tleonard@princeton.edu. This article is derived in part from a book forthcoming from Princeton University Press, *Illiberal Reformers: Race, Eugenics, and American Economics in the Progressive Era*.

History of Political Economy 47 (annual suppl.) DOI 10.1215/00182702-3130439

featured novel organizational forms—trusts, natural monopolies, industrial corporations, and industrial labor unions—and a rapidly increasing
economic interdependence wrought by the furious pace of economic
growth. Free markets, to the extent they ever could, could no longer self-
regulate. Progress, the economists argued, now required the visible hand
of a powerful regulatory state, guided by expert social scientists—a model
of economic governance progressives called *social control*.

In the third act, the economists joined their progressive allies in a cru-
sade to reform and remake American government. If a regulatory state
was to be the new guarantor of economic progress, it would need to be
built. By March 1917, the end of Woodrow Wilson's first term, it was.
Many additions remained to be made, but the "fourth branch" of government was established.[1]

The establishment of the fourth branch not only marked an epoch-mak-
ing change in the relationship of government to American economic life.
It also signaled a shift in political authority *within* the state, moving power
from the courts and parties to the new regulatory agencies of the executive, and from politicians and partisans to bureaucratic experts, who represented themselves as objective scientists above the political fray, administering progress for the good of all.

Progressive economists, who were the architects and framers of the
fourth branch, defined economic progress variously, emphasizing the goals
of justice, efficiency, national unity, and conflict reduction in different
measures. But nearly all agreed that the best *means* to their several ends
was social control—investigation and regulation by independent government agencies supervised by a vanguard of scientific experts dedicating
themselves to the public good. The task of the fourth-branch bureaus was
administration, not politics.

Social control, then, was less a set of well-defined goals than a method—
a bureaucratic approach to economic governance institutionalized in
administrative government. As Robert Wiebe (1967, 166) famously put it,
"The heart of progressivism was the ambition of the new middle class to
fulfill its destiny through bureaucratic means."

---

1. I use *fourth branch* to describe the independent government agencies, staffed and advised
by experts, which, though nominally inside the executive branch, were chartered specifically to
be free of political influence, employing a permanent civil service rather than political appointees. The term, though certainly not the concept, is somewhat anachronistic applied to the
Progressive Era.

2. Economics in the Nation's Service
as Well as Its Own

The Progressive Era founders of American economics neither wrote nor pretended to write only for the applause of their peers. They intended to influence affairs, which required a market for the economic expertise they were retailing. In the broadest sense, two clients were available circa 1890, business and government.[2]

Corporations did not begin hiring social scientific experts until roughly the beginning of the First World War. Prospects in government were better, but only marginally. The federal government's single social welfare program, the Pension Office, which paid pensions to Civil War veterans and their survivors, was seen not as a model for the regulatory state but as a cautionary tale. A sprawling bureaucratic colossus, the Pension Office had nearly one million beneficiaries by 1900, supported a vast rent-seeking industry of attorneys and examining physicians, and was widely regarded as politically corrupt, inefficient, and unfair.[3]

The Interstate Commerce Commission (1887), formed to regulate the railroad industry, and the US Bureau of Labor Statistics (1885) had only just opened. The great Progressive Era creation of the fourth branch, with its multiplication of investigatory and regulatory agencies, and with its adversarial approach to business, was visible on the horizon, but only barely.[4]

If barely visible, the fledgling economists saw the vocational opportunity and cast their lot with the regulatory state, which was to be the great benefactor of American economics. Francis Amasa Walker's 1888 presidential address to the American Economic Association (AEA) presciently understood that an alliance with the regulatory state would allow the nascent profession to be in the nation's service as well as its own (Walker 1889).

Walker's premises were epistemic and vocational. He believed, first, that the new economics could tell government something that it did not already know, that is, the new economics could successfully guide government in deciding which investigations and interventions were merited.

2. Opportunities for economists in other organizational settings, such as charities, labor unions, or foundations, were still many years away.

3. See Skocpol 1992.

4. On the Progressive Era rise of a newly adversarial relationship between government and business, see McCraw 1984a.

Of what use was economic expertise to government otherwise? Walker believed, second, that economic expertise in the service of the regulatory state would advance the professional fortunes of the discipline.

There were two implications of consequence. The first Walker left implied: economists had to establish that their advice was objective, not partisan—*disinterested* was the term. Working for the national interest meant avoiding too close an association with any special interest, even one as important to progressive economics as labor. The second implication Walker made clear: American economics would have to shed any remaining crust of laissez-faire dogma. Laissez-faire, of the sort that had characterized midcentury American political economy into the 1870s, was a nonstarter as a professionalizing strategy. How much scientific expertise, Louis Menand (2001, 302) asks, was required "to repeat, in every situation, 'let the Market decide'"?

Having served in government in many roles, including two tours as superintendent of the US Census, Walker understood that, when economists possessed the political and scientific authority to advise on which policy interventions conduced to the public interest and which did not, theirs was a never-ending task, a task requiring the work "not of one mind but of many," and a task that, moreover, served to "heighten the popular interest in political economy, increase the number of its students, and intensify the instinct of union and cooperation." Rising to his theme of serving the state, Walker (1889, 29) enthused, "in such a work who would not wish to join?"

The 1890s, plagued by financial panic, prolonged economic depression, and labor strife, generated a groundswell of support for economic reform, and with it, political reform. This political turn lent ever-growing credibility to Walker's idea that advising or serving in government was a surer route to professional success than the traditional public-intellectual model of shaping public opinion by lecturing and publishing in the newspapers and periodicals.

As the economy recovered from the depths of the mid-1890s depression, the professional advantages of government as a client—*the* client—for professional economic expertise were almost taken for granted. In his presidential address to the AEA in 1899, Arthur T. Hadley (1900) put the prevailing view plainly: "Influence in public life . . . is the most important application of our studies." The greatest opportunity for economists, Hadley urged, lay "not with students but with statesmen." Hadley, who became president of Yale University the following year, saw economists' brightest future not "in the education of individual citizens, however widespread and salutary, but in the leadership of an organized body politic" (Hadley 1899, 206).

Edwin R. A. Seligman of Columbia University, in his own presidential address before the AEA in 1902, argued that the new industrial order made social control a national necessity, which meant, Seligman (1903, 69) reminded his receptive confreres, that economics would be the "basis of social progress," even "the creator of the future." On these grounds, the ordinarily circumspect Seligman dared to portray the expert economist as "the real philosopher of social life" and a figure worthy of public "deference to his views."

At the turn of the century, American economists had only begun to establish themselves as expert advisers to political decision makers. But even at that early moment, the discipline's leaders foresaw a political role that went beyond providing information and advice to the powerful. The expert economist could not only advise, but lead.

3. Market Failure

Behind social control, of course, was the idea that an unregulated economy no longer worked. Market failure was nothing new in Anglophone political economy. Its leading textbook in the latter half of the nineteenth century, John Stuart Mill's *Principles of Political Economy*, explored at length the many ways in which markets could go awry. Markets could fail to provide valuable public goods. Markets could, as in the cases of railroads and utilities, lead to monopoly. Markets could also impose spillover costs, such as pollution, on third parties without their consent (Medema 2007). There were also endemic agency problems, as when business managers pursued private ends rather than carry out their fiduciary duties. And, even when they did not fail in these ways, markets could distribute their benefits unequally or unfairly. There was nothing in capitalism, Mill made clear, that ensured a just distribution.

The progressive economists' German professors nonetheless disparaged Mill as the avatar of "English economics," their term for the classically liberal tendency of political economy in Great Britain. Mill's (1848, 515–16) text, after all, had concluded that "*laisser-faire* should be the general practice." But Mill was not naive about the shortcomings of free markets. He was, rather, skeptical that government interventions to remedy market failures would do more good than harm.

Agency problems afflicted government bureaucrats no less than business bureaucrats. A career civil servant, Mill warned that government was badly informed, its employees were mediocre and often corrupt, and, moreover, politics continually threatened the goals of efficiency and fairness alike. Market ills were serious, but government cures were all too likely to be worse, Mill maintained.

A Millian skepticism toward government's motives and competence was scarcely unfounded in late nineteenth-century America, the notorious heyday of spoils-system patronage and ward-heeling machine politics. But, at the turn of the twentieth century, American economists no longer shared Mill's skepticism. They were supremely confident in their own expertise as a reliable, even necessary, guide to economic reform, and optimistic also about the competence of the governments that would deploy it.

Freshly established in the academy, they spoke confidently of the scientific competence of their new discipline. Economic science could diagnose market ills and could prescribe remedies that would treat or even cure them. "Within certain limits," Richard T. Ely (1889, 38) announced in his pioneering textbook, "we can have just such a kind of economic life as we wish."

Yale's Hadley would have demurred at Ely's hyperbole, but his own 1899 presidential address to the AEA reflected American economics' sanguine mood, when it concluded that "economic science is now at the height of its prosperity" (194). Edwin R. A. Seligman's (1903, 69) presidential address confidently forecast that "like natural science, the economics of the future will enable us to comprehend the living forces at work . . . and control them and mould them to ever higher uses." Seligman's confidence was sufficient, recall, for him to portray economists—only barely established as professionals—as the "real philosophers of social life," superintending American economic life for the good of all.

In his 1910 presidential address to the American Association for Labor Legislation (AALL), Yale's Henry Farnam captured the extraordinary self-confidence of economists when he compared scientific progress in economics to scientific progress in surgery (Moss 1996, 16). Surgery, Farnam said, was once primitive and dangerous; it did patients more harm than good. "But increased knowledge," Farnam argued, "has made surgery bold. It is bold because it is instructed" (16).

Recent advances in medical knowledge—especially the revolutionary discovery that germs cause infectious disease—made surgery a positive benefit to society. Without identifying the comparable scientific revolution in economic science, Farnam announced that the same was now true for economic reform. Economists, Farnam told the gathered labor reformers, possessed scientific knowledge sufficient to ensure that their reform cures were "more effective and less dangerous."

Farnam's bold claim exemplified two defining attributes of the professionalizing economists: first, they claimed to be an established science before they were in firm possession of the kind of scientific knowledge possessed by the natural and life sciences they invoked as exemplars, and second, they were also sure that their disinterested expertise provided a reliable guide to the public good.[5] "The political economist," Ely's (1889, 100) textbook informed its readers, "is to the general public what the attorney is to the private individual."

The economists' outsized confidence in their own expertise as a reliable, even necessary guide to the public good was nearly matched by their extravagant faith in the transformative promise of the scientific state. On its face this was a puzzle, for progressive economists judged American political life to be as disorganized, inefficient, and corrupt as its economic life. The professionalizing economists, like all progressives, thus placed their fondest hopes for economic reform in an institution—American government and its party system—they judged wholly inadequate to the task (Rodgers 1982, 125).

Their solution to the contradiction was yet more reform, political reform. During the Progressive Era, then, government served a dual role for progressives—simultaneously an instrument and an object of reform. Progressive economists held up the state as the chief agency of economic improvement, but only by presupposing the necessary political reforms that would create a modern administrative state, organized on the efficiency-minded principles of scientific management, which would subordinate politicians, party bosses, and the patronage system to expert advisers situated in a permanent and professional bureaucracy of new investigatory and regulatory agencies—the fourth branch.

By 1917 the fourth branch was established. The US government now taxed personal incomes, corporations, and estates. It created the Departments of Labor and Commerce and dissolved prominent industrial combinations in steel, oil, tobacco, and sugar. It restricted immigration. Its

5. The formulation of the first point I owe to Dorothy Ross, "American Social Science and the Idea of Progress," 157.

Federal Reserve regulated money, credit, and banking. Its Federal Trade Commission supervised domestic industry, and its new Permanent Tariff Commission regulated international trade. State and federal labor legislation mandated workmen's compensation, banned child labor, compelled children to attend school, inspected factories, fixed minimum wages and maximum hours, paid pensions to single mothers with dependent children, and much more.

The progressive economists who blueprinted and framed the regulatory state agreed that industrial capitalism had made laissez-faire obsolete. But they had different (albeit related) views of the state's role in economic life, which arose from differing conceptions of what Progressive Era markets could do. Different conceptions of the state's role also meant different conceptions of what its economic experts do.

To put it overly dichotomously, right progressives, exemplified by John Bates Clark, conceived of the state's role as restoring healthy competition to the market, whereas left progressives conceived of the state's role as replacing the market. Right progressives conceived of market failure as departures from competitive prices that would obtain but for various market imperfections (Leonard 2003). The regulatory state's job, then, was to remedy imperfections and restore competitive prices.

Left progressives, in contrast, were more skeptical of economic competition to begin with. Market failure was not anomalous; under the conditions of industrial capitalism it was endemic. Even competitive markets, left progressives often said, were more destructive than vivifying. Left progressives criticized trade as wasteful "higgling," deemed price competition as "ruinous" or "cutthroat" in certain product markets, and depicted wage competition in labor markets as a destructive "race to bottom."

Unlike Clark and his neoclassical successors, the left progressives and their institutionalist successors defended a more thoroughgoing role for the state. The state expert does not merely police unfair and inefficient trade practices; the state expert *administers* trade, in the same way that the business expert—the scientific manager—administers a large business organization, via planning, management, and centralized direction.

It was the difference between market capitalism and managerial capitalism, which, in turn, derived from different premises of how economic efficiency was obtained. Whereas the right progressive expert aimed to make markets better, because well-functioning markets promote efficiency, the left progressive expert aimed to make management better, because well-functioning administration, which organized economic activity *outside* the marketplace, was seen as the source of greater efficiency.

4. Left Progressives and the Efficiency Vogue

The left progressives' enthusiasm for administration drew heavily on scientific management. During the decade from 1908 to the US entry into the First World War in 1917, Samuel Haber (1988, 131) writes, "*efficiency* and *good* came closer to meaning the same thing than in any other period of American history." When Jane Addams (1910) argued that labor legislation was necessary for "efficient citizenship," and the labor economist Helen Sumner (1910, 26) maintained that women's industrial employment endangered "efficient motherhood," they well captured the term's vogue.

Like *progressive*, *efficiency* was a virtue word, and its positive connotations extended beyond efficiency in the economic sense, which Louis Brandeis (1934, 51) defined as "greater production with less effort and at less cost, through the elimination of unnecessary waste, human and material." At the peak of the efficiency vogue, *efficiency* connoted modernity, organization, order, a scientific sensibility, and the other virtues associated with enlightened social control.

The late Progressive Era vogue for efficiency had roots in both the labor question and trust question. During the great industrial merger wave of 1895–1904, 1,800 major industrial firms were consolidated into 170 giant firms, and nearly half of the consolidated corporations controlled over 70 percent of their respective industries (Lamoreaux 1988, 1–2).[6] Was big business more efficient? The progressive economists answered with a resounding yes. As champions of efficiency, they also advocated making government more efficient by importing the modern management practices of big business.

Some historians have seen the progressives as inconsistent, simultaneously criticizing "business-made chaos" while scheming to "reorganize government along business lines" (Rodgers 1982, 126). The progressive economists, right or wrong, saw no inconsistency. In distinguishing the firm from the market, they distinguished managerial capitalism from market capitalism.

---

6. More than three-quarters of the mergers acquired a market share of more than 40 percent (Lamoreaux 1988, 2).

A large firm was a bureaucratic organization. When administered by expert managers applying scientific methods, the well-run firm was efficient, and its efficiency-enhancing techniques, moreover, could be applied to other forms of organization. A competitive market, in contrast, comprised many small firms and many customers. A competitive market was not an organization and could not be managed. Market decisions were decentralized and its outcomes were unplanned, and *this,* left progressives argued, was the source of economic disorder and waste.

Left progressive economists attacked the free market system, but they did not oppose greater industrial scale. On the contrary, they regarded the new consolidated enterprises as exemplary "islands of conscious power in an ocean of unconscious cooperation," which, unlike the small merchants and producers they were displacing, were more likely to be scientifically managed and efficient.[7] Cooperation, not competition, was the source of efficiency.

Expertise lay at the heart of this conception of business efficiency. Efficiency did not arise spontaneously with growth in the size of a business. Efficiency required scientific management. Indeed, large-scale enterprise became viable only after the visible hand of expert management proved more efficient than the invisible hand of market forces (Chandler 1977, 339).

Columbia University's Wesley Clair Mitchell (1874–1948), one of Thorstein Veblen's students and later founder of the National Bureau of Economic Research, made this distinction plain in his 1913 magnum opus, *Business Cycles.* Coordination *within* a firm was "the result of careful planning by experts," whereas coordination *among* independent firms was not planned at all—market orders arose spontaneously. Expert management, or coordination inside the firm, Mitchell said, yielded "economy," whereas market coordination among firms created "waste." Thus, the growth in the size of firms brought about by the great merger wave increased economic efficiency, because it increased the scope of expert management, the source of greater cost efficiency, while it reduced the waste of market exchange. In Mitchell's formulation, economic waste was not business made; it was market made.

Progressive economists regarded big business as a permanent feature of the new economic landscape. "It is useless to abuse and attack the trusts,"

---

7. Dennis Robertson (1923, 85) memorably described firms as "islands of conscious power in this ocean of unconscious cooperation, like lumps of butter coagulating in a pail of buttermilk."

John R. Commons said in a column titled "Opinions of New Yorkers" in the September 14, 1889, edition of the *New York Times*; the trusts must be discussed "from the viewpoint of inevitability." "The true line of policy," said Princeton's William F. Willoughby (1898, 94), "is to recognize that consolidation of industrial enterprises is inevitable." Commons and Willoughby were labor reformers, both of whom became president of the American Association for Labor Legislation, and they judged big business to be, on balance, good for workers (Willoughby 1898).

In fact, most progressive economists judged industrial consolidation as not only inevitable but also desirable. Greater size, they argued, reduced costs in two ways. Firms merged by vertical integration eliminated market-made waste, sometimes derided as "higgling of the market." No cost-increasing transactions with middlemen were required if Carnegie Steel mined its own coal and iron ore, and transported raw material to its mills using its own barges and railcars. Second, larger industrial scale (and access to lower-cost financing) provided factory workers with technically superior capital equipment, which increased labor productivity, lowering the per-unit cost of production. As Simon Patten concluded, the "combinations were much more efficient than were the small producers whom they displaced" (quoted in DiLorenzo 1985, 84).

Consolidation did more than reduce costs. It also promised higher revenues, insofar as it eliminated what Jeremiah Jenks (1901, 21) called "the wastes of competition," an idea shared by several progressive economists. Competition in industries with high fixed costs—paradigmatically, railroads—drove rival firms to set prices equal to their very low variable costs of production. Pricing at variable cost meant firms could not recover their fixed costs, thus selling at a loss, which injured profits and wages alike—a phenomenon called "ruinous" or "cutthroat" competition. The horizontal merging of formerly rival businesses reduced ruinous competition by raising prices high enough to recover full costs.[8] All in all, William F. Willoughby judged, the cost and price advantages of the consolidated firm meant that it ordinarily offered its workers better working conditions, increased safety, more regular hours, and higher wages.[9]

---

8. Alfred Chandler (1982, 366–67) finds that output prices in consolidated industries fell during the first two decades of the twentieth century. Horizontal combinations resulted in oligopoly, not monopoly, and the competition-reducing effects on price of horizontal combination was more than offset by the cost-reducing effects of manufacturing economies of scale.

9. William F. Willoughby (1898, 89) said, "The environment under which the laborers carry on their work is far superior in the larger establishments."

Progressive economists certainly were not apologists for big business. They worried about monopoly, which for them meant the consolidated firm's power to restrict output and charge consumers prices above full cost. Like most progressives, they feared the potential of big business to corrupt politics. And some, like John Bates Clark, believed that less competition in industry inhibited technological innovation. But progressives distinguished monopoly from size per se, and because of this, were not antimonopoly in the populist, small-proprietor sense of the term.

Indeed, the 1895–1904 decade of industrial consolidation goes some way toward explaining the puzzle of why, in 1905, William A. White could say "it is funny how we have all found the octopus," when, as Daniel Rodgers (1982, 124) puts it, "less than a decade earlier . . . his like had denied that animal's very existence." The consolidated industrial firm "discovered" by economic reformers circa 1905 was, in fact, a new beast. The market values of the new behemoths, exemplified by US Steel's initial capitalization of $1.4 billion in 1901, were one hundred, even one thousand, times larger than the largest American manufacturing enterprises of the 1870s.

The new industrial giants also organized themselves differently, increasingly adopting the corporate form. Outside of banking, transportation, and utilities, the business corporation had been rare before the 1890s. Only one manufacturing company was listed on the New York Stock Exchange in 1890 (Higgs 1991, 476–77). The decade of industrial consolidation also marked the advent of the industrial corporation.

The consolidated industrial corporation was, moreover, different from the animal conjured in the 1880s by western, agrarian populism, as represented by William Jennings Bryan. The Bryanite populists' antimonopolism, which continued an American political tradition dating back to Andrew Jackson, was more than a protest against the high rates that railroads charged shippers or banks charged farmers. Economic populism also opposed big business because of its competitive threat to small-scale enterprise, a small-is-good position that persisted in American antitrust law into the middle of the twentieth century. For the populists, size *was* monopoly. And though progressives and populists found common ground elsewhere, progressives generally rejected economic populism's defense of what they saw as inefficient and outmoded small producers and merchants.

On the question of trust policy, all three major presidential candidates in the 1912 election offered impeccable reform credentials. The Republican Taft administration had broken up Standard Oil and American

Tobacco, indeed had initiated more antitrust proceedings (in fewer years) than had Theodore Roosevelt, the "trustbuster" who was in 1912 heading the Progressive Party ticket. Woodrow Wilson, the New Jersey governor and Democratic Party nominee, was vigorously antitrust.

There were differences among progressives concerning trust policy. The leading strand of progressive business regulation, represented by Roosevelt, argued that big business should be regulated by big government, but not dismantled. Rooseveltian progressives imagined the federal government as a powerful, neutral defender of the public interest in securing the lower production costs provided by large scale, with vigorous regulation to ensure that the trusts did not abuse their pricing power or corrupt politics.

The aim of Rooseveltian antitrust was not to punish bigness but to punish bad behavior—unfair trade practices or corruption of politics. The job of antitrust regulation was to make big business good rather than to make it small. Rooseveltian progressives regarded breaking up the big firms as impractical and destructive of the efficiencies that large scale provided.

Richard T. Ely (1900, 213), for example, argued that naturally evolved big businesses were "a good thing, and it is a bad thing to break them up; from efforts of this kind, no good has come to the American people." Progressive political journalists used blunter language. Walter Lippmann (1914, 124), writing in *Drift and Mastery*, sneered at the small proprietor celebrated by populist antitrust:

> If the anti-trust people . . . [did] what they propose, they would be engaged in one of the most destructive agitations that America has known. They would be breaking up the beginning of collective organization, thwarting the possibility of cooperation, and insisting upon submitting industry to the wasteful, the planless scramble of little profiteers.

Lippmann's *New Republic* colleague, Herbert Croly (1909, 359), said that the small businessman should be "allowed to drown."

The barons of big business found such rhetoric congenial. They too invoked the language of cooperation, efficiency, and elimination of "ruinous competition" to defend their consolidated giants against government breakup. "The day of the combination is here to stay," John D. Rockefeller proclaimed, and "individualism has gone never to return" (Nevins 1959, 169).

Louis Brandeis represented the minority position that mainstream antitrust assailed, and, until he was appointed to the US Supreme Court in

1916, he had an influential client in President Wilson. Brandeis was skeptical about the greater efficiency said to obtain with large scale. The industrial giants were supplanting small business not with lower costs, he said, but with unfair practices. Brandeis also worried that the Rooseveltian approach might lead to business capture of its regulators, or worse. Leaving the behemoths intact, Brandeis warned, could enable rather than impede a plutocratic corruption of democracy.

Brandeis's condemnation of what he called "the curse of bigness" made him an outlier among economic reformers, a sophisticate with populist conclusions. Thomas McCraw (1984b, 94) aptly characterized Brandeis as less "the people's lawyer" than "the small businessman's lawyer." Brandeis (1934) was skeptical that Jeffersonian ends could ever safely be entrusted to the Hamiltonian means of Roosevelt and the other economic progressives who, in his view, uncritically placed their faith in the ongoing virtue and wisdom of big government.

Brandeis's skepticism that Hamiltonian means could reliably serve Jeffersonian ends was rare indeed among economic progressives. Most economic progressives were, like Herbert Croly, supremely confident that Hamiltonian means could be made to serve progressive ends, provided the "wise minority" was in the saddle.

5. Taylorism: Bible of the Efficiency Gospel

The bible of the 1910s gospel of efficiency was Frederick Winslow Taylor's international best seller, *The Principles of Scientific Management* (1911). A century later, scientific management, or *Taylorism*, ordinarily serves as a term of abuse. Taylorism is today most often associated with dehumanizing work practices, time and motion studies, a preoccupation with worker malingering, and the deskilling of labor. The Taylor system, on this reading, treated workers as mere cogs in the industrial machine.

But the original progressive economists and their reform allies regarded scientific management altogether differently. Taylor's program appealed to a great many American progressives, who saw in Taylorism a scientific method for improving workers' jobs and wages, and a system for making factory work and other forms of organization more efficient. Taylor's biographer rightly judged *The Principles of Scientific Management* "a progressive manifesto."[10]

10. Daniel Nelson, quoted in Kanigel 1997, 504.

Taylor's great champion was Louis Brandeis, who called Taylor a genius and made Taylor's national reputation by using scientific management theory to criticize the railroads in the *Eastern Rate* case of 1910. Brandeis, who represented the shippers opposed to the rate increase that the eastern railroads sought from the Interstate Commerce Commission, invoked Taylor to argue that railroads would not need higher rates if only they would manage their costs more efficiently, using the principles of scientific management. Brandeis's star witness, the efficiency expert Harrington Emerson, testified that the railroads were wasting about $22 million per day (in 2014 dollars) (Alexander 2008, 79).[11] "The coming *science of management* in this century," Brandeis gushed, marked "an advance comparable only to that made by the coming of the *machine* in the last" (quoted in Kanigel 1997, 504).

John R. Commons called scientific management "the most productive invention in the history of modern industry" (quoted in Haber 1964, 148). Commons (1921, 272) later claimed, after leading a platoon of Wisconsin graduate students through a study of thirty industrial firms, that capitalism could be cured, but only through the intervention of expert management. Theodore Roosevelt saw the efficiency gains from scientific management as a vital example of national conservation. Scientific management, said Roosevelt, "is the application of the conservation principle to production. . . . We couldn't ask more from a patriotic motive, than Scientific Management gives from a selfish one" (quoted in Gilbreth 1912, 2).

Muckraking journalists, who made their living treating business claims dubiously, piled on the Taylor bandwagon with alacrity. Ida Tarbell, who made her reputation with a damning critique of Standard Oil, referred to Taylor as a creative genius, telling her readers that "no man in history has made a larger contribution to . . . genuine cooperation and juster human relations" (quoted in Kanigel 1997, 104–5). Ray Stannard Baker, another leading muckraker, serialized Taylor's *Principles of Scientific Management* in his *American Magazine*, introducing it with a fawning profile of Taylor titled "The Gospel of Efficiency" (1911). Political journalists also embraced Taylorism; the *New Republic*'s Walter Lippmann, for example, told his readers that scientific management would "humanize work" (Haber 1964, 94).

Florence Kelley, like many leading progressives, joined the Taylor Society, which, during the 1920s, served as a refuge for future New Dealers

11. Emerson referred to Taylor's early paper "Shop Management" (1903) as "one of the most important papers ever published in the United States" (quoted in Gilbreth 1912, 6).

such as Rexford Tugwell and John Maurice Clark. Tugwell (1932), a member of Franklin D. Roosevelt's "Brains Trust," later said that "the greatest economic event of the nineteenth century occurred when Frederick W. Taylor first held a stop watch on the movements of a group of shovellers in the plant of the Midvale Steel Company" (quoted in Nyland 1996, 987). Taylor's disdain for "pre-scientific management," and the emphasis that Taylor's system placed on the technological aspects of production over the financial side of business, eventually won over Thorstein Veblen, originally a skeptic.

The superlatives showered on Taylor reveal how attracted progressives were to his vision of management by experts. Taylor offered them an irresistible package: efficiency, workplace harmony, and social justice, all realized via the expert application of science. A properly scientific approach to management, Taylor promised, one that brought system and scientific rigor to the heretofore prescientific and disorderly enterprise of running a factory, would not only increase production but also promote industrial peace and greater fairness. As Samuel Haber (1964, x) observed, efficiency in the 1910s promised more than increased production; it also promised social harmony and cooperation.

Scientific management represented itself as the product of science—the application of engineering methods to business management. Rather than follow arbitrary rules of thumb, the industrial engineer would, via observation and experiment, methodically determine optimal work techniques, scientifically discovering the "one best rule." It was, Taylor (1911, 65) said, a "science of shoveling." That the science in scientific management was far more applied than theoretical in emphasis only heightened its appeal to economic reformers.

Scientific management also promised to advance workplace fairness. When Taylor substituted scientific planning for what he saw as the arbitrary power of bosses (shop foremen), progressives hailed the substitution of the "leadership of the competent" for the leadership of the bosses (Haber 1964, x). Scientific management, said Herbert Croly, replaced "robber barons" with "industrial statesman," a term that captures the progressive faith in technocratic leadership while revealing something of what Croly meant by *industrial democracy* (quoted in Haber 1964, x).

"In the past," Taylor (1911, 7) declared, "the man has been first, in the future, the system must be first." Of course, claims about system notwithstanding, Taylor, like all planners, was not eliminating authority. He was merely relocating it, by placing real authority, especially the authority to hire and fire, with the firm's planning department. Taylor did indeed reduce the power of the shop-floor foremen, but he did so by giving it to the efficiency experts (Haber 1964, 25).

Greater harmony between labor and capital, Taylor promised, would come via two channels: one, better work techniques and increased monitoring of worker effort, and two, the conflict-reducing consequences of increased output. The former ultimately proved to be the undoing of Taylorism. Production workers resisted greater management monitoring of their work effort. Nor did they gratefully receive the tutelage of efficiency experts, with its presumption that, as one contemporary reviewer of Taylor put it, "the best method is the one the individual laborer cannot discover for himself, and hence it is the function of management to discover and apply it" (Jones 1911, 834).

When the Taylor system was installed at the Watertown (Massachusetts) Arsenal, workers staged a walkout and successfully petitioned the War Department for its removal (Drury 1915, 138–41). Taylor's governing premise—that more supervision and less autonomy would be welcomed by workers, if only the new authorities were scientifically trained experts rather than shop-floor foremen—was, in retrospect, preposterous, but it successfully flattered the technocratic prejudices of economic progressives.

Most alluringly, in an era with four new strikes called every day, the efficiency gains claimed by scientific management held out the prospect of reducing labor-management conflict. Increased industrial production, Taylor said, would make it possible for "both sides [to] take their eyes off the division of the surplus until this surplus becomes so large that it is unnecessary to quarrel over how it shall be divided" (quoted in Haber 1964, 27). Taylor believed that both workers and management wrongly regarded labor conflict as endemic to industrial capitalism, when, in fact, the true cause of labor conflict was the inefficiency of traditional production methods. Once higher wages and profits showed them that they shared the common enemy of inefficiency, workers and management, Taylor believed, would be induced to work cooperatively.

This last Taylorite notion—applied scientific knowledge, when imparted through improved structures of political and economic governance, would treat and even cure conflict—was at the core of American progressivism. As reformers rather than revolutionaries, progressives tended to regard industrial conflict not as the necessary outcome of incorrigibly opposed economic interests but as a preventable mistake caused by misapprehension of what those interests were—a mistake, moreover, that experts could perceive and remedy.

However much Taylor's claims read as hyperbole today, in the 1910s scientific management offered progressives an almost irresistible vision— a scientific, expert solution to the labor question. Factory work would be made more efficient and more humane. Workers' wages would be increased, and the new industrial giants would be governed not by profit-grubbing capitalists but by socially minded scientific experts.

6. Scientific Management of Humankind

Progressives enthusiastically and rapidly seized on industrial efficiency as an exemplar, imagining that scientific management could increase efficiency not just on the shop floors of factories but in all corners of an industrial society plagued by waste, conflict, and injustice. Following Brandeis's 1910 intervention on behalf of Taylor, a flood of reform volumes on efficiency appeared, preaching greater efficiency in government, in charity, in education, in medicine, in religion, in the home, and in human beings themselves. The times, argued the progressive sociologist Charles Horton Cooley, demanded nothing less than a "comprehensive 'scientific management' of mankind, to the end of better personal opportunity and social function in every possible line" (quoted in Quandt 1970, 139).

The idea of applying business planning methods to improve government enjoyed great currency among economic progressives, not least because government was their central agency of improvement. Many American cities established efficiency bureaus, spearheaded by New York City's Bureau of Municipal Research, which was cofounded in 1906 by Edwin R. A. Seligman, to promote, as its motto read, "the application of scientific principles to Government."[12] Its many publications bore the title "efficient citizenship." Milwaukee's city government established the Bureau of Economy and Efficiency in 1910 and tapped John R. Commons to run it. Carl Sandburg (1911), covering efficiency for *La Follette's Weekly Magazine*, ingenuously described Commons "as one of those rest-

---

12. This was the Bureau of Municipal Research motto inscribed on the cover of its publication, *Municipal Research*.

less, persistent geniuses of toil," whose work combating waste in Milwaukee was "blazing a way out of the civic wilderness."

The New York Bureau of Municipal Research was retained by other cities, as a kind of consultancy, to review the efficiency of their budgeting methods, operations, and finances. When, in 1911, the New York Bureau opened its Training School for Public Service, the first ever dedicated to training civil servants for the task of public administration, it recruited Taylor for lectures and required all its students to read his *Principles of Scientific Management* (Nyland 1996, 992). Commons likewise brought to Milwaukee nationally known scientific management gurus, experts such as Harrington Emerson, Brandeis's star witness in the *Eastern Rate* case.

The cause of making government more efficient gained impetus with its ever-expanding size and scope. A number of American cities replaced mayors with technocratic city managers, who promised not politics but management. Cities, like industrial firms, could be scientifically administered, provided partisanship and politics were successfully pushed to one side, as Frederic Howe claimed the state of Wisconsin had done.

State governments also founded efficiency bureaus, and President William Howard Taft created the United States Commission on Economy and Efficiency, which operated from 1910 to 1913. The Institute for Government Research, a proto–think tank chartered in 1916 (and in 1927 consolidated into the Brookings Institution), was founded by advocates of greater government efficiency.

President Taft imported as a commissioner Frederick D. Cleveland of the New York Bureau and also tapped the Princeton economist William F. Willoughby, president of the American Association for Labor Legislation and a leader of the progressive movement for more efficiency in government. Willoughby (1919, 4) held up administrative government as the way to achieve "the same standards of efficiency and honesty which are exacted in the general business world." Popularly controlled government was too "prone to financial extravagance" and no longer up to the rigors of governance now that government had entered nearly "every field of activity."

Willoughby argued, in the name of efficiency, that US government power should be consolidated under the executive branch. The American founders' separation-of-powers doctrine, which decentralized power by design, was just as obsolete as small shops and artisanal producers of the early nineteenth-century economy. Willoughby's contempt for constitutional checks and balances was widely shared among progressive political scientists of the day. Columbia's Charles Beard, who in 1915 was named director of the New York Bureau's Training School for Public Service, disparaged the separation of government powers as "the political science of negation" (quoted in Rodgers 1987, 182).

The new university discipline of political science, just beginning its emergence from social science departments, referred to the scientific study of improving government as public administration. Woodrow Wilson, long before entering politics in 1910, the beginning of the efficiency vogue, was a pioneering theorist of public administration, which sought to centralize and rationalize American government. "The field of administration," Wilson wrote in 1887, "is a field of business . . . removed from the hurry and strife of politics. . . . It is a part of political life only as the methods of the counting-house are part of the life of society; only as machinery is a part of the manufacture product" (209–10). Like its social control sibling in economics, public administration was technocratic in spirit. By professionalizing government service, experts insulated from politics could make public policy less partisan and more efficient.

In these respects, Wilson the academic was quintessentially progressive: he not only believed that a science of public administration could improve American government; he also believed that intellectuals do not merely serve the public interest but *lead* the public interest, by their superior ability to identify the social good.[13] Having been among the vanguard of professionalizing economists in the late 1880s and 1890s, Wilson also saw that laissez-faire politics was a bar to the disciplinary professionalization of political science, no less so than laissez-faire economics had been a bar to the professionalization of economic science. In this sense, Progressive Era political reform was of a piece with Progressive Era economic reform. Under the banner of efficiency, it moved real power from untrained partisans and bosses to expert administrators, regulatory bodies, and the executive branch (Eisenach 2006, viii–ix).

7. Right Progressive Views of Market Failure

Right progressive views of economic policy were informed by marginalist economics, a late nineteenth-century theoretical innovation led in America

13. Wilson, in the 1912 presidential election, presented himself as the people's champion, but his concept of democracy was, like the social controllers, limited. Stockton Axson, his brother-in-law, observed: "His instinct for democracy involved the idea that, because a democracy is free, it is the more necessary that it be led. His faith in the people has never been a faith in the supreme wisdom of the people, but rather in the capacity of the people to be led right by those whom they elect and constitute their leaders."

by John Bates Clark. *Marginalism* describes the views of economists who endorsed both marginal analysis of consumption (marginal utility) and of production (marginal productivity). Clark's marginal productivity theory, definitively gathered in his magnum opus, *The Distribution of Wealth*, postulated that properly competitive markets pay workers wages equal to the value of their contribution to output. When workers received wages worth less than the marginal worker's contribution to output, owing to a lack of competition or other market failure, they were exploited and deserved more.

When Clark argued that a wage equal to the value of marginal product was not only efficient but also just, his critics were many. His former student, Thorstein Veblen, derided Clark's theory as "neoclassical," an epithet meant to imply that marginalist economics was just laissez-faire dressed up in a new theoretical costume. But Clark (1890, 44) offered what rival progressive theories of wage determination did not, an analytically determinate answer to the vital question of whether workers were getting paid what they should: "to every man his product, his whole product, and nothing but his product."[14]

Clark's answer was also, at least in principle, measurable. Measure the value of the additional goods produced by the last worker hired, Clark said, and you knew what a fair wage was. Whatever the merits of Clark's distributive ethics, and they were vigorously disputed, other progressive conceptions of fair wages were embarrassingly vague, offering little guidance to wage investigators and regulators (Persky 2000). "We know," Clark (1894) could say of his competitive-wage standard, "at what we should aim."[15]

Clark's marginalism, moreover, theoretically connected labor markets to markets for goods—just as competitive prices were efficient in product markets, so too were competitive wages efficient in labor markets. When big business priced its products above the competitive price, it was both unfair and inefficient, just as it was unfair and inefficient when big business paid its workers wages below competitive levels. Clark's marginalist economics used the same general theory to address the labor question as well as the monopoly question.

Clark was naive in his hope that the public would seize on his conception of marginal-product wages as a natural solution to the labor question.

14. Clark's critics were legion, but nearly all missed one flaw in Clark's argument: even if it were true that wages were fair when they equaled the value of the worker's contribution to output, it did not follow that the distribution of productive ability among workers was also fair. That is, a fair wage did not entail a fair income distribution.

15. This is his presidential address to the AEA, "Modern Appeal to Legal Forces."

And his conservative critics, men like J. Lawrence Laughlin, were no less numerous than those, like Veblen, on the left. But economists gradually came to see the professional, political, and conceptual advantages in it.

Clark's marginal-productivity theory of wages was reformist without being radical; it offered, as Clark (1914, 5) had it, a "golden mean" between letting the state do nothing and having it do everything. It also offered a determinate and, in principle, measurable goal for wage regulation, all part of a general theory of price determination that applied to the labor market as well as the market for goods.[16] Politically, competitive wages also seemed to provide a compromise position between the slogan "more for labor" and the laissez-faire view that labor deserves whatever it gets.

No less than his left progressive colleagues, Clark's primary concern was that American economic arrangements be made ethically defensible (Homan 1927, 41). "The supreme question is a moral one," Clark (1912, 72) said plainly: "Is labor generally getting its due?" Clark also placed the expert economist at the heart of the regulatory system, for he believed that competitive wages and prices required state investigation and regulation. The economic expert was required to determine whether big business was engaging in anticompetitive practices, be it collusion to fix prices, predation to drive out competitors, or contracts to bar customers from dealing with its rivals. Experts would also be needed to ensure that the tariff was not so high as to create monopoly and to ascertain whether and when big business was pricing its goods above competitive levels or paying its workers less than competitive wages.

Moreover, Veblen's epithet of "neoclassical" notwithstanding, Clark did not share his classical predecessors' thoroughgoing skepticism about government's willingness and competence to enact successful economic regulation. "We are dependent on action by the state for results and prospects which we formerly secured without it," Clark (1907, 380) made clear. "Though we are forced to ride roughshod over *laissez-faire* theories, we do so in order to gain the end which those theories had in view, namely, a system actuated by the vivifying power of competition, with all that that signifies of present and future good" (380).

Clark was quintessentially progressive in his belief that the expert economist could identify what was socially good, could accurately measure departures from competitive prices, could successfully determine

16. In Mary Furner's terminology, Clark was more a corporate liberal than democratic statist. See Furner 1990.

fair wages independent of the representatives of labor and industry, could monitor and enforce regulatory compliance, all the while maintaining a single-minded focus on the social good and an Olympian objectivity unsullied by bias, capture by regulated parties, or systematic error.

8. Conclusion

If I have too starkly dichotomized left and right progressive conceptions of economic expertise, it is in order to illuminate subtle but historically important differences, not to imply that Progressive Era boundaries of left and right were fixed among the progressive economists. Ideological boundaries were fluid, and economic theory was plural. Moreover, both shifted with changing economic and political conditions, and with the changing vocational opportunities for expert economists serving the state.

All this said, I find the left and right progressive heuristic useful. Though space precludes elaboration, it helps us, for example, understand American economics before the Second World War as contingent, shifting professional alliances organized around these rival but overlapping views of what the administrative state can and should do in commercial life. Institutionalist economics (Rutherford, this issue) carried forward much of the left-progressive program, and neoclassical economics carried forward much of the right-progressive program.

During the Progressive Era, left and right progressives regularly found common ground, as they did in the American Association for Labor Legislation (AALL), a "child of the AEA" formed in 1905. The AALL featured social gospel firebrands like Richard T. Ely and John R. Commons, and was run by several of Commons's protégés, while also enlisting men such as AALL cofounder Henry Farnam; Yale's Irving Fisher, sixth AALL president; and Harvard's Frank Taussig, a longtime affiliate. The AALL's major campaigns successfully fought to eliminate industrial hazards such as phosphorous poisoning of match workers, to compensate workers injured in industrial accidents, and to fix minimum wages. Fisher led the AALL's unsuccessful campaign to compel government provision of health insurance.

At other times, left and right progressives moved apart. Clark's right progressive conception of economic policy as policing and remedying market failures was too circumscribed for many left progressives, especially for those who regarded economic competition as more destructive than vivifying. Equally important, recurring catastrophe in the first half of the twentieth century—notably two world wars, the Dust Bowl, and two economic depressions, one Great and one small—created new vocational opportunities. War and economic crisis have invariably enlarged the size, scope, and influence of the fourth branch and of economists who advise and staff it.

Mobilization for the First World War offered left progressives the chance to pursue their grander, more statist schemes of intervention, and they seized it. The US War Industries Board (WIB) introduced Americans to scientific management methods applied by the government to the entire economy; it coordinated most government purchasing, determined the allocation of economic resources, established priorities in output, restricted the alcohol trade (a dress rehearsal for Prohibition), and fixed prices on commodities in over sixty industries (Fogel et al. 2013). The chief of the WIB's Central Bureau of Planning and Statistics was the economist Edwin F. Gay, dean of the Harvard Graduate School of Business Administration and a former president of the Massachusetts branch of the AALL. Gay was a champion of Taylorism who once described scientific management as "the most important advance in industry since the introduction of the factory system and power machinery."[17]

Gay and other economists, notably his friend Wesley Clair Mitchell, who ultimately directed the WIB's Price Division, put their scientific management ideas into government practice, first, by gathering and systematizing economic information (Cuff 1989). Mitchell's Price Division, for example, produced an immense study of American wholesale prices, data crucial for directing wartime production from Washington.

When Grosvenor Clarkson, WIB member and historian, called the WIB an "industrial dictatorship," he exaggerated, but for the purposes of paying a compliment, namely, that the WIB established that the "whole productive and distributive machinery of America could be directed successfully from Washington (quoted in McGerr 2003, 287, 285). Economic mobilization for war was, in Clarkson's characterization, "a story of the conversion of one hundred million combatively individualistic people into a vast cooperative effort in which the good of the unit was sacrificed to the good of the whole." In appraising the advantages that war collectivism provided to the progressive movement, Clarkson volunteered that they "almost [made] war appear a blessing instead of a curse" (quoted in McGerr 2003, 299).[18]

---

17. Quoted in the *American Magazine* (1911, 563).
18. My discussion of the WIB is indebted to McGerr 2003, especially pages 283–99.

The WIB's success at war mobilization affirmed the progressive faith in expertise and legitimized the idea of scientific management applied to the entire economy. John Dewey, for one, believed that the success of war collectivism was the most important result of the First World War. It demonstrated, Dewey said, that expert central planners could direct a vast economy from Washington. In but a few months, Dewey ([1918] 1929a, 517) wrote, "the economists and businessmen called to the industrial front" had done more to demonstrate the practicability of social control than had a generation of "professional Socialists." The great success of American wartime economic planning, Dewey ([1918] 1929b, 557) said, was a "revolution" in economics, impossible to ignore.

President Wilson saw it differently and dismantled most of the economic planning apparatus. More statist regulation would have to await the New Deal. But the fourth branch remained, in state governments and in the US government, newly (and permanently) fortified by the wartime tax regime. Even after demobilization, federal spending, adjusted for inflation, was nearly triple its prewar levels.[19]

If American economists were not yet the "real philosophers of social life" Edwin R. A. Seligman had dared to portray them as in 1902, they had successfully seized the professional opportunity presented by the demands of war and reconstruction, and consolidated while expanding their new national role as expert advisers and policymakers. Wesley Clair Mitchell (1924, 33), reflecting in 1924, observed that the Great War had restored to "economic theory the vitality it had after the Napoleonic wars." The First World War had been a global catastrophe in countless ways, but it proved to be a boon for American economic expertise in the service of the state.

References

Addams, Jane. 1910. "Charity and Social Justice." *North American Review* 192 (656): 68–81.

Alexander, Jennifer Karns. 2008. *The Mantra of Efficiency: From Waterwheel to Social Control*. Baltimore: Johns Hopkins University Press.

Brandeis, Louis D. 1934. *The Curse of Bigness: Miscellaneous Papers of Louis D. Brandeis*. Edited by Osmond K. Fraenkel. New York: Viking.

Chandler, Alfred. 1977. *The Visible Hand*. Cambridge, Mass.: Belknap Press of Harvard University Press.

19. In 1914 US government expenditures were $735 million. In 1922 they were $3,324 million. Adjusted for inflation (about 58 percent [1914–22]), US government spending nearly tripled. See *US Historical Statistics*, Series P 99–108, Series L 1–14.

Clark, John Bates. 1890. "The Law of Wages and Interest." *Annals of the American Academy of Political and Social Science* 1 (1): 43–65.

———. 1894. "Modern Appeal to Legal Forces in Economic Life." *Publications of the American Economic Association* 9 (5–6): 9–30.

———. 1907. *Essentials of Economic Theory*. New York: Macmillan.

———. 1912. "The Federal Commission on Industrial Relations: Why It Is Needed." In *Proceedings of the Academy of Political Science, Vol. II, 1911–12*, 71–74. New York: Columbia University.

———. 1914. *Social Justice without Socialism*. Boston: Houghton Mifflin.

Commons, John R. 1921. *Industrial Government*. New York: Macmillan.

Croly, Herbert. 1909. *The Promise of American Life*. New York: Macmillan.

Cuff, Robert. 1989. "Creating Control Systems: Edwin F. Gay and the Central Bureau of Planning and Statistics, 1917–19." *Business History Review* 63:588–613.

Dewey, John. (1918) 1929a. "Propaganda." In *Characters and Events: Popular Essays in Social and Political Philosophy*, edited by Joseph Ratner, 2. New York: Henry Holt.

———. (1918) 1929b. "The Social Possibilities of War." In *Characters and Events: Popular Essays in Social and Political Philosophy*, edited by Joseph Ratner, 2. New York: Henry Holt.

DiLorenzo, Thomas J. 1985. "The Origins of Antitrust: An Interest-Group Perspective." *International Review of Law and Economics* 5 (1): 73–90.

Drury, Horace B. 1915. "Scientific Management: A History and Criticism." PhD diss., Columbia University.

Eisenach, Eldon, ed. 2006. *The Social and Political Thought of American Progressivism*. Indianapolis, Ind.: Hackett.

Ely, Richard T. 1889. *Introduction to Political Economy*. New York: Chautauqua.

———. 1900. *Monopolies and Trusts*. New York: Macmillan.

Fogel, Robert William, Enid M. Fogel, Mark Guglielmo, and Nathaniel Grotte. 2013. *Political Arithmetic: Simon Kuznets and the Empirical Tradition in Economics*. Chicago: University of Chicago Press.

Furner, Mary. 1990. "Knowing Capitalism: Public Investigation and the Labor Question in the Long Progressive Era." In *The State and Economic Knowledge: The American and British Experiences*, edited by Mary O. Furner and Barry E. Supple, 241–86. Cambridge: Cambridge University Press.

Gilbreth, Frank. 1912. *Primer on Scientific Management*. New York: D. Van Nostrand.

Haber, Samuel. 1964. *Efficiency and Uplift: Scientific Management in the Progressive Era, 1890–1920*. Chicago: University of Chicago Press.

———. 1988. "Efficiency." In *Historical Dictionary of the Progressive Era, 1890–1920*, edited by John D. Buenker and Edward R. Kantorovich, 130–31. Westport, Conn.: Greenwood Press.

Hadley, Arthur T. 1899. "The Relation between Economics and Politics." *Yale Law Journal* 8 (4): 194–206.

———. 1900. "Economic Theory and Political Morality." *Publications of the American Economic Association*, 3rd ser., 1 (1): 45–61.

Higgs, Robert. 1991. "Origins of the Corporate Liberal State." *Critical Review: A Journal of Politics and Society* 5 (4): 475–95.

Homan, Paul T. 1927. *Contemporary Economic Thought*. New York: Harper.

Jenks, Jeremiah W. 1901. *The Trust Problem*. New York: McClure, Phillips & Co.

Jones, Edward D. 1911. Review article. *American Economic Review* 1 (4): 833–36.

Kanigel, Robert. 1997. *The One Best Way*. New York: Viking.

Lamoreaux, Naomi R. 1988. *The Great Merger Movement in American Business, 1895–1904*. Cambridge: Cambridge University Press.

Leonard, Thomas C. 2003. "'A Certain Rude Honesty': John Bates Clark as a Pioneering Neoclassical Economist." *History of Political Economy* 35 (3): 521–58.

Lippmann, Walter. 1914. *Drift and Mastery: An Attempt to Diagnose the Current Unrest*. New York: Mitchell Kennerly.

McCraw, Thomas. 1984a. "Business and Government: The Origins of the Adversary Relationship." *California Management Review* 26 (2): 33–52.

———. 1984b. *Prophets of Regulation: Charles Francis Adams, Louis D. Brandeis, James M. Landis, Alfred E. Kahn*. Cambridge, Mass.: Harvard University Press.

McGerr, Michael. 2003. *A Fierce Discontent: The Rise and Fall of the Progressive Movement in America, 1870–1920*. New York: Free Press.

Medema, Steven G. 2007. "The Hesitant Hand: Mill, Sidgwick, and the Evolution of the Theory of Market Failure." *History of Political Economy* 39 (3): 331–58.

Menand, Louis. 2001. *The Metaphysical Club*. New York: Farrar, Straus and Giroux.

Mill, John Stuart. 1848. *Principles of Political Economy, with Some of Their Applications to Social Philosophy*. Vol. 2. London: John W. Parker.

Mitchell, Wesley Clair. 1924. "The Prospects of Economics." In *The Trend of Economics*, edited by Rexford Tugwell, 3–34. New York: Knopf.

Moss, David. 1996. *Socializing Security: Progressive-Era Economists and the Origins of American Social Policy*. Cambridge, Mass.: Harvard University Press.

Nevins, Allan. 1959. *John D. Rockefeller*. New York: Scribner.

Nyland, Chris. 1996. "Taylorism, John R. Commons, and the Hoxie Report." *Journal of Economic Issues* 30 (4): 985–1016.

Persky, Joseph. 2000. "The Neoclassical Advent: American Economics at the Dawn of the 20th Century." *Journal of Economic Perspectives* 14 (1): 95–108.

Quandt, Jean B. 1970. *From the Small Town to the Great Community: The Social Thought of Progressive Intellectuals*. New Brunswick, N.J.: Rutgers University Press.

Robertson, Dennis. 1923. *Control of Industry*. New York: Harcourt, Brace.

Rodgers, Daniel T. 1982. "In Search of Progressivism." *Reviews in American History* 10 (4): 113–32.

———. 1987. *Contested Truths: Keywords in American Politics since Independence*. New York: Basic Books.

Ross, Dorothy. "American Social Science and the Idea of Progress." In *The Authority of Experts*, edited by Thomas L. Haskell, 157–75. Bloomington: Indiana University Press.

Sandburg, Carl. 1911. "Making the City Efficient." *La Follette's Weekly Magazine*, September 11, 6–7, 14–15.

Seligman, Edwin R. A. 1903. "Economics and Social Progress." *Publications of the American Economic Association*, 3rd ser., 4 (1): 52–70.

Skocpol, Theda. 1992. *Protecting Soldiers and Mothers: The Political Origins of Social Policy in the United States*. Cambridge, Mass.: Belknap Press of Harvard University Press.

Sumner, Helen. 1910. "The Historical Development of Women's Work in the United States." *Proceedings of the Academy of Political Science in the City of New York* 1 (1): 11–26.

Taylor, Frederick Winslow. 1911. *Principles of Scientific Management*. New York: Harper.

Tugwell, R. G. 1932. "The Principle of Planning and the Institution of Laissez-Faire." *American Economic Review* 2:75–92.

Walker, Francis Amasa. 1889. "The Recent Progress of Political Economy in the United States." In *Report of the Proceedings of the American Economic Association*, 17–40.

Wiebe, Robert. 1967. *The Search for Order, 1877–1920*. New York: Hill and Wang.

Willoughby, William F. 1898. "The Concentration of Industry in the United States." *Yale Review*, o.s., 7:72–92.

———. 1919. "The Modern Movement for Efficiency in the Administration of Public Affairs." Introduction to *Organized Efforts for the Improvement of Methods of Administration in the United States*, by Gustavus Adolphus Weber. New York: D. Appleton.

Wilson, Woodrow. 1887. "The Study of Public Administration." *Political Science Quarterly* 2 (June): 197–222.

Institutionalism and the Social Control of Business

Malcolm Rutherford

Institutional economics occupied an important place in American economics from 1918 until the Second World War and after, although in a more marginalized position (Rutherford 2011). Institutionalism clearly embodied and carried forward many ideas previously developed in the Progressive period by writers such as R. T. Ely and H. C. Adams, writers classified as "left progressives" by Thomas C. Leonard in his essay in this volume. The themes of social control and of the administrative state were, if anything, even more apparent in the institutionalist literature than in the work of the earlier progressives, one of the paradigm texts within institutionalism being J. M. Clark's *Social Control of Business* (1926).[1]

Clark's specific reference to *business* as the object of social control is significant and relates to the particular influence of Thorstein Veblen on institutionalist thinking. Veblen characterized the economic system of America in the early 1900s as a system of business or pecuniary institutions. Business institutions include firms and markets and the surrounding legal institutions of property rights. In Veblen's (1904) view the business firm had undergone significant development in the recent past, because of the introduction of new large-scale technology, the development of new methods of corporate finance, and the growth of the

Correspondence may be addressed to Malcolm Rutherford, Department of Economics, University of Victoria, Victoria, BC, P.O. Box 1700, Canada V8W 2Y2; e-mail: rutherfo@uvic.ca.
    1. The first edition of this book was published in 1926, a second in 1939.

History of Political Economy 47 (annual suppl.) DOI 10.1215/00182702-3130451

methods of salesmanship and advertising. The point that Veblen and the institutionalists made was that the activities of business firms were no longer adequately controlled by the existing institutions of the market. In Adam Smith's world the activities of businesses were to be channeled in the direction of the social advantage through the action of competitive markets with relatively little additional regulation. But for institutionalists, businesses had developed new methods of profit making, had increased in scale, and could manipulate consumer wants. At best, Smith's ideas applied only to an economy of "petty trade" and could not provide an adequate foundation for the understanding and control of large-scale industry and "big business." As Walton Hamilton (1932, 593) expressed it, "The fundamental issue stands out in clear cut relief": there is a lack of harmony between the technology of industry and the form of its organization and control. "An economic order in which the productive processes belong to big business and the arrangements for its control to petty trade cannot abide." The task is to "devise a scheme adequate to the direction of great industry. In a world of change a society cannot live on a wisdom borrowed from our fathers."

Institutionalists did not use the terminology of market failure, but in the many references to the need for new methods for the social control of business, there is the clear implication that the existing institutions of the market are inadequate to the task of guiding business activity in socially desirable directions. In this broad sense, institutionalists found market failure to be widespread, in fact *endemic* to the existing system of business. However, in their analysis institutionalists did not use the competitive model as a standard, as a way to judge departures from an ideal, as that particular ideal was seen as no longer applicable or relevant. For example, in a 1940 work on competition, Clark attempts to define a practical policy objective of "workable competition" to replace the perfectly competitive ideal.

Institutionalist discussion thus takes place in a framework of identifying "economic problems" and possible policy solutions without specifying an ultimate ideal state. Institutionalists adopt a pragmatic position wherein the attempt to achieve some end in view (solve a specific problem situation) will lead over time to the improved specification of ends as well as means. The approach taken is problem centered, instrumental, and pragmatic, with the idea of the discipline of economics as engaged in an ongoing process of investigation and problem solving. Hamilton talked about teaching "the art of handling problems" and of attempting to produce students who could make "contributions to an intelligent direction of social change" (quoted in Rutherford 2011, 153). This is to be the role of the economist as expert investigator and policy adviser. However, there is a clear recognition that the world is complex, evolving, and far from completely understood. This viewpoint did not stop institutionalists from making policy recommendations. Policies are to be regarded as experiments and subject to appraisal on the basis of the results of attempting to implement them. Done carefully, such experiments will themselves add to knowledge about how the world works. Even Wesley Mitchell (1923, 18), who was relatively cautious about giving explicit policy advice, argued that "social progress" could be gained through "wise policy experiment":

If we never act in social matters until we have perfect assurance regarding the consequences which will follow, we shall never act at all. Social experimentation, based on clearly thought-out hypotheses and accompanied by careful record-keeping, is one of the essential processes in increasing social knowledge and gaining social control.

What, then, were the major problems with business that required new methods of social control to be experimented with? Over the length of the period considered here, there were certainly changes in the specific problems identified. Walton Hamilton's *Current Economic Problems* (1919) includes the problems of business cycles, war, international trade, railway regulation, monopoly, immigration, economic insecurity, unionism and industrial conflict, and control within industry. J. M. Clark in the first edition of his *Social Control of Business* focuses on microeconomic issues and takes as his example of "one major field" for social control the problem of public utilities and trusts. In the second edition (1939), Clark, in reaction to the Great Depression, introduces a whole new section: "The New Era: Depression and Comprehensive Control." K. William Kapp's *Social Costs of Private Enterprise* (1950) introduces the consideration of the problems of air and water pollution, but in the context of a broad notion of social cost that explicitly relates back to the work of Veblen and Clark.[2]

Despite the length and breadth of the institutionalist literature, and the variety of specific problems considered, a number of general themes stand out. First, there are consumption decisions, particularly with respect to

2. In 1937 Kapp received a fellowship from the Frankfurt school, then located at Columbia University as the Institute for Social Research. While in the United States, Kapp was influenced greatly by Veblen and J. M. Clark. The second edition of Kapp's book on social costs was called *The Social Costs of Business Enterprise* (1963) to indicate his debt to Veblen and to the institutionalists. See the essay by Sebastian Berger in this volume.

problems relating to advertising, status goods, and a lack of information. Second, there are arguments about the idea that economic control through business institutions often leads to waste; that business organization does *not* necessarily result in maximum productive efficiency; and that making money is not necessarily the same thing as making useful goods. Business institutions are also linked to waste in the form of business cycles and related problems of unemployment. Third, some forms of competition can be wasteful or damaging, for example, arms-race types of competition. Competition can result in a race to the bottom in terms of wages and working conditions, and under certain circumstances competition can result in a disorderly rather than an orderly industry. Fourth, private business often succeeds through a strategy of shifting costs onto other people, workers, or whole communities. This came to include environmental externalities, but was always defined in broader terms. Fifth, there are many things of social benefit that private business will not provide or will underprovide, particularly in the realm of education, science, and technology. These themes recur throughout the institutionalist literature considered here, from Veblen to Kapp, and are remarkably consistent. They all concern questions of the efficiency of business and markets in the allocation and use of resources, but each also has an ethical dimension, particularly in regard to the distributional and social justice consequences (both intra- and intergenerational) of the operation of the system.

Consumer Valuations

The institutionalist view of the consumer is one that emphasizes the consumer's computational constraints, limited information, and the significance of business advertising and sales effort in molding consumer preferences. One key line of argument starts from Veblen's (1898) critique of the hedonistic view of humankind, of individuals with given utility functions nicely calculating pleasures and pains. For Veblen, the individual is best conceived of as a bundle of habits and propensities, rather than as a utility maximizer. Consumption habits are affected by social consumption norms, comparison with others, and by advertising and salesmanship (Veblen 1899). Veblen, however, simply substitutes his psychology of propensity and habit for utility maximization. A more logical criticism is provided by J. M. Clark. Clark argues that decision making requires effort and is therefore costly. A "good hedonist" should take account of these decision costs, but this in turn creates further informational and decision-making costs with the result that perfect optimization would be impossible. Clark's (1918, 25) "good hedonist" would "stop calculating when it seemed likely to involve more trouble than it was worth, and, as he could not in the nature of the case tell just when this point has been reached, he would make no claim to exactness for his results." Like Veblen, Clark took this to mean that consumption decisions would be based largely on habits and social norms. Custom and habit are methods of economizing on decision costs and may embody the results of deliberation and previous experience. However, habits and customs are "quasi-static" and slow down the responses of consumers to changes in prices or quality. In a rapidly changing world, habit and custom can be quickly outmoded, becoming a poor guide for decision making (124).[3]

A second line of argument focuses more specifically on informational problems in the making of consumption decisions. In a modern economy a consumer is faced with a vast array of goods to choose between, a lack of information on the exact characteristics of many of these goods, and a difficulty in estimating the contribution any item might make to household welfare. Many of these issues appear in Wesley Mitchell's famous essay "The Backward Art of Spending Money" (1912). For Mitchell, consumption activity is beset with problems including a pervasive lack of reliable information available to the consumer, the constraints on specialization within the household, the importance of nonpecuniary values to household decision making, and the lack of a well-defined or measurable household objective function. In this way, Mitchell presents the household task of spending money as undeveloped or "backward" when compared with the business task of making money. Mitchell's essay anticipated a huge literature developed in the 1920s and 1930s on ways to "improve buying" including consumer protection through law, such as pure food and drug laws and truth in advertising laws, standardization of measures, impartial testing agencies, and consumer education (Kyrk 1933). Honest labeling, truth in advertising, and impartial testing of goods "are all appropriate objects of state policy" (Clark 1926, 177).[4]

Institutionalists from Veblen on have also shown a concern with the role of business advertising and salesmanship in shaping preferences. In Veblen's (1904, 55) view, advertising attempts to establish a differential

3. In line with this stress on the role of social norms and habits, the empirical work on consumption done by institutionalists in the 1920s and 1930s was designed to investigate the conventional "standard of living" of various different social groups (Kyrk 1923; McMahon 1925; Peixotto 1927).

4. This line of argument implies a market failure in the provision of reliable information to consumers, consumer-information-sharing aspects of a public good, and the need for intervention in the form of provision of information and consumer protections.

monopoly based on "popular conviction" and seeks to divert expenditure from one business to another. Most advertising is competitive in nature and has the characteristics of an arms race. Competitive advertising is indispensable to individual business concerns, as they will lose market share if they do not advertise, so all firms must engage in advertising if only to counteract the advertising of their rivals. In addition, Veblen (1904, 56–57) emphasizes the tendency of advertising to be deceptive and misleading—his primary example being such goods as patent medicines—and he talks of the "organized fabrication of popular convictions." As most advertising has little or no genuine informational content, it has little or no value to the community at large, and Veblen sees it as misinforming rather than informing consumer choice and wasteful from a social point of view.[5]

In later works Veblen highlights the massive increase in the resources allocated to packaging and other forms of sales efforts. These expenditures on publicity and salesmanship result in what Veblen (1923, 305) calls the "quantity production of consumers" for the goods in question. These ideas of business advertising and sales efforts creating consumers and markets, and undermining of the concept of consumer sovereignty, is also found in the work of J. M. Clark, Kapp, and J. K. Galbraith. Clark (1918, 20) points out that the standard welfare analysis assumes that "demand should be independent of anything producers do, except the making of goods and the fixing of prices." Business, however, does not take the consumer's aims as given but seeks to guide them into particular channels. Furthermore, the guidance of choice is a significant economic activity and one that "cannot be regarded as itself guided by formed scales of choices" (23). Thus, the "maximum gratification of existing wants" is "meaningless" as a standard to judge a system in which resources are being devoted to the guidance of those wants (166). Kapp (1963, 245) argues that advertising that stimulates compulsive and nonrational behavior through deceit and half-truths is a "denial of the integrity of the individual." Galbraith (1967) presents what he calls the "revised sequence" of firms managing consumer preferences. In this revised sequence the consumer's satisfactions are subject to manipulation, and the traditional welfare implications assigned to the consumer's choices are undermined. Ironically, one of the best examples of the creation of a market through advertising, De Beers's development of the market for expensive diamond

---

5. Veblen does allow that advertising may contain useful information for consumers, but argues that most advertising has only slight informational benefit.

engagement rings, was itself deeply informed by Veblen's analysis of conspicuous consumption, emulation, and status goods (Epstein 1982).

Finally, an important part of Veblen's (1899, 30) analysis of consumption points to the significance of a propensity to emulation and invidious comparison. Although each social group has its own conventional standard of living, individuals are concerned with their relative standing in society, and in the modern world that means relative standing in pecuniary terms. What this means is that there is a tendency to "conspicuous consumption" in order to display relative standing. Consumption activity has a signaling function. Such conspicuous display may be engaged in by those of high pecuniary standing or by those wishing to appear to have such standing. Conspicuous consumption clearly has utility for the individuals undertaking it and will be happily catered to, and promoted, by business enterprises, but, in Veblen's (1899, 97–101) view, has no social value and can be characterized as wasteful. Veblen's argument here is based on an ethical judgment that ostentatious display is not a socially worthy end or a use of resources that enhances "life and well-being on the whole" (98). This implies that, even in the absence of advertising or outside manipulation of preferences, not all consumer wants are deserving of the same status as legitimate ends for productive activity. Left to its own devices, business will devote resources to the production of whatever consumers demand regardless of such considerations.

Wastes of Business Enterprise

The concept of waste and an abiding concern with efficiency was a central element in the progressive literature. This was given an important additional dimension as a result of the experience of production during the First World War. Physical production rose sharply and the standard of living for the "underlying" civilian population rose, despite the diversion of so many men into the armed forces. Stuart Chase (1925) noted the 25 to 30 percent increase in physical output over the prewar level, a performance attributed to wartime planning, standardization, and prioritization of production of necessities. This seemed to imply that normal peacetime business was wasteful of productive resources. Chase argued that there were four main channels of waste: (1) waste in consumption including military goods, speculation, adulteration, vice, quackery, superluxuries, fashion, and advertising; (2) waste of workforce because of unemployment, industrial disputes, preventable accident and sickness, and idleness;

(3) waste in production and distribution because of a failure to use the best management and engineering practice, lack of coordination, duplication, restriction of output, and excessive selling costs; and (4) waste of natural resources, particularly in the cases of oil, timber, and soil, stemming from ignorance and a short-sighted pursuit of present profit. There was also a significant amount of attention given to the common pool problems in the oil industry in Texas and California (Chase 1925, 247–52; Stocking 1925). In some of these cases the problem is traced to lack of information or a failure to use modern "scientific" methods of management.

The progressive interest in scientific management has been noted in Leonard's essay in this volume, and this carries over to some extent, but in the institutionalist literature it is more often assumed that businesses have indeed employed efficiency experts or engineers (Veblen 1904). The waste associated with the business control of industry is presented as a systemic issue that stems from conducting business for profit, and profit seeking by individual firms may not be consistent with efficient production or over-all coordination. Making money does not necessarily directly translate into making goods (Mitchell [1923] 1950). These are issues that stand apart from the usual discussions of externalities, although one can find a number of them discussed under the broader heading of "social costs," most notably by Kapp (1950, 1963).

The main issues discussed by Veblen (1921, 108) under the heading of waste include not only the "production of superfluities and spurious goods" and the costs of advertising and salesmanship (including multiplication of shops, sales agents, advertising, fancy packaging, multiplication of brands, and adulteration of goods) but also the "systematic dislocation, sabotage and duplication" because of business strategy, and chronic unemployment of men and other resources because of business restriction of output under-taken to maintain profitable prices in the face of vast increases in produc-tivity. Thus, Veblen's arguments about business waste do not relate to lack of information or technique among businesspeople but to the financial incentives facing them under modern market conditions.

As noted above, Veblen argues that the resources devoted to sales effort, such as competitive advertising, excessive packaging, and so on, represent a waste. Businesses in these fields are seen by Veblen (1923, 302–3) as competitors in a closed market, "from which it follows that any device or expedient which approves itself as a practicable means of cutting into the market, on the part of any one of the competitive concerns, pres-ently becomes a necessity to all the rest on pain of extinction," a situation that would now be analyzed in terms of a prisoner's dilemma leading to a jointly and socially suboptimal outcome.

In addition to this, Veblen conceives of many other aspects of business enterprise as a strategic game. A business can seek to profit by inflicting damage on a rival, possibly by building duplicate facilities, by following predatory pricing strategies, or by attempting in other ways to obstruct or interfere with a rival's normal business activity. Business strategy is commonly "a struggle between rival business men," and the outcome often depends on "which side can inflict or endure the greater pecuniary damage" (Veblen 1904, 32). Much of this relates to attempts to create business coalitions and mergers. The tools of corporation finance are a key element in this, but the ready availability of equity markets and credit instruments gives rise to further opportunities for manipulation, predation, and the search for "free income" (166–76; Veblen 1919, 63–84).

Veblen was an early expositor of the problems of insider dealing, financial manipulation (manipulation of information and stock prices), conflicts of interest between the various classes of equity holders and bondholders, and the fact that the group of owners in control of a corporation may have only a transitory interest in the company and not in the company as a going concern (Veblen 1904, 174–76). Veblen was reacting to the activities of people such as Jay Gould, Andrew Carnegie, and J. P. Morgan, but he anticipates some of the less attractive aspects of the activities of present-day finance houses and private equity firms. In the 1920s and 1930s people such as Veblen (1923), W. Z. Ripley (1927), and Adolf Berle and Gardiner Means (1932) gave a great deal of attention to conflicts of interest between ordinary shareholders and those in control of the corporation, the lack of information given to shareholders, the inadequacy of published corporate accounts, and the opportunities for speculation, insider dealing, and outright fraud. J. M. Clark points out that the corporation provides many opportunities for abuse. Members of the corporation need "protection against each other," and small investors may have poor information about what they are buying with shares of stock. The relation is one of "trusteeship," and chances to make money at the expense of the company are "varied and tempting" (Clark 1926, 175–76). In the aftermath of the 1929 crash, concerns such as these resulted in the Securities Act of 1933 and the establishment of the Securities and Exchange Commission.

Further to this, Veblen analyzed the incentives for firms to use debt financing to trade on a thinner equity, despite the greater risks involved, and the increasingly common practice of issuing equity on the basis of intangible assets that are difficult to value and subject to significant and rapid fluctuation. Such developments were part of the expansion of debt and equity markets in the early 1900s. In Veblen's view these practices worked to increase the fragility of the economy. Veblen's (1904, 112–14) analysis of business cycles runs largely in terms of extensions of debt financing, based on expected earnings and made during an upswing, eventually becoming out of line with realized earnings, resulting in bankruptcies and liquidations.

Several aspects of Veblen's discussions of cycles were taken over by Wesley Mitchell. For Mitchell (1913, 1927), the problem of cycles emerges in the institutional context of developed business and financial institutions, hence the name "business cycle." Individual firms planned their own activities, but the economy as a whole was unplanned, resulting in cycles being generated from the profit-seeking activities of businesses, the procyclical behavior of banks, and various leads and lags in the movement of wages and prices. The Great Depression stimulated further institutionalist work on cycles and depressions, with a number of writers adopting views of the causes of depression that placed more emphasis on the roles of price inflexibility on the part of large corporations and shifts in the distribution of income toward profits, resulting in underconsumption. In the hands of J. M. Clark (1939), this led to a greater stress on fiscal policy and deficit spending as a solution, while others such as Rexford Tugwell (1932) advocated for a shift to government planning.[6] These debates played out over the course of the New Deal, with the planners losing out to a more Keynesian style of policy.

Another aspect of business waste discussed by institutionalists is found in what Veblen called business "sabotage." Sabotage involves the restriction of output to maintain profitable prices. Veblen (1904, 241) is not simply applying this idea to an individual firm with monopoly power but the manner in which the key industries of the entire industrial system are operated through "business coalitions" and other "working arrangements." Veblen's point is that the productive capacity of industry using modern technology is so large that if it were given free rein, prices would

6. Some of this literature is discussed by Roger E. Backhouse in this volume. A variety of views on price inflexibility were forwarded by J. M. Clark, F. C. Mills, Gardiner Means, and others. The price inflexibility thesis was sometimes combined with an underconsumptionist view taken from J. A. Hobson. This is most obvious in the work of Tugwell and in the Brookings studies on income and economic progress (Rutherford 2011, 292–98).

fall to unprofitable levels. To maintain profitability, output is restricted and industry is characterized by a normal state of excess productive capacity and unemployment (Veblen 1921, 8–9). The idea of the "capacity to produce" being significantly above actual output even in normal times became a common point of criticism of business in the 1920s and 1930s (Slichter [1924] 1971, 330; Chase 1925, 189–90; Nourse and associates 1934).[7]

Problems of Competition

In orthodox economics, problems of competition usually mean that there is insufficient competition, but in the institutionalist literature several arguments indicate that problems might arise from too much rather than too little competition.

Veblen's analysis of business indicates that competition can be socially wasteful (as with competitive advertising) or lead to firms seeking to inflict damage on rivals. Competition is not necessarily benign in its form. J. M. Clark (1926, 179) discusses some aspects of this in terms of those forms of competition where the actions of different firms or individuals neutralize each other. Examples he gives are competitive armaments, competitive advertising, the waste of "cross freights," and the competition involved in invidious consumption (179–80).

Even where competition is focused on lowering production costs, strong competitive pressures on firms can lead to a race to the bottom in terms of wages, working conditions, and product safety. This idea is apparent in the work of progressive economists such as H. C. Adams, but can also be found in the institutionalist literature in the work of Walton Hamilton and J. M. Clark (Rutherford 2011, 58; Clark 1926, 172). The suggested solution is to provide a set of minimum standards in terms of wages, hours of work, and health and safety that will serve to define the minimum level or ethical "plane" of competition. Later, Clarence Ayres (1966) advocated for guaranteed minimum income schemes.

Further, under certain cost conditions, such as firms having high levels of overhead and declining marginal costs, competition can lead to "cut-throat" competition and to prices below average total cost (Clark 1923). Such competition has the potential to become "ruinous" and to create

---

7. Concerns such as this linked the work of Veblen and Chase to the various engineering movements that arose at the same time. The common theme was the waste involved in business practice.

"chaos" rather than stability. For Clark, following on from writers such as A. T. Hadley, such conditions applied to railways; Hamilton applied similar arguments to the bituminous coal industry. Hamilton characterizes that industry as beset by persistent excess capacity, irregular operation, low wages, unsafe working conditions, and strikes and labor unrest, a state of affairs in contrast with that suggested by the theory of competitive markets. Hamilton locates the basic problem in technological advances increasing capacity and creating a cost structure with high overheads and decreasing costs. Under these conditions competition leads to price cutting, low or even negative profits, and low wages. This is combined with uncoordinated investment decisions and bankruptcy laws that allow for reorganizations that retain the mining capacity in the industry. The industry is characterized more by "chaos" than by an orderly state of normal profits and capacity matched to demand (Hamilton and Wright 1925).[8] Clark (1923, 23–24, 416–50) argues that to maintain profitability, firms facing such conditions will adopt strategies such as price discrimination and will seek to develop formal or informal constraints on competitive price-cutting. In a world of significant overhead costs, price differentials are not "imperfections" in the market but part of its "normal" operation, and competition is "necessarily a thing of self-imposed restraints" (459–61).

Clark also discusses "predatory" and "unfair" competition. The former involves firms attempting to generate monopoly power by deliberately driving out competitors by predatory pricing strategies, while the latter might involve the use of false information, bribery, intimidation, discrimination, and so on. The important point here is that "evidently, the public cannot afford to rest on a simple belief that all competition is good. The situation requires careful differentiation between different types of competition, coupled with wise restraints temperately exercised" (Clark 1926, 153).

Competition implies many firms, each small relative to the size of the market. Numerous institutionalists, including Veblen, Willard Thorp (1924), and Lawrence Frank (1925), argued for the efficiency gains of larger scale. Such gains came not only from production economies related to technology but also from the elimination of the transaction costs (or costs of doing business) involved in the use of markets:

> The amount of "business" that has to be transacted per unit of product is much greater where the various related industrial processes are

---

8. Hamilton argued for a consolidation of the coal industry under the control of workers and consumers (Hamilton and Wright 1928).

managed in severality than where several of them are brought under one business management. A pecuniary discretion has to be exercised at every point of contact or transition, where the process or product touches or passes the boundary of different spheres of ownership. Business transactions have to do with ownership and changes of ownership. The greater the parcelment in point of ownership, the greater the amount of business work that has to be done with a given output of goods or services, and the slower, less facile, and less accurate on the whole, is the work. This applies both to the work of bargain and contract . . . and to the routine work of accounting and of gathering and applying information and misinformation. (Veblen 1904, 46–47)

Explicit recognition of negotiation and bargaining costs and their reduction through integration can also be found in Clark 1923, 137. Veblen (1904, 46) sees such savings as a "partial neutralization of the wastes due to the presence of pecuniary motives and business management." Larger scale and industrial integration, then, can greatly increase efficiency, hence the generally negative attitude of institutionalists toward attempts to maintain competition by limiting firm size, but large scale can also create market power, monopoly, and the prospect of business sabotage. What is required is some middle ground between "pure oligopoly and the ruinously low prices likely to result from unlimited market chaos" (Clark 1940, 253), and this is precisely what Clark (1940) develops in his concept of "workable competition." This does not necessarily involve meeting as many of the conditions of perfect competition as possible: "If there are, for example, five conditions, all of which are essential to perfect competition, and the first is lacking in a given case, then it no longer follows that we are necessarily better off for the presence of any one of the other four" (242). The crucial thing is that prices be made independently under conditions of rivalry (Clark 1961, 18).

The problems of competition are not just found in product markets but also in labor markets, in this case primarily because of unequal bargaining power. The problems of labor unrest and industrial violence had long been characteristic of labor relations in the United States, and institutionalists looked to the recognition of trade unions, collective bargaining, and systems of mediation and arbitration as solutions to these problems. Institutionalists promoted a variety of labor legislation to this end, culminating in the Wagner Act of 1935. The Wagner Act provided employee rights to form trade unions and engage in collective bargaining, prohibited "unfair" labor practices, and established the National Labor Relations Board.

Shifting of Costs

Institutionalist arguments about cost shifting were most developed by J. M. Clark and, later, by K. William Kapp. Clark (1926, 178) discusses the issue under the heading of "unpaid costs of industry." Kapp (1963, 11) argues that "the fact that private entrepreneurs are able to shift part of the total costs of production to other persons or to the community as a whole, points to one of the most important limitations of the scope of neoclassical value theory." Kapp was aware of the increasing mention of externalities in neoclassical economics in the 1950s and 1960s, but nevertheless maintained that it was still not recognized that externalities "are not isolated cases but widespread and inevitable phenomena under conditions of business enterprise (8n2).

Even in the first edition of his book, published in 1950, Kapp devoted whole chapters to the shifting of costs involved in environmental issues such as air and water pollution. This makes Kapp one of the first economists to give sustained treatment to such environmental externalities. In terms of air pollution, Kapp's main concerns were with health effects, effects on vegetation and soil, and on the corrosion and deterioration of other materials. Kapp suggests that environmental policy should be based on objective standards of maximum acceptable concentration of pollutants in the atmosphere. In terms of water pollution he discusses the impacts of municipal and industrial waste discharges, including sewage, acids, salts, chemicals, pesticides, brines, radioactive materials, and heat (Kapp 1963, 78), and their effects on human health, animal and plant life, and water quality.

Cost shifting is, however, not limited to environmental costs. Under the same heading Kapp considers the overextraction of renewable and nonrenewable resources, including cases of open access and common pool resources. Also included by Kapp is the shifting of costs onto consumers in the form of shoddy goods, adulteration of goods, and designed obsolescence. Further, both Clark and Kapp give a great deal of attention to what might be called the human costs of industry, including occupational diseases, industrial accidents, costs involved in female and child labor, and technological and cyclical unemployment (Kapp 1963).

The issue of industrial accidents was given vast importance in the earlier institutionalist literature. Institutionalists such as Ezekiel Downey and John R. Commons were closely involved in the development and setting up of systems of workmen's compensation. The issue of industrial accident raises a further issue. In cases of damages an individual should be able to sue for compensation under common law, and this should give the individual bargaining power in the setting of employment contracts. But, as is pointed out by Clark (1926, 178), the individual may not be able to translate this "technical legal protection" into actual effective protection because of lack of bargaining power. Moreover, the ability to sue for damages under common law had been seriously compromised by court decisions and interpretations that had shifted responsibility to the worker or consumer. In the 1930s Hamilton (1931, 1937) directed particular attention to the impact of the courts adopting the doctrines of contributory negligence and caveat emptor. More recently, Andrei Shleifer and Edward L. Glaeser (2012, 143–54) have argued that these *judicial failures* were an important reason for the rise of the regulatory state.

The cost imposed on the worker and on society at large by unemployment is treated by Clark as a part of his broader concern with overhead costs. He argues that labor involves an overhead cost: "There is a minimum of maintenance of the laborer's health and working capacity which must be borne by someone, whether the laborer works or not. . . . If the maintenance is not forthcoming the community suffers a loss through the deterioration of its working power" (Clark 1923, 16). That the cost of labor is a variable cost to a business is "simply because the terms of the wage contract are drawn in that way" (16). In standard theory, the overhead costs of capital are recognized as having to be met, but human overhead costs are neglected (Clark 1922, 133–34). Recognizing the overhead-cost component of labor, Clark makes a series of recommendations to help stabilize employment and provide a minimum standard of living. Clark's (1923, 381) suggestions include efforts by firms to regularize employment, union-management agreements to specify the minimum amount of employment to be provided, and unemployment compensation of a sort that links the employer's premiums to "the disbursements which his own enterprise occasions." Institutionalists such as Commons and his students were closely involved in the effort to introduce unemployment compensation at both the state and the federal levels.

Social Goods

The underprovision of public, or social, goods by private business is clearly understood in the institutionalist literature. Clark (1926, 178–79) talks of cases of "inappropriable services," covering all cases "in which the person who renders a service cannot, for any reason, appropriate it in such a way as to be able to sell it to the recipient." Much of the institutional-ist discussion of public goods concerns scientific research and scientific knowledge. Where the benefits of research are distant or uncertain, research may not be undertaken by private research labs even if the poten-tial benefits are large. The benefits may be too distant, or too uncertain, or spread out thinly over a large number of people. Some knowledge may not be patentable, and even where patents are possible, the patent system itself may not encourage wide diffusion. Hamilton was especially concerned with the patent system. Knowledge is more important than real property, natural resources are largely what the current state of knowledge makes them, and modern industry is "nothing more than our accumulated techni-cal knowledge" (Hamilton 1949b, 339). Abundant production and rising standards of living rest on the advance of knowledge and its dissemination.

Patents have as their purpose the promotion of technological advance, but Hamilton's investigations indicated to him that the existing patent sys-tem had numerous failings in achieving that end. Research and invention has become a matter of corporate research and development laboratories. In the hands of corporations the patent system can easily be used to create control of an industry. A flood of closely related products can be patented, blocking out other competitors; patents can be used to "fence" in an inven-tion, "block" the work of rivals, or "trawl" for information; patent protec-tion can be extended in time by patenting successive modifications; spe-cial terms and conditions can be written into patent licenses, dividing the market between producers by quota, or territory, or product, and setting prices for various users; patents can be pooled, resulting in a closed and collusive market; and international agreements involving patents can pro-vide the basis for trade agreements between firms and international car-tels (Hamilton 1941; Hamilton and Till 1948). Hamilton wished to see a move to stricter standards of patentability and a shift to a system of com-pulsory licensing.

Under the heading of social goods might be included the interests of future generations. As Clark points out, commercial calculation discounts the future in such way as to place virtually no value of any benefits more than two generations ahead. But "if, as has been suggested, the interests of posterity" should take precedence over those of the current generation, "then this scale of values is false from a social standpoint, and the state has a duty to see that the needs of future generations are not unduly sacri-ficed to present profits" (Clark 1926, 180).

Conclusion

The institutionalist view of the operation of a business economy is clearly one that provides a great deal of space for government interventions of various sorts. In this connection it is interesting to note the full extent of J. M. Clark's list of legitimate areas for government action. Under "strict individualism" Clark argues that the following can be justified: public defense; protection of persons and property; regulating the appropriation of goods that are not yet private property; controlling inheritance and bequest; and the raising of public revenues. The "further grounds" for public action or "social control" Clark (1926, 170–84) finds in the following: monopoly or oligopoly; maintaining the level of competition; cases where the individual is not able to make sound judgments (including cases of complex decisions, irrevocable decisions, and cases where there is a lack of reliable information); cases where issues of agency apply; cases involving the victims of natural disasters and technological change; the provision of a social minimum; economic guidance in general; ensuring equality of opportunity; cases of unpaid costs of industry; cases of public goods or inappropriable services; cases where actions neutralize each other (arms races); unemployment of labor and capital; the interests of posterity; and any other discrepancies between private and social accounting.

It is true that more orthodox economists have also recognized many of these same issues and difficulties, but there is an important distinction. The orthodox approach presents these as exceptions or side effects of the market system. This is a direct result of the use of the perfectly competitive model as a reference point. For institutionalists, who do not use the perfectly competitive model as a reference, these problems are part and parcel of a market system based on pecuniary gain. They are as much a part of profit-seeking behavior as socially beneficial innovations and cost reductions; the issue is entirely one of the effectiveness of the institutions regulating the market (and there are always institutions of one sort or another regulating the market) in directing profit-seeking behavior to socially desirable ends. In K. William Kapp's (1963, 268–70) words, "the system of business enterprise must be regarded as an economy of unpaid costs," and orthodox economics a system of thought that tends to "eliminate the less congenial aspects of reality from the sphere of economic inquiry."

Another way to state this position is found in the many references in the institutionalist literature to the idea of "affectation with a public interest."

This phrase refers to a legal doctrine originally used to justify the regulation of a private business by the American courts in the 1870s. The courts themselves ultimately gave this doctrine a highly restricted meaning (Hamilton 1930), but institutionalists such as Clark (1926, 137, 177, 185) continued to argue that business activity was indeed affected with a public interest. In Clark's (1926, 50) words, "It is sufficiently clear that industry is essentially a matter of public concern, and that the stake which the public has in its processes is not adequately protected by the safeguards which individualism affords"; "every business is 'affected with a public interest' of one sort or another" (185). This public interest in the conduct of business serves to justify a broad range of government intervention and social control of business.

The tools of this social control consist of legislation, regulatory commissions, and government agencies, and institutionalists were instrumental in the passage of labor legislation, public utility regulation, consumer protection legislation, unemployment insurance, social security, agricultural support programs, securities and banking regulation, and more. Institutionalists were particularly heavily involved in the New Deal administration, which vastly, and permanently, expanded the role of the state and the role of economists in government. Not all the reforms they advocated came to pass, single-payer health insurance, for example, but they were successful in bringing into being a significant part of their program of social control.

There are, however, significant variations in the extent of the statism proposed by institutionalists. At one extreme, Rexford Tugwell (1932) and Mordecai Ezekiel (1936) advocated for governmental "planning" to control investment, coordinate production, and balance the growth of production with consumption, but most institutionalists favored more modest forms of intervention. At the other end of the spectrum, Wesley Mitchell was extremely cautious about explicit policy advocacy, preferring to simply provide "scientific" findings as inputs into the political policymaking process. In Mitchell's case, his caution was undoubtedly due partly to his desire to protect his National Bureau of Economic Research from accusations of political bias. Institutionalists such as John R. Commons and Walton Hamilton did not assume that social control required an extensive direct role for government, and both proposed policies that involved voluntary organizations or forms of organization that minimized the role of direct government intervention. Commons's (1901) advocacy of collective bargaining and Hamilton's proposals for the coal and health care industries are cases in point (Rutherford 2011, 66–72).

In this respect, institutionalists were not without their concerns with political processes. Commons (1934, 755–56) characterized legislative processes as "logrolling" and had a lifelong concern with the adequate representation of interests in politics. Clark was also aware of the potential limitations and downsides of government intervention. He stressed the value that people place on their liberty, the value of voluntary organization as opposed to compulsion, and the importance of leaving as much room for individual judgment as possible. Moreover, political processes of decision making are themselves far from perfect, are costly, and are subject to "perversion" because of the influence of private interests (Clark 1926, 184–89).

It is important to understand that the emphasis on administrative agencies in the institutionalist literature derives largely from *distrust* of "government by traditional political parties" (Commons 1950, 33, 262). For Commons (1939), these administrative agencies would constitute a "fourth branch of government," set up in a way that enabled them to engage in investigation and pragmatic and experimental rule making, with the aim of solving conflicts and improving conditions within the fields assigned to them. The economist experts who staff these agencies are seen by Commons as engaging in applied social science and as very different from purely political appointees subject to bias and corruption. Nevertheless, this highly optimistic (almost utopian) view of commissions relies on commissions remaining objective and nonpartisan. Appointees, however, are made by political entities and may have their own political biases, and the commission itself may be captured by the industry it is intended to regulate. Interestingly, it was Walton Hamilton who was one of the first to express concern with industry capture. As a result of his observations of the workings of the NRA,[9] Hamilton expressed concerns over the way that regulatory commissions worked in practice. Commissions "have closed public utilities to outsiders," agricultural regulation served the interests of producers but not of workers or consumers, and the NRA "staged a full dress performance of the hazards of the administrative process" in which wide powers were granted only to become "sanctions under which the strategic group could lord it over the industry" (Hamilton

9. Hamilton was heavily involved in the consumer representation aspect of NRA code making. See Rutherford 2011, 77–87.

and Till 1940). Over time he became increasingly disturbed by the extent of interest group influence on the regulatory process. The failures of the market to properly control business in the public interest had resulted in a move toward regulation. But regulation broke down the older division between state and economy. The most used form of regulatory device, the commission, was particularly susceptible to capture by the interests it was supposed to be regulating, and the campaign for regulation ultimately produced "its own counterrevolution" (Hamilton 1949a, 1957). Concerns such as these were later taken up and expanded by Chicago economists who were to spearhead the revival of a promarket and anti-interventionist position, but for institutionalists the market and politics, economy and state, cannot be untangled; the challenge lies instead in further institutional innovation (Hamilton 1957).

References

Ayres, Clarence E. 1966. "Guaranteed Income: An Institutionalist View." In *The Guaranteed Income*, edited by Robert Theobald, 161–74. New York: Doubleday.

Berle, Adolf A., and Gardiner Means. 1932. *The Modern Corporation and Private Property*. New York: Macmillan.

Chase, Stuart. 1925. *The Tragedy of Waste*. New York: Macmillan.

Clark, John M. 1918. "Economics and Modern Psychology." 2 pts. *Journal of Political Economy* 26 (January): 1–30; (February): 136–66.

———. 1922. "The Empire of Machines." *Yale Review*, n.s., 12:132–43.

———. 1923. *Studies in the Economics of Overhead Costs*. Chicago: University of Chicago Press.

———. 1926. *Social Control of Business*. Chicago: University of Chicago Press.

———. 1939. *Social Control of Business*. 2nd ed. Chicago: University of Chicago Press.

———. 1940. "Towards a Concept of Workable Competition." *American Economic Review* 30 (June): 241–56.

———. 1961. *Competition as a Dynamic Process*. Washington, D.C.: Brookings.

Commons, John R. 1901. "A New Way of Settling Labor Disputes." *American Monthly Review of Reviews* 23 (March): 328–33.

———. 1939. "Twentieth Century Economics." *Journal of Social Philosophy* 5 (October): 29–41.

———. 1950. *The Economics of Collective Action*. New York: Macmillan.

Epstein, Edward Jay. 1982. "Have You Ever Tried to Sell a Diamond?" *Atlantic*, February 1. www.edwardjayepstein.com/diamond.htm.

Ezekiel, Mordecai. 1936. *$2,500 a Year: From Scarcity to Abundance*. New York: Harcourt Brace.

Frank, Lawrence K. 1925. "The Significance of Industrial Integration." *Journal of Political Economy* 33 (April): 179–95.

Galbraith, John Kenneth. 1967. *The New Industrial State*. Boston: Houghton Mifflin.

Hamilton, Walton H. 1919. *Current Economic Problems*. Chicago: University of Chicago Press.

———. 1930. "Affectation with Public Interest." *Yale Law Journal* 39 (June): 1089–112.

———. 1931. "The Ancient Maxim Caveat Emptor." *Yale Law Journal* 40 (June): 1133–87.

———. 1932. "The Control of Big Business." *Nation*, May 25, 591–93.

———. 1937. "The Living Law." *Survey Graphic* 26 (December): 632–35, 735.

———. 1941. *Patents and Free Enterprise*. Temporary National Economic Committee, Monograph No. 31. Washington, D.C.: Government Printing Office.

———. 1949a. "The Genius of the Radical." In *Years of the Modern*, edited by John W. Chase, 63–91. New York: Longmans, Green.

———. 1949b. "A New Patent Policy." *Current History* 17 (December): 338–41.

———. 1957. *The Politics of Industry*. New York: Alfred A. Knopf.

Hamilton, Walton H., and Irene Till. 1940. "Antitrust—the Reach after New Weapons." *Washington University Law Quarterly* 26 (December): 1–26.

———. 1948. "What Is a Patent?" *Law and Contemporary Problems* 13 (Spring): 245–59.

Hamilton, Walton H., and Helen R. Wright. 1925. *The Case of Bituminous Coal*. New York: Macmillan.

———. 1928. *A Way of Order for Bituminous Coal*. New York: Macmillan.

Kapp, K. William. 1950. *The Social Costs of Private Enterprise*. Cambridge, Mass.: Harvard University Press.

———. 1963. *The Social Costs of Business Enterprise*. New York: Asia Publishing.

Kyrk, Hazel. 1923. *A Theory of Consumption*. Boston: Houghton Mifflin.

———. 1933. *Economic Problems of the Family*. New York: Harper and Brothers.

McMahon, Theresa S. 1925. *Social and Economic Standards of Living*. Boston: D. C. Heath.

Mitchell, Wesley C. 1912. "The Backward Art of Spending Money." *American Economic Review* 2 (June): 269–81.

———. 1913. *Business Cycles*. Berkeley: University of California Press.

———. 1923. "Unemployment and Business Fluctuations." *American Labor Legislation Review* 13:15–22.

———. (1923) 1950. "Making Goods and Making Money." In *The Backward Art of Spending Money*, 137–48. New York: Augustus M. Kelley.

———. 1927. *Business Cycles: The Problem and Its Setting*. New York: NBER.

Nourse, Edwin G., and associates. 1934. *America's Capacity to Produce*. Washington, D.C.: Brookings Institution.

Peixotto, Jessica B. 1927. *Getting and Spending at the Professional Standard of Living*. New York: Macmillan.

Ripley, W. Z. 1927. *Main Street and Wall Street*. Boston: Little, Brown.

Rutherford, Malcolm. 2011. *The Institutionalist Movement in American Economics, 1918–1947: Science and Social Control.* Cambridge: Cambridge University Press.

Shleifer, Andrei, and Edward L. Glaeser. 2012. "The Rise of the Regulatory State." In *The Failure of Judges and the Rise of Regulators*, by Andrei Shleifer. Cambridge, Mass.: MIT Press.

Slichter, Sumner H. (1924) 1971. "The Organization and Control of Economic Activity." In *The Trend of Economics*, edited by Rexford G. Tugwell, 303–55. Port Washington, N.Y.: Kennikat.

Stocking, George Ward. 1925. *The Oil Industry and the Competitive System: A Study in Waste.* Boston: Houghton Mifflin.

Thorp, Willard L. 1924. *The Integration of Industrial Operation.* Washington, D.C.: Census Bureau.

Tugwell, Rexford G. 1932. "The Principle of Planning and the Institution of Laissez Faire." *American Economic Review* 22 (March): 75–92.

Veblen, Thorstein. 1898. "Why Is Economics Not an Evolutionary Science?" *Quarterly Journal of Economics* 12 (July): 373–97.

———. 1899. *The Theory of the Leisure Class.* New York: Macmillan.

———. 1904. *The Theory of Business Enterprise.* New York: Scribner's.

———. 1919. *The Vested Interests and the State of the Industrial Arts.* New York: B. W. Huebsch.

———. 1921. *The Engineers and the Price System.* New York: B. W. Huebsch.

———. 1923. *Absentee Ownership and Business Enterprise in Recent Times.* New York: B. W. Huebsch.

Economic Power and the Financial Machine: Competing Conceptions of Market Failure in the Great Depression

Roger E. Backhouse

Prior to the emergence of global climate change, the Great Depression was arguably the biggest market failure in the history of the United States. It was a catastrophe not just because of the economic chaos and hardship it produced but because it threatened the liberty that was fundamental to American democracy. The rise of Nazi and fascist regimes in Western Europe showed, according to Franklin Delano Roosevelt, that if private power grew to a point where it became stronger than the state, a democracy's liberty was threatened. The subservience of government to a private power was fascism. Democracy was also threatened whenever the business system did not generate enough employment and an acceptable standard of living. These dangers, he claimed, both confronted the United States:

> Among us today a concentration of private power without equal in history is growing.
>
> This concentration is seriously impairing the economic effectiveness of private enterprise as a way of providing employment for labor and capital and as a way of assuring a more equitable distribution of income

Correspondence may be addressed to Roger E. Backhouse, Department of Economics, University of Birmingham, Edgbaston, Birmingham B15 2TT, UK; e-mail: reb@bhouse.org.uk. This article was written as part of a project, supported by a Major Research Fellowship from the Leverhulme Trust, to write an intellectual biography of Paul Samuelson. I am grateful for the editors and conference participants, in particular Malcolm Rutherford, for helpful comments on previous drafts of the article.

History of Political Economy 47 (annual suppl.) DOI 10.1215/00182702-2007-3130463

and earnings among the people of the Nation as a whole. (FDR to Congress, April 29, 1938, USTNEC 1938, 185)

The letter to Congress in which he made this assessment went on to document the increase in the concentration of income and wealth that had taken place during the Depression, arguing that increased industrial concentration threatened the competition on which the free enterprise system depended. He clearly had Germany in mind when he went on to write, "Private enterprise is ceasing to be free enterprise and is becoming a cluster of private collectivisms; masking itself as a system of free enterprise after the American model, it is in fact becoming a concealed cartel system after the European model" (186). Unless the concentration of economic power could be reversed, American democracy, resting on a foundation of liberty, was in grave danger.

Roosevelt may not have used the language of market failure, but it would have been an apt label for his diagnosis of the problem still facing the United States after almost a decade of depression. His view that markets had failed was long-standing (see Stabile and Kozak 2012, chap. 8), but these ideas reflected a substantial literature on the limitations of markets that had developed in the 1920s and 1930s. This literature, generally focusing on the way American business had evolved in the late nineteenth and early twentieth centuries, contended that the competitive conditions required for markets to work well no longer prevailed, and during the 1930s these ideas were adduced as explanations of the Great Depression and the inability of traditional, market-based policies to solve the problem.

One reading of this literature is that it was doing no more than provide an explanation of why prices were inflexible—the "classical" theory of depression criticized by John Maynard Keynes in *The General Theory of Employment, Interest, and Money* ([1936] 1972). However, it is misleading to bracket this literature with the "classical" view attacked by Keynes, for it was rooted in American institutionalism and came with no bias toward laissez-faire. Price inflexibility was incidental to this literature, whose main concern was the functioning of large corporations and the markets in which they operated, and the structural problems this created for market organization. The story told here is of how this literature, in which market failure was associated with monopoly power, came to be melded with ideas about the failure of what Roosevelt called the financial machine to equilibrate saving and investment: about how institutionalists came to adopt a more Keynesian perspective on the cause of the Great Depression. The outcome was thus the emergence of an American Keynesianism with institutionalist roots. Concern with monopoly power did not disappear, but it came to be associated with industrial economics rather than with what increasingly came to be considered macroeconomic problems. The institutionalist literature did, however, leave a mark on postwar Keynesian macroeconomics in that it was widely taken for granted that competition was imperfect, in clear contradiction to the position taken by Keynes.

This article outlines these theories as they were developed in the academic literature and as they were drawn on in a major inquiry, authorized by Roosevelt's letter to Congress. It then traces some of the ways in which this literature, though it was eclipsed by Keynes's competing vision of the market failure that led to the Depression, nonetheless fed through into postwar economics. It fed directly into the literature on industrial organization, in which Joe Bain and the architects of what came to be known as the Harvard school attempted to analyze the relationship between market structure and economic performance. The Chicago attacks on the Harvard school, associated with George Stigler, developed a perspective on industrial policy that began as a critique of the institutionalist literature. The link with postwar macroeconomics is less direct, but it can be seen in the widespread practice of justifying reverse-L-shaped aggregate supply curves with an account of oligopolistic price setting. The article illustrates this using the textbook that, above all others, came to be linked with American Keynesianism—Paul Samuelson's *Economics* (1948)—which, to an extent not generally recognized, drew on the institutionalist literature discussed below.

The story told here is not completely new. Rutherford (2011, chap. 10) has written about the complexity of the institutionalist response to Keynes, drawing attention to the divide between those institutionalists who blamed depression on business profit-making and those who adopted underconsumptionist explanations (291n5); and the story parallels and overlaps with the one told by Frederic S. Lee (1990) in relation to the National Resources Committee. Similarly, Perry Mehrling (1997) has pointed out that Alvin Hansen's "conversion" came when he saw how he could accommodate certain Keynesian ideas within his earlier conception of the business cycle. However, such work has not drawn out the implication of this episode for thinking about the concept of market failure.

1. Questioning Competitive Markets: The 1920s

In the United States there is a long tradition of concern with the dangers posed by monopolies and cartels. This was reflected in the passage of the Sherman Antitrust Act in 1890, which made it illegal to attempt to create a monopoly in interstate or international trade, and the Clayton Act in 1914, which amended the Sherman Act by making illegal specific practices through which this was achieved (price discrimination, exclusive dealing contracts, mergers between competing companies, and interlocking directorates). This legislation and its use against perceived monopolies was a significant part of the background against which economists discussed the operation of markets after the First World War.

One of the most significant books to emerge during the 1920s was Frank Knight's *Risk, Uncertainty, and Profit* (1921). This book is best known for its distinction between risk and uncertainty, and for its rigorous account of the conditions necessary for perfect competition. Knight's motivation for developing the theory of perfect competition was to show that the prerequisites for perfect competition, and hence the traditional theory of value, to be valid were not satisfied in the real world. The most important assumption was perfect knowledge, and a large part of his book was devoted to exploring the implications of uncertainty. This took him into dynamics, for in a world in which there was no change, there was unlikely to be much uncertainty.

A lot of Knight's book was theoretical, dealing with abstract and even philosophical ideas. However, his concern was with how markets worked, for he wanted "to isolate and define the essential characteristics of free enterprise as a system or method of securing and directing cooperative effort in a social group" (Knight 1921, viii). Knight claimed that his book "probably" emphasized the defects of free enterprise, but before concluding that any other system was better, it was necessary to examine alternative forms of social organization. The only conclusion to which he admitted was that "in the ultimate society, no doubt, every conceivable type of organization machinery will find its place" (ix). Markets have problems, but so too might other forms of social organization.

Whereas the fundamental problem for Knight was uncertainty, John Maurice Clark (1923), who had helped Knight turn his thesis into a book, took a different view. For him, the fundamental problem was "overhead costs"—those costs that cannot be attributed to specific units of output and that businesses have to incur irrespective of the quantity of goods they produce. This undermined traditional views about markets because, as

Clark (1923, 32) put it, "there is no natural system of prices in the old sense. Cost prices do not mean anything definite any more." In other words, the existence of overhead costs meant that supply and demand did not determine unique prices, and prices did not correspond either to the cost of producing goods or to the value of goods to consumers: they varied over the business cycle according to the level of prosperity (chap. 23). Competition reduced price differentials, but it did not eliminate them completely. Because of this, decisions had to be made about how overhead costs should be apportioned, raising questions about how objectives of efficiency, incentives, and fairness were to be balanced against each other.

The implication was that competition was "a varied and elastic thing" (461):

> Competition is necessarily a thing of self-imposed restraints, governed by the folkways of the business community even more actively and consciously than by the underlying restraints imposed by government. . . . Agreements, understandings and the sentiment against "spoiling the market" all play a part in restraining competition, and are limited in their turn by some of the various forms of potential competition. Some of the forces of potential competition do not begin to act until the earnings of the capital engaged in the business are materially above the minimum rate necessary to attract free capital; while some of the forces of active competition continue to act even after prices are below the level necessary to cover operating expenses.

Clark argued that these were not merely imperfections in the market but were "essential to its 'normal' operation" (460). He even included government expenses in the overhead costs industry had to bear, for government furnishes "vital, if intangible, factors of production; and produces far more than it costs" (463).

Though making no assumption about the number of firms—he claimed to be presenting a general theory of competitive processes—Clark saw competitive markets as characterized by the type of indeterminacy usually attributed to oligopoly. Mechanical forces of supply and demand did not determine prices but merely determined the constraints within which human psychology would operate. Markets would not equate supply and demand, for there were times when both labor and capital were idle.

> In times of depression, prices of goods and rates of wages do not come down to the point where demand for the ultimate factors of production would be equal to supply. They are pegged at higher levels which hark

back to the more active times which trade has enjoyed, and hopes to enjoy again. There is a sag, but it is like the sag of a rope stretched across a chasm, and does not reach bottom. These sustaining forces take varied forms . . . especially in connection with the ultimate costs of labor, and cut-throat competition. (465)

The reference to "cutthroat competition," alluding to his arguments about how businesspeople normally sought to avoid such potentially ruinous practices, makes it clear that he was not simply alleging that wages were sticky. They might be sticky, but this was an inherent feature of competition in a world where prices had to be significantly greater than variable costs if firms were to survive.

The result of this was that markets might break down—they might fail. The economic system, involving an endless process of learning through trial and error, was "the very opposite of fool-proof": "it requires nothing short of superhuman qualities of vision, foresight, correlation and co-operation to make it work without disastrous break-downs" (480). This raised questions for democracy, for democracy required that this "super-human vision . . . must be grasped by the many and this correlation must be democratically conceived and brought into being" (480).

Edward Chamberlin's *Theory of Monopolistic Competition* (1933), like Knight's book originally a thesis supervised by Allyn Young, was published in the midst of the Great Depression, but its conception was in the 1920s, for the thesis on which it was based had been submitted to Harvard in 1927. His starting point was the claim that economists, among whom he cited Knight and Clark, were confused about perfect competition. The reason for their confusion, he argued, was that "supposedly perfect competition is really imperfect" (Chamberlin 1933, 4). He set out to construct a synthesis of the theories of monopoly and perfect competition, ending up with a complex theory of market structure. Markets could be distinguished according to the number of sellers, but account also had to be taken of product differentiation and selling costs, such as advertising. Chamberlin was trying to create an economic theory appropriate for the modern world in which these were central phenomena of business activity. His search was for a more realistic theory. "Competitive theory," he argued, "is unreal in large part because it fails truly represent the forces at work in the economic system" (176).

A more radical appraisal of markets, published after Chamberlin's thesis, though before his book, was *The Modern Corporation and Private Property* (Berle and Means 1932). In differentiating between sources of income—the returns for providing capital, managing a business, and bearing risk and uncertainty—Knight had drawn a clear distinction between management and ownership of business. In a project funded by the Social Science Research Council, launched in 1928, not long before the height of the stock market boom that preceded the Great Crash, but published only after the world had moved into depression, a lawyer, Adolf Berle, and an economist, Gardiner Means, developed the idea that ownership and management were different into a critique of the market system as it had evolved in the United States. The corporation, they argued, was both a way of holding property and a means whereby economic life was organized. It permitted the concentration of wealth and its control by a small number of people—the managers of large corporations. Investors had surrendered control over their wealth and had "effectively broken the old property relationships and has raised the problem of defining these relationships anew" (Berle and Means 1932, 2). They documented the history of the corporation and the concentration of economic power that had taken place. Even though wealth had become more concentrated, ownership of modern corporations was widely dispersed, leaving managers in control. The significance of this stemmed from the different interests of owners and managers. The law might be able to look after the rights of the property owner, but it was not able to regulate the way managers ran the businesses under their control.

Arguing that existing theories were inadequate, Berle and Means called for a new concept of the corporation. Taking Adam Smith as representing traditional theory, they argued that the separation of ownership from control had rendered traditional theory obsolete. Modern corporate enterprise was not the same as the forms of private enterprise with which Smith was familiar, and in the modern corporate world, involving cooperation and the exercise of "authority almost to the point of autocracy" within business, "individual liberty is necessarily curtailed" (Berle and Means 1932, 349). The profit motive had become distorted, and competition was no longer effective:

> Today competition in markets dominated by a few great enterprises has come to be more often either cut-throat and destructive or so inactive as to make monopoly or duopoly conditions prevail. Competition between a small number of units each involving an organization so complex that costs have become indeterminate does not satisfy the condition assumed by earlier economists, nor does it appear likely to be as effective a regulator of industry and of profits as they had assumed. (351)

These works are enough to show that, even during the prosperity of the 1920s, economists were questioning whether there might be structural reasons why markets could not be fully competitive and might fail to deliver the benefits they were supposed to bring. In the 1930s, such explanations were to become a prominent explanation of the Depression.

2. The Depression and Market Failure: The 1930s

When the world was hit by the Great Depression, many economists naturally turned to theories of the business cycle for their diagnoses of what had gone wrong. However, the downturn clearly indicated a failure of American capitalism, and some economists argued that this failure amounted to a market failure: it was the result of a breakdown of competition—of a failure of competition to produce the results that, according to traditional theory, it should produce. In other words, they turned not to interactions between different parts of the economy but to the way individual markets functioned, drawing on ideas developed in the 1920s and earlier. These two perspectives on the Great Depression can be seen in the programs of the American Economic Association (AEA) soon after the stock market crash of 1929. At the first session after the crash, a roundtable discussion on the causes of the economic problem was titled "The Theory of Dynamics as Related to Industrial Instability" (Taussig et al. 1930). At the 1931 meeting, when it was becoming much clearer that it was no ordinary depression, the equivalent session included a diagnosis by Joseph Schumpeter (1931), to which five economists responded (Adams et al. 1931), producing a wide-ranging discussion of possible causes of the cycle. However, at the same meeting, the causes of the Depression were also addressed in a session in which eight economists discussed "the decline of laissez faire" (Handman et al. 1931). Though labeled "economic history" and covering several centuries of thinking, it appears to have been motivated, at least in part, by current problems. The link between markets and depression is clearest in Alvin Hansen's contribution (Handman et al. 1931, 8–9), talking about the problems of price rigidity, especially for a country still on the gold standard, in a rapidly changing world. Hansen argued that "social control" of business posed a dilemma, for while it might be possible to achieve greater stability than was available under free enterprise, the price would be slower technical advance and a more static market.

These two approaches can also be identified in the following year's AEA meeting, in 1932. Hansen, Harry Jerome, and Sumner Slichter intro-

duced a discussion of the role of technological change in creating unemployment, a topic squarely in the tradition of American business cycle
theory. Alongside that were sessions on "private enterprise in economic
history" and "economic organization and the control of industry." Though
concerned with markets and market structures, this was as clearly
addressed to the problem of depression as was the session on technological change. The first paper, by Henry Harriman (1932, 67) of the New
England Power Company, argued that freedoms that might have been justified in the relatively simple society of the previous century could no
longer be tolerated, for "the unwise action of one individual may adversely
affect the lives of thousands." His argument was that producers would be
willing to "gauge their output to the consuming capacity of their country,"
but they were unable to do so because of the "ever-present risk of incur-
ring penalties under anti-trust laws which . . . are not in consonance with
the present-day needs of industry" (67). He suggested a scheme whereby
businesses coordinate their activities so as to get away from "the present
harsh and unremunerative competitive system" on condition that all such
agreements were regulated by a government authority. This theme was
taken up in the following paper in which Rexford Tugwell (1932, 75), then
one of Roosevelt's advisers, argued that because "war in industry is just as
ruinous as war among nations," there was a need for national planning.
Such planning should be thought of as technical rather than political—as
a "normal extension and development of the kind of planning which is a
familiar feature of contemporary business" (76).

Such arguments were reinforced by some of the measures Roosevelt
introduced in his first term. In the face of falling prices and a collapse of
business profits, the National Industrial Recovery Act (NIRA) of June
1933 suspended the antitrust laws and supported measures to sustain
prices. Companies were required to establish codes of fair competition,
fixing prices and wages, establishing production quotas, and restricting
entry. The NIRA was followed by the creation of the National Recovery
Administration (NRA), which helped draw up such codes of practice,
with firms that participated being allowed to use a Blue Eagle emblem to
indicate their compliance. The NRA came to an end in May 1935, when it
was declared unconstitutional, initiating an ongoing conflict between
Roosevelt and the Supreme Court.

Means extended the ideas he had developed with Berle in a series of
articles in the mid-1930s. The theoretical foundations for his work were
presented in an article that argued for bringing economics together not
with law (as in the collaboration with Berle) but with political science. The

reason was that political science dealt with the organization of economic activity through administrative means. He claimed that by 1929, "the control of something approaching half of industrial activity had become an administrative matter handled within 200 great administrative units" (Means 1935a, 62). Markets were failing to restrain their power, which had been further increased in the Depression. When such a high proportion of economic activity was organized outside the marketplace, it did not make sense to rely solely on market coordination. Because economists had few tools for analyzing nonmarket organization, they should turn to political scientists for assistance.

Because the behavior of large corporations was unlike that of more traditional businesses, the market had "become rather a disorganizing than an organizing influence," as the administrative actions of large firms set prices (62). Prices were increasingly inflexible, which undermined the effectiveness of the market as a device for coordinating economic activities. "A Ford Company," Means wrote, "can throw a whole countryside into depression by its single decision to alter radically the character of its output." The system had become unstable through relying on the market to coordinate activities that were not organized through markets.

Means, now in the Department of Agriculture, applied these ideas to monetary policy, arguing that it was no longer appropriate to treat all prices as being flexible. He substantiated his claim that some prices were set administratively by using wholesale price data to classify items according the frequency with which their prices changed. This revealed large differences between commodities: there were 125 items that changed price almost every month, and, at the other end of the scale, there were 95 that changed price less than five times in eight years (Means 1935b, 402). The former were the ones to which traditional theory applied; the latter were determined administratively. There was also a clear correlation, albeit with wide dispersion, between the frequency of price changes and the fall in prices from 1929 to 1932. Prices that changed infrequently had fallen around 10 percent, while ones that changed often had fallen 50 percent (with wide dispersion about both of these figures [Means 1935b, 404]). There was also a connection with production, as industries with inflexible prices saw the largest falls in output.

The problem of excess capacity was tackled in a major project started in 1932 by the Brookings Institution. Directed by Edwin Nourse, the project's first volume, *America's Capacity to Produce* (Nourse et al. 1934) established, on the basis of industry-by-industry statistical analysis, that there was excess capacity of around 20 percent. In the last in the series of four volumes arising from the project, one of Nourse's collaborators, Harold Moulton (1935), concluded that by 1932 as much as 40 percent of capacity was unused. Moulton, the author of *Income and Economic Progress*, claimed that this failure was not the result of technical barriers on the production side but the failure of consumption to keep pace with productive capacity. The root cause of this lay in the fact that too much income was flowing to high-income groups (who saved a high proportion of their income), leading to excessive saving. Saving was not translated into productive investment because the demand for investment was determined by consumption spending, which was not rising sufficiently fast, a very Hobsonian argument. The remedy was to be sought in making the distribution of income more equal. To achieve this, Moulton discussed employment in public enterprises, ideally self-financing but some financed by taxation, wage increases, profit sharing, and price reductions. The last of these was thought particularly important:

> There is one type of distributive reform which in our judgment outranks all the others in its promise of attaining the goal we seek. This is in the gradual but persistent revamping of price policy so as to pass on the benefits of technological progress and rising productivity to all the population in their role as consumers. . . . To seek the acceleration of economic progress by means of price reduction is not to attack the system of private capitalism but rather to return to the very logic upon which that system was justified and extolled by both lay and professional students of the economic process during the days when the system was assuming its present general character. (Moulton 1935, 161–62)

To achieve economic progress it was necessary to do more than protect the interests of specific interests and groups: economic progress had to include "all our people, the unskilled laborer as well as the master of a trade, those seeking to develop a new business as well as those entrenched in an old one—the masses not the classes" (163).

Another powerful statement of the case that capitalism had to be reformed if it was to survive came from Henry Simons, at Chicago, whose "Positive Program for Laissez Faire: Some Proposals for a Liberal Economic Policy," first published in 1934, constituted a strong attack on monopoly. Rather than adopt the almost corporatist strategy of accepting monopoly as a fact of modern life and seeking to make large corporations operate in the public interest, he argued that competition needed to be restored. His approach was explicitly libertarian in that he sought to defend liberty and democracy against their communist and fascist critics and against their real enemies, "the naive advocates of managed economy or national planning" (Simons [1934] 1948, 41). The goal of economic policy should be to allow prices—central to the free enterprise system— to be determined independently of government. Instead of tinkering with relative prices, thereby interfering with the efficient operation of the free enterprise system, governments should take positive actions to maintain competitive conditions in industry, for the problem facing society was monopoly.

> There is an intimate connection between freedom of enterprise and freedom of discussion. . . . Political liberty can survive only within an effective competitive economic system. Thus, *the great enemy of democracy is monopoly, in all its forms*: gigantic corporations, trade associations and other agencies for price control, trade-unions—or, in general, organization and concentration of power within functional classes. Effectively organized functional groups possess tremendous power for exploiting the community at large and even for sabotaging the system. . . . If the organized economic groups were left to exercise their monopoly powers without political restraint, the result would be a usurpation of sovereignty by these groups—and, perhaps, a domination of the state by them. (44)

Given his mention of communism and fascism, such language suggests that Simons had in mind political developments in those parts of Continental Europe where corporate interests became tied up with the state and the attack on democracy.

Simons therefore proposed measures designed to eliminate monopoly— what he called "a complete 'new deal' with respect to the private corporation" (58). These including reserving to the federal government the power to license private corporations, prohibiting companies engaged in making or selling commodities or services from owning securities of any other such corporation, limiting the total property that any one corporation could own, restricting the types of securities that could be issued, preventing interlocking directorships, and implementing measures to reduce the waste of advertising (58–59, 71). Where monopolies were inevitable (utilities and railroads), they should be nationalized and run by the state.[1]

---

1. Simons also advocated tax reform, a change in the nature of property rights so as to reduce the degree of inequality, and a series of measures to reform the monetary system.

By adopting such a program, the state would effectively discharge its responsibilities to support a free enterprise system. "The so-called failure of capitalism (or of the free-enterprise system, of competition)," Simons claimed, "may reasonably be interpreted as primarily a failure of the political state in the discharge of its minimum responsibilities under capitalism" (43). Markets could succeed only if the state ensured that competition prevailed, a task that required a radical reform.[2]

A similar attitude toward monopoly was found in Arthur E. Burns's *Decline of Competition: A Study of the Evolution of American Industry* (1936), an exhaustive six-hundred-page historical study of competitive practices in the United States, which clearly illustrates this way of thinking. In response to economists' arguments about the benefits of competition, "read as beguiling briefs for laissez faire," Burns argued that competitive capitalism had been given a thorough trial in the period stretching from the Civil War to the NIRA.[3] However, despite attempts to give it legislative support, "capitalism failed to preserve its competitive quality" (Burns 1936, 1). The concentration of industry in the late nineteenth century through dramatic and ruthless methods was widely blamed on the "pathological tendencies of a few individuals," and legislation was introduced to restrain such people (2). The possibility that such practices were inherent in a competitive, individualistic system was ignored. The twentieth-century attempts of the Supreme Court, "armed with the phrases 'restraint of trade' and 'monopoly,'" to compel "normal" competitive behavior proved ineffective. "Intent" to restrain trade was hard to establish, and statistical measures, such as long periods of price stability, were inconclusive evidence.

Drawing on Chamberlin 1933 and Robinson 1933, Burns argued that there was no clear distinction between monopoly and competition, and elements of monopoly were an increasingly important and inescapable part of the economic system:

Elements of monopoly have always been interwoven with competition but the monopoly elements have increased in importance. They can no longer be regarded as occasional and relatively unimportant aberrations from competition. They are such an organic part of the industrial

2. The substantial role Simons saw for the state no doubt explains why later Chicago economists, though they might see him as a predecessor, did not consider him a supporter of free markets.

3. Burns cites Alfred Marshall's *Industry and Trade* (1919) as an example of the caveats economists made concerning laissez-faire.

system that it is useless to hope that they can be removed by law and the industrial system thus be brought into conformity with the ideal of perfect competition. (Burns 1936, 3)

A major factor was a reduction in the number of sellers in many industries. Part of the problem was developments in technology making for large-scale organization, but concentration was also encouraged by the developments in corporate law highlighted by Berle and Means, which favored corporations over individuals, and by patent laws. Antitrust law had failed because, in outlawing certain practices, it had simply caused businesses to suppress competition in ways not covered by the law. Burns reviewed many of these practices in detail: price discrimination, nonprice competition, and the integration of industrial operations.

The extent to which Burns departed from mechanical views of the way that markets worked, believing that there was significant indeterminacy in pricing policies, leaving room for business psychology, is shown by his eventual conclusion. Critical of the NIRA and NRA, he came down in favor of social control of business through the courts. "Reasoned decisions publicly available are the best means of providing for the evolution of an effective technique of control and for the minimization of resistance to policy" (Burns 1936, 590).

Though Moulton had sketched out what needed to be done to ensure economic progress, none of the four volumes produced by the Brookings team proposed specific policies to achieve these goals. This was tackled three years later by Nourse and Horace Drury in *Industrial Price Policies and Economic Progress* (1938). Taking up Moulton's conclusion, they started from the premise that the best way to improve economic welfare was "through a consistent policy of expanding real incomes by lowering the prices of goods and services wherever advances in techniques and organization make such a course practicable" (Nourse and Drury 1938, 2). After reviewing the way that prices were formed in a wide range of markets and in different businesses, they presented a detailed account of the history of competition in the United States, supporting the conclusions reached by Berle, Means, and Burns, whose books were cited approvingly, that in many industries competition no longer worked as it had in the past. In some industries, such as agriculture, the market determined prices, and there was no need for action. However, many industries were characterized by administered prices, determined not by the market but by the industrial executive. These prices were the problem.

The "administered prices" of the big corporation are expressions of the thinking of particular men who occupy executive positions. They reflect the way in which those individuals suppose that the economic process works. A big corporation is a potent instrument in the hands of a stupid man to carry into effect a price policy which may stunt its growth or lead to its actual death. It is, in the hands of one who under- stands the laws of economic growth, an equally powerful instrument for the carrying out of a price program which will stimulate and develop the market, lead to capacity operations, and thereby contribute to that general prosperity on which the given business will feed in the future. (Nourse and Drury 1938, 270–71)

Though there might be a role for regulating prices, there was in Nourse's conclusions an assumption that business behavior needed to be changed. Industrialists might bemoan the stupidity of labor union officials, yet they could be equally stupid in their pricing policies. The clear implication was that if industrialists could be persuaded that there were better policies, they would find it in their interests to adopt them. Businesspeople benefited from free enterprise, but in return they acquired obligations to society.

If the American business man demands the right of freedom of eco- nomic enterprise, society in granting it to him may properly ask that he use that freedom aggressively in the public interest. . . . If he cannot meet it [this challenge,] the system of free enterprise under private cap- italism is doomed to a condition of invalidism, low vitality, and unpro- ductiveness. (275)

By the time Roosevelt wrote to Congress, there was thus an extensive literature arguing that stagnation and depression were the result of compe- tition having broken down, implying the need for policies that ran counter to the policies of maintaining prices that he had pursued in his first admin- istration. The problem was not ruinous competition putting firms out of business but inadequate competition, resulting in households having insufficient incomes to buy the goods being produced.

3. The Concentration of Economic Power

In response to the president's letter, Congress established a Temporary National Economic Committee (TNEC), made up of members of both the Senate and the House of Representatives, to investigate the concentration of economic power. Staff from various government agencies produced a series of monographs, and the TNEC heard evidence from many witnesses. One of the most widely discussed hearings was the one in which Lauchlin Currie and Alvin Hansen gave evidence (see Sandilands 1990, 83–84; Stein 1969, 167–68). Hansen was the first, and during the morning of May 16, 1939, after explaining about flows of savings and investment, he argued that the Depression had been brought about by a decline in investment that could be linked to population growth having been much lower in the 1930s than it had been in the 1920s. A fall in investment, and hence unemployment, could arise from a mere slowdown in the rate of expansion. His evidence was primarily statistical, full of technical details about how magnitudes were measured.

Before Currie gave evidence in the afternoon, the committee chair, Senator Joseph O'Mahoney, emphasized the importance of the topic by reading out a letter Roosevelt had sent that day, saying that he was concerned not only with idle men and factories but also with "the vast reservoir of money and savings [that had] remained idle in stagnant pools" (USTNEC 1940, 3519, 4009). Roosevelt expressed his hope that the committee would analyze ways in which "the financial machine" could be made to work more efficiently. Currie's evidence provided further statistics, focusing explicitly on "income-producing expenditures that offset saving," material that was clearly directly related to Roosevelt's concerns. Hansen was then recalled to interpret Currie's statistics. His crucial point was that, to have full employment, all savings, even money that was hoarded, had to be offset by some form of spending.

Though such justification may not have been necessary, especially given Roosevelt's letter, Hansen justified paying attention to saving and investment by arguing that it was wrong to focus exclusively on commodity markets:

Too frequently when the functioning of the price system is under consideration attention is focused almost exclusively upon the commodity markets.

To leave an inquiry into the functioning of the price system, with a consideration of commodity prices alone would in my judgment overlook a sector in our economy, which is more important than any other for an understanding of the operation, the maladjustments and the instability of modern economic life. I refer in particular to that area which relates to the flow of savings and to the flow of new investment into the expansion of productive equipment. (USTNEC 1940, 3497)

He made no comments on the merits of the idea that there was a much more generalized market failure linked to a decline of competition, but merely drew the committee's attention to the importance of what Roosevelt had called the financial machine. A later critic (Stigler 1942, 5) pointed out that the TNEC had failed to hear any other opinions on monetary economics and that both Hansen and Currie completely ignored monopoly. Given his previous work, Berle might have been expected to address the problem in his testimony (USTNEC 1940, 3809–35), but he did not. He was called as an expert on corporate finance, and his evidence concerned the role of bank credit and corporate bond markets in influencing investment. His evidence on the concentration of corporate capital, and problems faced by small businesspeople in raising capital, fit well with the arguments with Means about the changing structure of industry, and with creating new financial institutions that might make the system run more efficiently.

Even if Hansen and Currie were the star witnesses (Stein 1969, 168), their testimony covered only eighty-eight of the thirty-three thousand pages published by the TNEC.[4] Elsewhere, in both monographs produced by employees of the government agencies involved, some supervised by academic economists, and the record of the hearings, extensive attention was paid to problems of industrial structure and factors that might have caused competition to become ineffective. Monographs were devoted to the structure of industry, pricing policies (with a separate monograph on basing-point pricing), antitrust policy, patents, taxation, wages, profits, income distribution, life insurance, and the motion picture industry. Hearings covered patents, technology, and the concentration of economic power, monopolistic practices, insurance, investment, and profits, as well as specific industries.[5] These were summarized in the TNEC's final report (USTNEC 1941a).

The report began by documenting the extent of monopoly in the United States. After an explanation of some of the problems involved in defining monopoly, statistics were presented on the degree of concentration in different industries, along with a discussion of the practices that firms used to maintain their market positions. It concluded that concentration had increased over the previous fifty years, and even in industries that were

4. There is an ambiguity in the number of volumes in that some volumes numbered separately were printed as single physical volumes. The page count is taken from Stigler 1942, 1.

5. Neither list is comprehensive. For a complete set of volumes, go to archive.org/search .php?query=temporary%20national%20economic%20committee.

normally competitive, "competition is constantly breaking down" (UST-NEC 1941a, 26). However, it was not inevitable that this should happen: the report rejected the argument that the efficiency of large-scale production inevitably led to monopoly, which was the result of formal agreements, secret understandings, combinations, interlocking directorates and stockholdings, restrictive practices, coercion, intimidation, violence, and property rights that gave their owners exclusive privileges, patents, and tariffs (28).

After a chapter on the concentration of production, the report turned to "managed industrial prices" (chap. 3). Though expressed in different language, this was Means's argument about administered prices.

> For the prices of a vast range of industrial commodities and even of some agricultural products are controlled to a material extent by the policy decisions of business executives acting individually or in concert. Unlike such products as wheat . . . the prices of such commodities as steel, aluminum, automobiles, cigarettes, and bread are all subject to a substantial degree of control by a limited number of executives in a few large companies. (67)

Such businesspeople all faced constraints on their ability to set prices, but they were continually trying to widen the limits within which they had discretion over prices. The result was that the businessperson had become "the economic planner of our society."

Attention was also paid to technological change. Economic theory held that increased productivity would lower prices, increasing the consumer's purchasing power. However, "this theory presupposes that all prices are 'market' prices" (USTNEC 1941a, 118). But in many industries, where prices were "influenced" (there was no settled terminology for this phenomenon), businesses were able to retain some of these gains. Prices remained high and employment fell fastest in these industries. Technological advance thus created gains and losses. Anticipating later chapters, a summary of these losses was immediately followed by the observation that "evidence of the lack of balance between investment and consumption necessary for the maintenance of a 'balanced economy' is unmistakable" (USTNEC 1941a, 141).

The report transitioned to the discussion of saving and investment by moving from the analysis of the concentration of production to the "concentration of ownership of corporate assets, earnings and profits" and the concentration of ownership of wealth in general. This led to an analysis of the concentration of savings (in a chapter written by Oscar Altman) that began, quoting from Currie's testimony, by explaining that what mattered was not whether savings were invested or consumed but whether they were hoarded and not returned to the income stream. Hydraulic metaphors abounded, as when the chapter talked of the "reservoirs" in which savings were collected (214). The capital market was the name used to refer to the set of institutions that transferred funds from savers, increasingly concentrated, into the hands of investors.

When it turned to the concentration of investment, another chapter written by Altman, the report pointed to two functions performed by investment. Not only did investment increase productive capacity; it also maintained the flow of purchasing power. This was illustrated with a diagram taken from a TNEC monograph by Martin Taitel (USTNEC 1941a, 225; USTNEC and Taitel 1941, 128), shown here as figure 1. Though its circularity is only implicit, this is virtually a circular flow diagram, for it shows how national income in one period generates national income in the next. However, where postwar circular flow diagrams were to focus on the flow of income, with the capital market considered a side channel, here the "capital pool" was central, with a detailed analysis of the relationship between the stock of capital and flows of saving and investment.

Altman's statistics showed that over the previous two decades, the fraction of investment funded by business saving—by companies' internally generated funds—had increased dramatically, and he argued that this was an underestimate of the true figure. This gave scope for the issues raised by Berle and Means about the separation of ownership and control to be important.

> When businesses invest their own funds it must not be assumed that the actual savers are identical with those who make the investment decisions. . . . It is the managers who decide how much should be set aside for reserves and expansion. . . . In theory the stockholders have the right to determine whether investment of the earnings of the property should be made at all, and how much. Actually, in most cases, they play no effective part in the decisions. (USTNEC 1941a, 231)

For market mechanisms to work, investment would have to respond to profit rates, but there was evidence that this did not happen. Though he conceded that little was known about the extent to which "social, personal and political elements" determined investment decisions, there was evidence that "high rates of profit do not of themselves attract new investment, nor low rates deter it" (USTNEC 1941a, 246). The most important

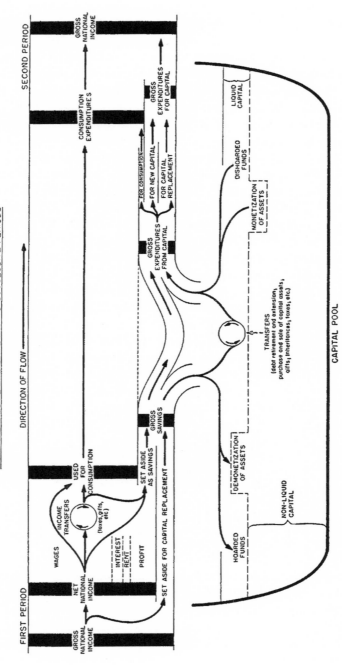

Figure 1 Selected features of the flow of funds

factors affecting new investment were the level of output and the need to introduce new technologies.

The Depression, Altman concluded, had arisen because concentration of income and wealth had raised the level of saving, and hence the need for investment. At the same time, concentration of wealth reduced the outlets for investment: "Concentration limits the extent to which capital expenditures can or will be made for capital goods to take business away from existing facilities" (247). It is the last phrase that is crucial here, for it is the result of a decline in competition.

This set the stage for the chapter arguing for policies to stimulate investment, written by Paul Sweezy and strongly influenced by Hansen, whose testimony was quoted at length at the outset. There was some evidence that investment might be insensitive to interest rates, but this did not apply to all sectors of the economy. Housing and small business investment were responsive to interest rate cuts, so measures should be taken to focus on them. For much of industry, however, monopoly was a barrier in that monopolies would be reluctant to undertake new investment till older investments had worn out. "In short," Sweezy wrote, "under monopoly new methods tend to succeed old methods; under competition, new methods tend to replace old methods" (USTNEC 1941a, 278). The report therefore concluded with chapters on housing, small businesses, and consumers in more detail, and a closing chapter on fiscal policy.

4. The Legacy

When investigating the economic thinking spawned by the Great Depression, historians have focused on the constellation of events known as "the Keynesian revolution" and the emergence of ways of thinking about "macroeconomic" problems. According to Keynes, there was a very specific market failure: a market economy had no mechanism to ensure that sufficient investment would be undertaken to absorb the savings that would be generated at full employment. His aim was to argue that, despite the existence of mass unemployment, the key market failure was in the capital market, not the labor market. For over three decades, this was the framework within which the causes of depressions were debated: was wage rigidity necessary for involuntary unemployment to occur, or was there some other reason why free market economies would typically fail to achieve full employment?

The present article adds an important element to the conventional story of the Keynesian revolution. Many American economists sought to explain the Great Depression as a failure of competition. Though they were not "Keynesians," they hardly fit Keynes's stereotype of a "classical" economist, using arguments about how concentration of market power could interfere with market processes and produce inequalities of wealth that would, in a Hobsonian manner, reduce aggregate spending. The catastrophic failure of the market system was due, at least in significant part, to the growth of monopoly, which prevented traditional market mechanisms from working. Though the phrase was not used at the time, the nearest being the phrase "failure of capitalism," cited by Simons, this amounted to an argument that there had been a general market failure. Markets worked when there was effective competition, but competition was not working, not because individual businesspeople were crooks, but because of deeply rooted structural factors. Wage rigidity was a part of this story, but only a small part.

The proceedings of the TNEC are particularly important because these two perspectives on the Depression—that it was the result of a failure of the financial machine to translate savings into investment, and that the Depression was the result of a widespread breakdown in competition— came together in their hearings. Historians who have considered this episode have focused on the way that Hansen and Currie captured the attention of the committee. However, while that is correct, simply focusing on a clash between "Keynesian" and older views obscures how a new form of what, for want of a better term, might be called "American Keynesianism" arose out of the literature that associated market failure with the breakdown of competition. Hansen, whose arguments are particularly influential, was rooted in the "institutionalist" traditions out of which the literature on the decline of competition emerged, his Keynesianism being dominated by structural factors, such as the decline in population growth and changes in the flow of innovations, both factors in arguments about the growth of monopoly.

Even more significant, the TNEC report presented arguments for fiscal policy as a response to the problems caused by the concentration of economic power. Concentration of wealth affected saving and concentration of power within industry affected investment, and arguments about ownership and control provided a foundation for the Keynesian stress on the distinction between saving and investment. Keynesianism had been encompassed into a worldview that owed more to American institutionalism than to Marshall's Cambridge.

It is easy to trace the links between the literature discussed here and postwar industrial economics. Edward Mason, who, along with Joe Bain, was one of the leading figures in what became known as the "Harvard" school of industrial economics, had helped supervise the monograph on the central topic of "price behavior and business policy" (USTNEC 1941b), as well as acting as a consultant on another volume. The TNEC's quantitative approach, based on classifying industries, finds a clear echo in the work of Mason and Bain and their colleagues. Stigler's (1942) questioning of the TNEC's conclusions about the extent and implications of monopoly represents an early statement of the "Chicago" view of monopoly. As this literature developed, it lost its connections with the business cycle and the attempt to explain the Great Depression in terms of a failure of competition. At the same time, explanations of the Depression were increasingly seen in Keynesian terms. As Rutherford has shown, institutionalists increasingly adopted Keynes.

However, the perspectives discussed in the present article did leave a mark on American Keynesianism as it developed after the Second World War. Accounts of the history of macroeconomics often focus on what Perry Mehrling (1997) has called "monetary Walrasianism," a term that accurately describes mathematical modeling in the tradition of John Hicks, Oskar Lange, Franco Modigliani, and Don Patinkin, in which macroeconomics is grounded on theories of competitive markets. It is well known that much work did not fit this framework, being less formal, and often based on the assumption that firms were imperfectly competitive, facing costs that were roughly constant up to full capacity. What is not often acknowledged is that this approach was rooted in the analysis of markets discussed in the present article. It is no coincidence that some of the most influential interpreters of Keynes in the early 1950s were not monetary Walrasians but had institutionalist roots: for example, Dudley Dillard's *Economics of John Maynard Keynes: The Theory of a Monetary Economy* (1948) and Hansen's *Guide to Keynes* (1953). John Kenneth Galbraith, a very influential Keynesian on account of his public profile, went so far as to develop, in a series of highly popular books, theories of market failure that clearly owed much to institutionalist theories of market failure developed during the 1930s (see Parker 2005).

The debates discussed in the present article also left their mark on the work of Paul Samuelson, whose widely used textbook, *Economics: An Introductory Analysis* (1948), did much to define postwar American Keynesianism. Samuelson was personally and intellectually close to Hansen during the decade after Hansen's testimony to the TNEC. He was recruited by Hansen to act as a consultant to the National Resources Planning Board, working with Altman, author of two of the crucial chapters in the final report, and testified several times before the committee, making proposals that were taken up in several monographs. The project on which Samuelson worked—using statistics on the distribution of income to obtain forecasts of postwar consumption—was entirely in the spirit of the TNEC's analysis of concentration. He had Harvard teachers (e.g., Mason), other students (e.g., Sweezy), and MIT colleagues (e.g., Douglass Brown and Charles Myers) who were heavily involved in the TNEC's deliberations. Much of this affected his thinking on macroeconomics and carried over into his textbook.

The TNEC was cited only three times in his textbook, once on the structure of American industry, once on industrial insurance schemes, and once to criticize the mistaken belief of those testifying to it that the US economy was entering a period of stagnation. However, its influence is pervasive. His discussion of business organization and the modern corporation documented industrial concentration under the heading "the evil of monopoly" (Samuelson 1948, 126–27). He acknowledged that business was controlled by managers, not by its owners, and he saw managers as having sufficient monopoly power to have some discretion in setting prices. Imperfect competition was more than a theoretical possibility. After discussing competitive markets, he wrote,

> The practical importance of pure competition is not great enough to justify its further discussion. The competitive firm need only look at the newspaper price quotations of the Board of Trade to know all there is to know about price, demand, and revenue. . . . Realistically speaking, we must recognize that modern business firms—even the largest—are unable to calculate their marginal revenue and marginal cost. They cannot determine their optimum price and output with nice exactitude. . . . There seems nothing to do about this unsatisfactory situation but to try to specify a number of different competitive and monopolistic patterns characteristic of various important industrial situations. (Samuelson 1948, 509, 510, 511)

His first such category, "chronically overcrowded sick industries," carries stronger overtones of institutionalist industrial economics than the economic theory found in the mathematical models of markets in his *Foundations of Economic Analysis* (Samuelson 1947).

Samuelson's account of the determinants of saving and investment are too brief to be sure how far he accepted Altman's and Taitel's analysis, but he did cite large corporations when explaining that saving and investment were undertaken by different people and for different reasons (Samuelson 1948, 254). His emphasis on the investment opportunities provided by new products, new resources, and greater population clearly echoed Hansen, and, though he discussed the determination of interest rates, there was no systematic account of the effect of interest rates on investment: he allowed for the possibility that investment might vary with the level of national income but not that it might vary with the rate of interest.

Were these merely remarks in an introductory textbook, they might have little significance, despite Samuelson's preeminence. Their significance arises because such a position was standard outside the world of mathematical economics. In the 1960s, it was routine to assume constant costs, another regularity established in the prewar literature and markup pricing (Samuelson 1948, 509) to argue that prices would be largely independent of output. Arguments about "cost-push" inflation, which were widespread in the 1950s and 1960s, were based on the assumption that prices were determined substantially independently of output, an assumption that made sense in a world where corporations had sufficient monopoly power to have discretion over the prices they set (see Forder 2014; Backhouse and Forder 2013). Though consistent in its own terms, it was a view of the world that later generations of economists, committed to mathematical modeling of rational individuals, failed to understand.[6]

5. Concluding Remarks

Though they used different language, the Great Depression was, for most economists of the time, a clear example of market failure. For much of the 1930s, many American economists argued that the growth of market power had led to a failure of competition and that this had caused capitalism to fail. At the end of the decade, such explanations of the Depression

---

6. A good example of this is the notion of cost-push inflation. This was based on the assumption that supply and demand did not completely determine prices, with the result that there were limits within which noneconomic, possibly sociological, factors could influence inflation, independently of the level of aggregate demand. As macroeconomics changed in the 1970s, this view changed into one in which cost-push was no more than a label for changes originating on the supply side. The distinction between cost-push and demand-pull had lost its rationale, but survived.

were displaced by theories about the failure of what Roosevelt called "the financial machine" to translate savings into investment. The interplay of these two conceptions of market failure can be seen in the proceedings of the TNEC, and this shows that, although the Keynesian perspective came to dominate the TNEC's final report, it was merged with and presented as an extension of the view that the root cause of the problem was the concentration of economic power. The failure of the financial machine came to be seen as an extension of the more general view of market failure that had been widespread in the 1930s but which by the 1950s had dropped out of fashion, certainly among mathematical economists.

The adoption of Keynesian ideas by the supporters of the institutional movement contributed to the rapid decline of the movement during the 1940s. However, ideas about the market did feed into subsequent developments in economic analysis. In the 1940s and 1950s, discussions of the failure of competition were generally linked to microeconomics—to the failure of specific industries to perform well. The postwar debate between the "Harvard" and "Chicago" schools of industrial organization can be traced back at least to Stigler's critique of institutionalist analysis found in the TNEC reports. Postwar Keynesians focused not on market power but on deficient effective demand and the cause of depression, modeling this using the multiplier, the 45-degree line diagram popularized by Samuelson's textbook, and what came to be known as the Hicks-Hansen IS-LM model. However, the background of many leading Keynesians in the arguments about market power prevalent in the 1930s left their mark on the way these models were interpreted. They were seen not as grounded in theories of perfectly competitive equilibrium but as resting on ideas about the operation of imperfectly competitive markets that were not analyzed formally.

An important part of the story of the Keynesian revolution in America involves the taking up by institutionalists of Keynesian ideas, leading to the demise of institutionalism as a distinctive movement. In Hansen's case this involved realizing that Keynes was proposing arguments that could be related to his own theory of stagnation, and that the multiplier could be incorporated into his own theoretical framework. In the proceedings of the TNEC, a similar process took place, in which ideas about the failure of the saving/investment mechanism were incorporated into a more general theory of market failure; those ideas then dominated. This is not a complete account of the Keynesian revolution in America, which also involves a turn toward fiscal policy as the main weapon with which to combat unemployment, but it is an important part of the story.

References

Adams, A. B., C. Goodrich, J. Demmery, W. L. Thorp, and A. H. Hansen. 1931. "The Business Depression of Nineteen Hundred Thirty—Discussion." *American Economic Review* 21 (1): 183–201.

Backhouse, R. E., and J. Forder. 2013. "Rationalizing Incomes Policy in Britain, 1948–1979." *History of Economic Thought and Policy* 1 (1): 17–35.

Berle, A. A., and G. C. Means. 1932. *The Modern Corporation and Private Property.* New York: Macmillan.

Burns, A. R. 1936. *The Decline of Competition: A Study of the Evolution of American Industry.* New York: McGraw Hill.

Chamberlin, E. H. 1933. *The Theory of Monopolistic Competition.* Cambridge, Mass.: Harvard University Press.

Clark, J. M. 1923. *Studies in the Economics of Overhead Costs.* Chicago: University of Chicago Press.

Dillard, D. 1948. *The Economics of John Maynard Keynes: The Theory of a Monetary Economy.* New York: Prentice Hall.

Forder, J. 2014. *Macroeconomics and the Phillips Curve Myth.* Oxford: Oxford University Press.

Handman, M., A. P. Usher, G. W. Stocking, V. W. Bladen, B. Mitchell, W. Jaffé, A. H. Hansen, and C. Goodrich. 1931. "Economic History—the Decline of Laissez Faire." *American Economic Review* 21 (1): 3–10.

Hansen, A. H. 1953. *A Guide to Keynes.* London: McGraw Hill.

Harriman, H. I. 1932. "The Stabilization of Business and Employment." *American Economic Review* 22 (1): 63–74.

Keynes, J. M. (1936) 1972. *The General Theory of Employment, Interest, and Money.* Vol. 7 of *The Collected Writings of John Maynard Keynes.* London: Macmillan.

Knight, F. H. 1921. *Risk, Uncertainty, and Profit.* Boston: Houghton Mifflin.

Lee, F. S. 1990. "From Multi-Industry Planning to Keynesian Planning: Gardiner Means, the American Keynesians, and National Economic Planning at the National Resources Committee." *Journal of Policy History* 2 (2): 186–212.

Marshall, A. 1919. *Industry and Trade.* London: Macmillan.

Means, G. C. 1935a. "The Distribution of Control and Responsibility in a Modern Economy." *Political Science Quarterly* 50 (1): 59–69.

———. 1935b. "Price Inflexibility and the Requirements of a Stabilizing Monetary Policy." *Journal of the American Statistical Association* 30 (190): 401–13.

Mehrling, P. 1997. *The Money Interest and the Public Interest: American Monetary Thought, 1920–1970.* Cambridge, Mass.: Harvard University Press.

Moulton, H. G. 1935. *Income and Economic Progress.* Washington, D.C.: Brookings Institution.

Nourse, E. G., and H. B. Drury. 1938. *Industrial Price Policies and Economic Progress.* Washington, D.C.: Brookings Institution.

Nourse, E. G., F. G. Tryon, M. Leven, H. B. Drury, H. G. Moulton, and C. Lewis. 1934. *America's Capacity to Produce.* Washington, D.C.: Brookings Institution.

Parker, R. 2005. *John Kenneth Galbraith: His Life, His Politics, His Economics.* Reprint ed. New York: Farrar, Straus and Giroux.

Robinson, J. 1933. *Economics of Imperfect Competition.* London: Macmillan.

Rutherford, M. 2011. *The Institutionalist Movement in American Economics, 1918–1947: Science and Social Control.* New York: Cambridge University Press.

Samuelson, P. A. 1947. *Foundations of Economic Analysis.* Cambridge, Mass.: Harvard University Press.

———. 1948. *Economics: An Introductory Analysis.* New York: McGraw Hill.

Sandilands, R. J. 1990. *The Life and Political Economy of Lauchlin Currie: New Dealer, Presidential Adviser, and Development Economist.* Durham, N.C.: Duke University Press.

Schumpeter, J. 1931. "The Present World Depression: A Tentative Diagnosis." *American Economic Review* 21 (1): 179–82.

Simons, H. C. (1934) 1948. "A Positive Program for Laissez Faire: Some Proposals for a Liberal Economic Policy." In *Economic Policy for a Free Society*, 40–77. Chicago: University of Chicago Press.

Stabile, D. R., and A. F. Kozak. 2012. *Markets, Planning, and the Moral Economy: Business Cycles in the Progressive Era and New Deal.* Cheltenham: Edward Elgar.

Stein, H. 1969. *The Fiscal Revolution in America.* Chicago: University of Chicago Press.

Stigler, G. J. 1942. "The Extent and Bases of Monopoly." *American Economic Review* 32 (2): 1–22.

Taussig, F. W., F. C. Mills, B. Garver, F. H. Knight, R. W. Souter, L. L. Lorwin, and M. Ezekiel. 1930. "The Theory of Economic Dynamics as Related to Industrial Instability." *American Economic Review* 20 (1): 30–39.

Tugwell, R. G. 1932. "The Principle of Planning and the Institution of Laissez Faire." *American Economic Review* 22 (1): 75–92.

United States, Temporary National Economic Committee (USTNEC). 1938. *Investigation of Concentration of Economic Power: Hearings, Part 1–3, Economic Prologue.* Washington, D.C.: US Government Printing Office.

———. 1940. *Investigation of Concentration of Economic Power: Hearings, Part 9, Savings and Investment.* Washington, D.C.: US Government Printing Office.

———. 1941a. *Investigation of Concentration of Economic Power: Final Report of the Executive Secretary.* Washington, D.C.: US Government Printing Office.

———. 1941b. *Investigation of Concentration of Economic Power: Monographs 1–3, Price Behavior and Business Policy.* Washington, D.C.: US Government Printing Office.

United States, Temporary National Economic Committee (USTNEC), and M. Taitel. 1941. *Investigation of Concentration of Economic Power: Monograph 12, Profits, Productive Activities, and New Investment.* Washington, D.C.: US Government Printing Office.

Analyzing Market Failure:
Adam Smith and
John Maynard Keynes

Bradley W. Bateman

There is very little literature that discusses the work of Adam Smith and John Maynard Keynes together. They have largely escaped comparison. On the one hand, this might be surprising, since Keynes purposely set the "classical school" as the foil of *The General Theory* and Adam Smith is the first great classical economist. Thus, one might have expected that now that there has been over seventy-five years of literature on "Mr. Keynes and the classics" that the topic of Smith and Keynes would have been well explored. On the other hand, Keynes barely mentions Smith in *The General Theory*, making David Ricardo, instead, bear the brunt of his attack on the classical school.[1] In this, of course, Keynes followed many of his late nineteenth-century predecessors, not least the German historical school and Alfred Marshall, in making Ricardo the *analytical* starting point for the classics.

Correspondence may be addressed to Bradley W. Bateman, Randolph College, Lynchburg, VA 24503; e-mail: bbateman@randolphcollege.edu. I wish to thank Steven Medema for encouragement to pursue the topic of this essay. I owe a great debt of gratitude to Bruce Caldwell for helping me to improve the original version of the essay presented at the conference in April 2014 by pointing out a bad mistake I had made. My anonymous referee was generous with her comments.

1. We know that Keynes read Smith when he was still an undergraduate on a summer hiking trip and that he enjoyed Smith very much. Had Keynes chosen to create a caricature of Smith in *The General Theory*, it would have been only fair, of course, since Smith's portrait of the mercantilists in *The Wealth of Nations* is a particularly cartoonlike straw man. Perhaps ironically, the only reference to Smith in *The General Theory* comes in chapter 23, "Notes on Mercantilism, the Usury Laws, Stamped Money, and Theories of Under-Consumption," where Keynes treats Smith sympathetically and refers to him as "the forerunner of the classical school" (361).

History of Political Economy 47 (annual suppl.) DOI 10.1215/00182702-3130475
Copyright 2015 by Duke University Press

The paucity of literature comparing and contrasting Smith and Keynes might also be surprising because Smith is so often cast as the iconic defender of laissez-faire capitalism and Keynes as the great defender of the need for state intervention to sustain capitalism. It would seem natural, then, to compare and contrast them given their status in the public mind as the defenders of very different visions of capitalism.

In fact, however, they share at least one aspect in their analysis of capitalist society that points to a common understanding of the potential for market failure. But because this shared aspect of their analytical systems lies far outside the contemporary modeling assumptions, it defines a form of "market failure" that does not exist in contemporary economics.

Two Different Types of Economic Model

It is ironic that an analytical similarity in Smith's and Keynes's models led both men to see the same potential for market failure, since, in all likelihood, one of the main reasons for the thinness of the literature on Smith and Keynes is due to the utter incompatibility of their analytical systems. Despite being an empirically minded analyst, Smith had "no great faith in" political arithmetic, and his work has never been subjected to the kinds of efforts at mathematization that Ricardo's work has been (Smith [1776] 1937, 573).[2] This made it much more difficult to insert Smith into the literature on "Mr. Keynes and the classics," which was based for much of its run on the comparison of simple mathematical models to differentiate Keynes from his predecessors. Keynes was no great fan of the political arithmetic either, however; thus, the analytical differences between them are *not* about differences in their equations.

Both men painted with words, rather than equations, but they painted in very different styles. Smith's analytical system might most easily be recognized by the modern term *surplus school*, meaning that he built a model that examined how the economic system reproduces itself each year, focusing on how much had been carried forward from the previous year (what he referred to as a society's "stock") to support production in the next year. The crucial question for his analysis, then, became whether

---

2. The only effort I could find to reproduce Smith's basic system in *The Wealth of Nations* as a mathematical model is Eltis 1975. When Smith referred to "political arithmetic," he was, of course, referring to William Petty's empirical work and not to modern mathematical modeling. I am, thus, using the term loosely here to capture Smith's lack of faith in reducing economic discussion to "arithmetic."

a nation's stock was larger at the end of the year than it had been at the beginning of the year. If the size of a nation's stock increased, it then had a *surplus*, which could be used in the next year to support even more production.[3] This might also be thought of as an agricultural model of output, for it very much reflects the agricultural cycle of production and reproduction: the past year's output supports society during the current year while the next year's output is being produced. If your net output at the end of the year exceeds the stock at the beginning of the year, then you have the ability to plant, grow, or raise more the next year. Since we know that Smith was influenced by the physiocrats, it is not surprising that his basic model is one that mimics agricultural production and is based on a simple idea of the periodicity of production.

Like Smith, Keynes created a model that was largely written and based on "commonsense" ideas of how production takes place. By Keynes's day, however, the agricultural model of production no longer made sense, and his model seems much more familiar to us for being essentially industrial. For Keynes, production is instantaneous, or in real time. Rather than pay workers out of last year's output, and focus on whether enough is produced this year to support a larger workforce next year, workers in Keynes's model are paid their wages out of the current year's production.

One of the easiest ways to see the difference between their models is to focus on Smith's famous concepts of "productive" and "unproductive" labor. A productive laborer in Smith's schema is one who produces things that could end up in the "stock" available to support workers next year. An unproductive worker is one who is paid from last year's stock but does not produce anything that could add to next year's stock. Thus, farm laborers or those who work in a pin factory are productive laborers, but opera singers and teachers are unproductive laborers. The distinction is crucial for Smith because according to his analysis one of the most important things to know if one is making an inquiry into the nature and causes of the wealth of nations is whether the nation's stock is growing or whether there is a growing surplus to support more workers and more production in the future.[4]

Like us, Keynes was not much concerned with what laborers do when they are at work, only that they are employed and earning an income. Keynes makes no distinction between productive and unproductive labor because anyone who works for wages is making something, whether a

3. The term *surplus* is a modern term, not Smith's. But it is evocative, and I think it helps make the point here for the contemporary reader.

4. This is really the point of book 2 of *The Wealth of Nations*.

good or service, that adds to the national income. Keynes would have been happy to have more painters and opera singers, as long as they were being paid for their work. Smith respected some kinds of unproductive labor (he was an unproductive laborer, after all); but for his system, they were a drag on the economy and a lost chance for more growth. For Keynes, there was no unproductive labor.[5]

From Smith to Keynes

There is not a single narrative about how modern economics made the transition from Smith's type of surplus model to Keynes's type of instantaneous production model.[6] It might be more fair to say that the transition is simply no longer a subject of inquiry for most historians of economic thought, although most could point to the nineteenth-century controversy around the "wages fund" as a particularly important source of controversy leading to the transition.[7]

Classical economists following Smith argued that there was a limit to the total amount of wages that could be paid to workers in any given year, with the limit defined by the amount of "stock" created in the previous year. Once rent and profits were paid out of the "stock," the remainder defined a "wages fund" for classical economists. As this idea became increasingly politicized in the nineteenth century, it came under especially heavy fire from those who claimed that it was possible to pay workers more than some arbitrary amount defined by *past* production.

The mathematization of economics helped speed the change away from the agrarian model; the modern nexus between production and wages that Keynes employs in *The General Theory* emerged in the early mathemati-

5. Perhaps the best proof that unproductive labor was irrelevant to Keynes comes in the passage from *The General Theory* in which he states that if a nation wishes to increase employment, it could do so by burying money in bottles and then paying men to dig up the bottles. He is obviously saying here that this is less desirable than putting them to work making things, but his point is nonetheless correct for his purposes; work is work when you are unemployed.

6. There was perhaps a trailing form of what I call Smith's periodicity, or agricultural conception of production, in the great Austrian economists. From the late nineteenth century when the school was formed, at least through the work of Friedrich Hayek in the 1930s, Austrians developed a theory about the "roundaboutness" of capital that focused on successive periods of production and how the output of one period produced more that could be used in subsequent periods to sustain more production. While this theory still has its defenders, it has no real impact in modern economic theorizing.

7. The best treatment I know of this transition is in the little classic by William Barber, *A History of Economic Thought*; see the introduction to part 3: "Neo-classical Economics."

cal models of production that were pioneered in the second half of the nineteenth century. In those models, the return to all factors of production comes out of *current* output, not from a stock of goods and machinery that has been carried over from the *previous year.*

Likewise, another impetus to the analytical changes that followed the wages fund debate is that the second industrial revolution had so radically changed the "commonsense" understanding of what production is that Smith's agricultural model no longer made sense to people. Once vertically integrated production accelerated on a massive scale after 1860, an agricultural model of production no longer made any sense.

Thus, both the mathematization of economic analysis and the second industrial revolution were also at work in driving the change in how economists modeled production. But it is hard to escape the feeling that Karl Marx's adaptation of Smith's surplus model also helped propel this change. In *Capital*, Marx turned the surplus produced from one year to the next into the analytical device for explaining the exploitation of laborers in a capitalist economy. Marx argued that the surplus rightly belonged to the workers who had produced it through their labor, but that capitalists appropriated and used it to build their own fortunes. In fairness, this change was not a sudden shift from Smith's position; Ricardo and other early nineteenth-century classical economists had developed less optimistic ideas than Smith's about the possibility for how the surplus would affect the economy.

But no one else before Marx had used the classical surplus model to argue that workers were "exploited" and to show analytically how that exploitation could be measured. Thus, Marx had made the surplus model unattractive for economists who favored markets and capitalism. There clearly was a need for a new way to conceptualize production, and emerging marginalist conceptions worked particularly well: wages (and all other factor payments) came out of current production, not from a stock of output carried over from the past, and laborers (like all other factors) could be shown to be earning the value of what the marginal worker produced. No surplus value, no exploitation. The earliest issues of *History of Political Economy* have many articles about the marginalist revolution, and they largely focus on the more or less simultaneous emergence of marginalist analysis in Austria, England, and the United States. Since then, the narratives about the emergence of marginal thinking have become more complex and multinational (Ekelund and Hebert 2002). We can presumably take these scientific advances at face value as efforts to develop models that more clearly and persuasively depicted the operation of an industrial economy; but we do not need to attribute sinister motives to people to understand that the efforts were also welcomed as a way to deflect "surplus" reasoning and Marx's conclusions about exploitation in a market economy while laying the wages fund debate to rest.[8]

Analytically, however, the shift to marginalism in the mainstream also set up a fundamental affinity between Smith and Keynes that is not well understood and underpins their common vision of how markets might fail. Neither Smith nor Keynes was a marginalist, and neither used utility as the basis of his modeling. This obvious, but unexplored, link between them ended up leading both theorists to use a measure of employment as their primary measure of economic success.

Constructing Labor Metrics

The idea of using a measure of employment as the ultimate metric for economic success would strike most contemporary economists as odd. It is virtually impossible to escape a contemporary economic education without coming to accept that economic success is measured in terms of efficiency and utility. A good economic outcome is one that uses the least resources and produces the most satisfaction. This axiom is so central to economists trained in the mainstream (and even some who are not fully mainstream) that they manage to believe that it is a "value free" proposition. It is just a "fact" that this is the right way to measure economic success. Hence the usual definitions of market failure pivot on whether an "efficient" outcome has been achieved. Anything that prevents a market from coming to an "efficient" outcome is a cause of market failure. This might be because of a failure to fully specify legal rights, or because of monopoly power, or because of the presence of externalities, but the "failure" in market failure is a failure to achieve economic efficiency in the common understanding of economists. Ask most economists about evaluating an economic event in terms of how many people have lost jobs or how many gained a job, and they instinctively try to change the terms of evaluating the event.

But regardless of what contemporary economists think about how to measure economic success, Smith and Keynes both built systems in which

---

8. *Surplus* is in quotation marks here to differentiate it from the surpluses (consumer and producer) that Alfred Marshall introduced into marginalist analysis. Marshall's concepts are quite distinct from those of the classical schools and, to my knowledge, have never been used as the basis for arguments about the exploitation of labor.

a measure of employment defined economic success. The measures of employment they chose to define economic success were different and were determined largely by the unique features of their respective systems. But neither theorist chose utility (or efficiency) to measure economic success.

Smith seemingly had little choice in selecting how to measure economic output.

At least he did not have the choice to build a model that built on maximizing individual utility. Models of utility were not available until the nineteenth century, and so despite Smith's ([1776] 1937, 715) declaration that "consumption is the sole end and purpose of all production," he never modeled with utility. Indeed, one of the most surprising things to contemporary economists when they read Smith is his inability to use simple marginal utility theorizing to explain why diamonds are more valuable than water despite the greater importance of water to human subsistence.

Thus, despite his belief in the primacy of consumption as the end of economic activity, Smith did not have access to the analytical tool of utility. Instead, when he theorized about the wealth of the nation, he turned to labor to measure what was happening. "Labour, therefore, is the real measure of the exchangeable value of all commodities" (33). In today's economic jargon we would say that for Smith, output, is a monotonically increasing function of labor: the more laborers employed, the greater the output. Or, more to the point, the greater the nation's output, the more labor will have been employed. But Smith did not think in terms of monotonically increasing functions. Instead he thought in terms of labor and output.

While Smith employed a labor theory of value, however, and measured total output in terms of the amount of labor that went into making it, it must be said for clarity that the labor which Smith was concerned to employ more of was *productive* labor. Since unproductive laborers contributed nothing to the stock of society, he was not concerned to employ more unproductive laborers; his desideratum was to increase the amount of productive labor in a society because the wealth of the nation could be increased only by increasing the amount of stock, and only productive laborers could make that happen.[9] Thus, while a larger total output under Smith's labor theory of value necessarily means that more people will have been employed (or that more labor will have been performed), the people doing the work will have to have been *productive* laborers.

---

9. Of course, if a society employed productive labor and increased the amount of stock, it still might not have economic growth if the stock were consumed rather than turned toward productive activity in the next period.

Smith's use of a labor theory of value might stem from many sources. He was almost certainly influenced by Locke and his belief that a man's right to the fruits of his labor was central to individual liberty. "The property that every man has in his own labour, as it is the original foundation of all other property, so it is the most sacred and inviolable" (Smith [1776] 1937, 140). As a distinguished scholar of rhetoric, he may have also felt that he could be persuasive in making his arguments for market society by appealing to the "commonsense" idea that more people at work meant a more successful society. "The interest of the labourer is strictly connected with that of the society" (286). In the end, however, whatever layers of philosophy and rhetoric were entwined in his adopting a labor theory of value, his analytical insight that the wealth of a nation is directly tied to the employment of productive labor would seem to have driven his decision to make labor his metric for economic output and, hence, employment of productive labor his ultimate metric for economic success.

Unlike Smith, Keynes had ready access to utility modeling, but he consciously chose not to use it. Cambridge was a center for the consolidation of marginalist thinking and the home for the development of much of the applied utilitarian modeling that would define twentieth-century mainstream economics. But he explicitly rejected utility as an adequate descriptive model of human behavior or as a normative end for economic behavior. This was a direct result of the influence of the Cambridge philosopher G. E. Moore on his early thinking, and it had profound effects on him as an economist.[10]

Thus, while Keynes did not employ a labor theory of value, he also did not employ a utility theory of value.[11] What he did in *The General Theory* was build a model of the economy in which the dependent variable is the level of employment. This simple fact is often overlooked because Joan Robinson (1937) and J. R. Hicks (1937) offered alternative ways to depict his model shortly after he published his book, each of which changed the dependent variable to income. Their work helped underpin the neoclassical synthesis that quickly emerged as the standard way to depict Keynes's arguments and locked in the idea that national income is the dependent

10. Perhaps the best way to understand Moore's influence on Keynes is through Keynes's autobiographical essay, "My Early Beliefs." To understand this anti-utilitarian influence in his economics, see Bateman 1988 and 1996, and Backhouse and Bateman 2011.

11. Because Keynes never attempted to build a unified theory of value that built on a theory of market exchange, some would say that he did not have a theory of value. But see Goodwin 2006 for a full explanation of Keynes's values and their place in his economics, especially Goodwin's treatment of Keynes's concern with unemployment.

variable in a "Keynesian" model.[12] But Keynes did not publish a general theory of income; he published a general theory of employment.

The Potential for Market Failure

To understand how Smith and Keynes understood "market failure," it might be best to reiterate that this is not the same market failure that contemporary mainstream economists define by that term. It is, for both men, very definitely a failure of markets to work, but it might just as well be called a failure of market society.

Thus, it might also be termed *capitalism failure*, although that exact term would also be anachronistic for both thinkers. Smith never mentions the word *capitalism* in his writings, nor did anyone else until well into the nineteenth century. For Smith, it might, then, better be called a failure of "the system of natural liberty." For Keynes, it might be appropriate to speak of a "failure of *individualistic* capitalism," since he referred occasionally in his writings to the term *individualistic capitalism* and usually quite disparagingly. But contrary to one of the most common caricatures of Keynes, he was not an enemy of capitalism (Backhouse and Bateman 2011). He believed that a particular form of capitalism (individualistic) failed in particular ways, but he did not think that this meant that capitalism was without merit; in fact, he argued that it needed to be reformed and managed, but he did not argue for its abolition.[13]

Yet another term to describe their vision of market failure might be *macroeconomic market failure*. This would be accurate from a contemporary perspective, capturing both the sense that the failure is a systemic failure of the entire economy and differentiating it from the traditional usage of the term *market failure*, which is a decidedly microeconomic concept.[14] Again, the term would be anachronistic, since neither theorist

12. Twentieth-century economists have usually assumed that utility is a monotonically increasing function of income; hence the "simple" act of changing Keynes's model to a "general theory of income," rather than a "general theory of employment," made it compatible with neoclassical economics at a very fundamental level that is not obvious at first sight.

13. It is fascinating that Richard Posner, generally understood to be a defender of markets and capitalism, has faced some of the same misinterpretation of being anticapitalist as Keynes did after the publication of Posner's book *A Failure of Capitalism: The Crisis of '08 and the Descent into Depression* (2009).

14. Posner (2010) has done an excellent job of analyzing the poverty of the means by which self-styled defenders of market society have tried over time to assume away mass employment from macroeconomic models. Posner is himself a defender of market society, but he does not deny the existence of macroeconomic market failure.

used the macro-micro distinction, but it would nonetheless have some contemporary descriptive value.

For Keynes, market failure was evidenced in mass unemployment caused by the failure of investment. If investment collapsed, so would employment, and in this case it would have nothing to do with workers' behavior; it was *not* the result of wages that were too high, unionization, or the inefficient government protection of workers. Mass unemployment exists in his model because of the failure of capitalists to invest enough to sustain full employment.[15] Keynes believed that fundamental uncertainty, as opposed to insurable risk, could cause investment to collapse for two interrelated reasons.

Most fundamentally, Keynes believed that an event that causes incalculable uncertainty about the future can cause capitalists' confidence in future profits to collapse. This loss of confidence in the future will cause investors to step back and disengage. So, for instance, if the housing market were to collapse, and this led to uncertainty about the stability of the banking industry, then investors throughout the entire economy might radically cut back on, or even stop, investing while they waited to see what happened to the banking industry. Keynes explicitly denied that such uncertainty was calculable.

Keynes argued that such a collapse in confidence could be compounded because of what he called liquidity preference. Faced with an event that creates incalculable uncertainty about the future, Keynes argues that people will try to liquidate their financial assets. In other words, when they lose confidence about the future, they will try to convert as much of their wealth as they can to cash. If they hold bonds, which are the only alternative to holding cash in Keynes's simple portfolio model, they will try to sell the bonds to get cash. In trying to sell their bonds, the price of bonds will fall and interest rates will rise. These high interest rates will cause investment to fall even more. Unemployment will, likewise, rise further.

Nor did he believe that market society created any kind of self-correcting tendency for the kind of mass unemployment that would ensue if busi-

15. It is fascinating in the context of a conference on "market failure" to consider how the popular textbook writer Greg Mankiw (2001) portrayed unemployment in the second edition of his best-selling (pre–Great Recession) introductory textbook. In the chapter devoted entirely to unemployment, all his explanations of it are microeconomic, and all unemployment is caused by the actions of workers, with the sole exception of the case of efficiency wages. While acknowledging that unemployment is a potentially difficult experience, he does not allow that it can happen for any other reason than the level of wages, and never mentions mass unemployment or unemployment caused by insufficient aggregate demand.

nesspeople lost their confidence. Nothing in a capitalist society guaranteed that animal spirits, investment, and unemployment would bounce back.

Contrary to the myths about Keynes's work, he also did not believe that government expenditure could necessarily correct the situation once confidence had disappeared. "If the fear of a Labour government or a New Deal depresses enterprise, this need not be the result either of a reasonable calculation or of a plot with political intent;—it is the mere consequence of upsetting the delicate balance of spontaneous optimism" (Keynes 1936, 162–63). His recommendations about how to combat this kind of mass unemployment were limited and hinged on *preventative* measures that would keep businesspeople from losing their animal spirits in the first place.[16]

Smith also saw the potential for a lack of investment to affect employment, although he did not see the need for any kinds of measures to combat it. This is because he understood it as a *theoretical* possibility, but not something that would actually happen, or at least not often enough to cause serious problems.

It is easy enough to see why Smith believed that the possibility of a collapse in investment leading to unemployment was small. Ironically, perhaps, workers in Smith's world were protected from this kind of unemployment disaster, in part, because of the sociology of the emerging market society in which they lived. Smith believed that people's rationality and ability to understand their own best interests were shaped by the class to which they belonged in a market society. Thus, for instance, of landlords, he says, "that indolence which is the natural effect of the ease and security of their situation, renders them too often, not only ignorant, but incapable of that application of mind which is necessary in order to foresee and understand the consequences of any public regulation"; whereas, he says of a laborer, "his condition leaves him no time to receive the necessary information, and his education and habits are commonly such as to render him unfit to judge even though he was fully informed." But while landlords and laborers are made less competent by their roles in a market society, capitalists are made more competent. Smith argues that the employers of labor, the capitalists who must invest their stock to make the nation grow, are formed very differently: "As during their whole lives they are engaged in plans and projects, they have frequently more acuteness of understanding than the greater part of country gentlemen" (Smith [1776] 1937, 286–87).

16. For a discussion of what kinds of measures Keynes proposed to combat a loss of confidence among businesspeople, see Bateman 2006.

Smith's capitalists were shrewd men who would not sit on their stock. Thus, as the control of stock fell increasingly into the hands of capitalists and out of the hands of the landed gentry, Smith believed that it would happen less and less often that stock would be used to sustain unproductive workers. In fact, capitalists would be "perfectly crazy" not to invest their stock productively (309). He also believed that these men who were shaped to reason and plan better than others were subject to a kind of natural prudence.[17]

> It can seldom happen, indeed, that the circumstances of a great nation can be much affected either by prodigality or misconduct of individuals; the profusion or imprudence of some, being always more than compensated by the frugality and good conduct of others.
>
> With regard to profusion, the principle which prompts to expence, is the passion for present enjoyment; which, though sometimes violent and very difficult to be restrained, is in general only momentary and occasional. But the principle which prompts to save, is the desire of bettering our condition, a desire which, though generally calm and dispassionate, comes with us from the womb, and never leaves us until we go into the grave. . . . Though the principle of expence, therefore, prevails in almost all men upon some occasions, and in some men upon almost all occasions, yet in the greater part of men, taking the whole course of their life at an average, the principle of frugality seems not only to predominate, but to predominate very greatly. (371–72)

This is a neat solution to the potential problem of insufficient investment, and it points to one possible reason for Smith's confidence in the long-run growth of employment. Living in a time of the fundamental economic transition in Europe from feudalism to market society, Smith saw the progress of the "system of perfect liberty" as irreversible.[18] In fact, that is the point of book 3 of *The Wealth of Nations*; a country can slow the

17. Smith sometimes speaks in this passage as if all humans have a tendency to prudence, although he refers only to capitalists in his examples. We know that elsewhere in the book he speaks of landlords not being prudent, and he argues that laborers rarely have the opportunity to exercise their prudence. Thus, this tendency that comes with us "from the womb" seems to be applied only in discussing the behavior of the owners of stock.

18. There is no doubt that Smith's narrative in book 3 commits him to the inevitability of Europe's transition from feudalism to a more prosperous market society. He argues that nations can choose to follow the "natural path" or the "actual path," but they end up at the same place. Robert Heilbroner (1975) argues, however, that Smith felt that eventually all civilizations would end up with stagnant economies and a poor working class. This conclusion, however, had nothing to do with the investment behavior of capitalists.

progress of market society through bad policies and poor institutions, but one way or another, it will end up with market institutions and economic growth. And with those market institutions will come the rationality of the capitalist and the wise(r) investment of society's stock. For Smith, the problem is not hoarding or loss of confidence, as it is for Keynes: the problem is merely one of prodigality versus frugality, and he believes frugality wins easily. The landed gentry may have been willing to waste their stock on unproductive labor, but capitalists were not. Capitalists were reasonable, calculating people who would invest in productive labor and so spur the growth of output.

Another way to understand how the context of Smith's writing may have shaped his belief that a failure of wise investment would not lead to widespread unemployment is to point out that no one spoke of "mass unemployment" in Smith's time. Smith clearly talked about more and less employment, and he cared passionately about people who were denied employment through guild regulations or feudal laws, but the kind of mass unemployment that Marx or Keynes observed was not "visible" in the same way. Whether this was because the economy during the Scottish Enlightenment was still primarily agricultural, or whether it was an idea that people could experience but not yet "see," is not clear.

Yet another way that we can understand the effects of Smith's context is to place him in the broad sweep of Western political and social theory in the early modern period. This is exactly what Albert O. Hirschman does, of course, in *The Passions and the Interests* (1977). Faced with the bleak prospects for peace and prosperity at the beginning of early modernity and given the role that the church often played in conflicts, Hirschman argues that Western social theorists began to abandon theology and to construct secularized theories of society that might create hope for a better future from alternative sources. Initially, these theorists argued that human passions might countervail one another to create peace and prosperity, providing a check and balance against each other. By the late eighteenth century, however, Hirschman argues that theorists such as Smith had evolved this argument about countervailing passions to say that humans' passions were tamed by their interests.

Thus, Smith's capitalists are not only shrewd and rational but also stoic, even-tempered, and not subject to the kind of swings in confidence that Keynes's investors are. The landscape in which they must make their selections may improve and deteriorate, but capitalists are not likely (often) to hire unproductive labor or to sit on their funds. They plow ahead, through thick and thin, doing the best they can, working to increase their own stock, and thereby increasing the stock of the nation.

Smith sees the *potential* for failure, but his carefully crafted sociology of human behavior, together with his belief in the fundamental prudence of capitalists, prevents a Keynesian crash in his system. The possibility of widespread unemployment exists in both men's models, however, and it is driven by the same possibility: insufficient investment.

What Does It Mean for a Market to Fail?

The Great Recession that followed the collapse of Lehman Brothers in 2008 has resurrected many fundamental debates within macroeconomics and has also reshaped macroeconomic orthodoxy. Whereas, twenty years ago, there was a general consensus among macroeconomists that most discretionary fiscal and monetary policies were ineffective, in the years since the Great Recession started, there has been a consensus that discretionary fiscal and monetary policies have a place in sustaining output when aggregate demand collapses. There is no consensus on how much or what form of these policies is most desirable, but there has been a return for much of the profession to the idea that some form of discretionary macroeconomic policy can be effective and, hence, is desirable. The advocates of policy ineffectiveness are many fewer, if no less passionate, but they no longer command the outlook of the profession.

One of the most high-profile conversions has been that of Richard Posner, an expert on microeconomic policy questions and a long-standing advocate of free markets. In several books (2009b, 2010) and articles (2009a, 2009c), Posner has acknowledged that until the Great Recession he had never given serious credence to Keynes's arguments that fundamental uncertainty can cause involuntary mass unemployment in a capitalist society. In the progression of his books and articles, Posner carefully tries to articulate what is necessary to make capitalism function well while honestly acknowledging that capitalism can fail when there is a collapse of confidence. In this, he nicely reflects the reconfigured mainstream since 2008.[19]

But regardless of whether it is a plurality of economists, or a majority, who have embraced this idea, Posner's analysis represents clear evidence

---

19. For an argument that policymakers had begun to turn away from the theoretical "policy ineffectiveness" arguments well before 2008, see Bateman 2010.

that there are other forms of "market failure" than the traditional definition of an individual market that is somehow prevented from coming to an
efficient equilibrium. It just happens to be the case that one of those forms
is mass unemployment caused by a collapse of confidence. For those not
trained in economics, this is as plain as day, although it has been difficult
for economists for many decades to include this intuition in their tool kits.

For Keynes, involuntary mass unemployment was the greatest market
failure. Smith recognized the possibility of large-scale, involuntary unemployment, but felt that it was not likely to happen often, if it did happen.
Because neither theorist used the applied utilitarian modeling of late
twentieth-century microeconomics, they each ended up with a quite different type of analysis. Both theorists could see the possibility of defining
employment in and of itself as a market failure because they employed a
model in which the dependent variable in the analysis was some measure
of employment.

But despite the recent turn among economists toward recognition that
involuntary mass unemployment does sometimes occur in capitalist market society, and for reasons that have nothing to do with the traditional
range of causes of economic inefficiency, one suspects that many economists will still bristle at labeling this a "market failure." A macroeconomic market failure caused by fundamental uncertainty and a loss of
confidence will still lie outside what they conceive of as a legitimate market failure.

But there are other things working in favor of the possibility that macroeconomic market failure may enter the economist's lexicon. The possibility exists partly because one of the devices most used by macroeconomists who denied the possibility of macroeconomic market failure was
what Posner (2009b, 310) describes as an "exaggerated form of rationality"; now, however, those exaggerations are being undercut by empirical
work. These exaggerated assumptions might, of course, be seen as suitable descendants of Smith's beliefs about the stable, stoic psychology of
employers; but the continued use of those exaggerated assumptions seems
increasingly ridiculous for a science that would pretend to study the mac-
roeconomy to help it perform better. Not only have we now experienced a
Great Recession in which we have seen that such narrow conceptions of
rationality do not reflect well the behaviors that can sometimes drive the
economy; we can also see that the complex of reactions in 2008 is not
unlike the complex of reactions in 1929 that caused the Great Depression.

Capitalist reactions to fundamental uncertainty can cause immense economic damage.[20]

We are today experiencing a yeasty time in the theoretical understanding of human rationality. The growth of behavioral economics and the influence of psychological research on models of human rationality have by no means played themselves out. But the kinds of models of exaggerated rationality that have been used in the past in an attempt to prevent the serious analysis of macroeconomic market failure would not seem likely to emerge as the kinds of theories that economists will rely on in the future. Thus, completely apart from the impact of the Great Recession on how macroeconomic models are built, there are forces at work within the profession undermining models employing an all-seeing form of rationality in which people have much more information about the future than anyone can reasonably be said to possess.[21]

The undermining of older macroeconomic theories taking place as a result of the new explorations in human decision making may work in another completely different direction to undermine the traditional economist's understanding of market failure. As mentioned earlier, most economists still imagine the criterion of market efficiency to itself be a "value-free" form of positive analysis. But as economists work with more and more complex forms of human decision making, they are likely to conclude that their traditional form of applied utilitarian analysis is itself value laden. Whereas the value-laden nature of utilitarian analysis is evident to most noneconomists, it has not been obvious to economists. This is not to say that economists need to abandon their traditional ideas of microeconomic market failure, which can be quite helpful in analyzing markets, but that they may become more open to understanding that values enter into *any* definition of market failure. This may make them more able to accept mass unemployment as a form of market failure in and of itself, no less (or more) plausible or value-free than their own traditional microeconomic conception of market failure.

Simply accepting the existence of macroeconomic market failure, however, will not provide easy answers to how capitalism might work better. One reason is clear in Posner's (2010) analysis and draws on much that

20. Posner notes that the damage done by the use of an exaggerated concept of rationality does not mean that all (or any) economic activity is irrational. Far from it. In this, he echoes Keynes in acknowledging that a collapse in confidence does not have to be understood as irrational.

21. Or, alternatively, it seems unlikely that models that assume that a handful of actors who have rational expectations will always drive a capitalist, market economy to full employment.

economists already know. Avoiding the kind of liquidity crisis that fundamental uncertainty can cause requires effective financial regulation, but those who would be regulated have much to lose through tighter regulation, and it seems difficult to look at the experience since 2008 and believe that effective financial regulation is likely.

Perhaps an even greater difficulty, however, lies in the awkward reality that is evidenced in much of Posner's analysis of policies that were (or might have been) offered in response to the Great Recession. More than once in analyzing a proposed new piece of financial regulation, Posner opines that the regulation is not desirable because it may have a deleterious effect on business confidence.

Once we accept that a loss of confidence in the business community may have devastating effects on employment, or that sustaining the animal spirits of capitalists is necessary to the success of market capitalism, then any policy that the business community does not like can be argued to be bad for the economy because of its potentially deleterious effects on national income and employment. Thus, the widespread acceptance of the idea of macroeconomic market failure may actually threaten the existence of democratic market capitalism; the desire of a majority for any policy may be trumped in this new calculus by the need to give investors, capitalists, and entrepreneurs the policies that they want.

But before going too far down the road of always deferring to capitalists' policy desires, we might remember Smith's ([1776] 1937, 288) admonitions about the desires of capitalists as regards public policy:

> The proposal of any new law or regulation of commerce which comes from this order, ought always to be listened to with great precaution, and ought never to be adopted till after having been long and carefully examined, not only with the most scrupulous, but with the most suspicious attention. It comes from an order of men, whose interest is never exactly the same with that of the public, who have generally an interest to deceive and even to oppress the public, and who accordingly have, upon many occasions, both deceived and oppressed it.

References

Backhouse, Roger, and Bradley Bateman. 2006. *The Cambridge Companion to Keynes.* Cambridge: Cambridge University Press.

———. 2011. *Capitalist Revolutionary: John Maynard Keynes.* Cambridge, Mass.: Harvard University Press.

Barber, William J. 1967. *A History of Economic Thought*. Harmondsworth: Penguin.

Bateman, Bradley. 1988. "G. E. Moore and J. M. Keynes: A Missing Chapter in the History of the Expected Utility Model." *American Economic Review* 78 (5): 1098–1106.

———. 1996. *Keynes's Uncertain Revolution*. Ann Arbor: University of Michigan Press.

———. 2006. "Keynes and Keynesianism." In Backhouse and Bateman 2006.

———. 2010. "Keynes Returns to America." In *The Return to Keynes*, edited by Bradley Bateman, Cristina Marcuzzo, and Toshiaki Hirai, 13–31. Cambridge, Mass.: Harvard University Press.

Ekelund, Robert, and Robert Hebert. 2002. "Retrospectives: The Origins of Neoclassical Microeconomics." *Journal of Economic Perspectives* 16 (Summer): 197–215.

Eltis, Walter. 1975. "Adam Smith's Theory of Economic Growth." In *Essays on Adam Smith*, edited by Andrew S. Skinner and Thomas Wilson, 426–54. Oxford: Clarendon Press.

Goodwin, Craufurd. 2006. "The Art of an Ethical Life: Keynes and Bloomsbury." In Backhouse and Bateman 2006, 217–36.

Heilbroner, Robert. 1975. "The Paradox of Progress: Decline and Decay in the Wealth of Nations." In *Essays on Adam Smith*, edited by Andrew S. Skinner and Thomas Wilson, 524–39. Oxford: Clarendon Press.

Hicks, J. R. 1937. "Mr. Keynes and the 'Classics.'" *Econometrica* 5 (April): 147–59.

Hirschman, Albert O. 1977. *The Passions and the Interests: Political Arguments for Capitalism before Its Triumph*. Princeton, N.J.: Princeton University Press.

Keynes, J. M. 1936. *The General Theory of Employment, Interest, and Money*. London: Macmillan.

Mankiw, Greg. 2001. *The Essentials of Economics*. 2nd ed. New York: Harcourt.

Posner, Richard A. 2009a. "Capitalism in Crisis." *Wall Street Journal*, May 7.

———. 2009b. *A Failure of Capitalism: The Crisis of '08 and the Descent into Depression*. Cambridge, Mass.: Harvard University Press.

———. 2009c. "How I Became a Keynesian." *New Republic*, September 23, 34.

———. 2010. *The Crisis of Capitalist Democracy*. Cambridge, Mass.: Harvard University Press.

Robinson, Joan. 1937. *Essays in the Theory of Employment*. London: Macmillan.

Smith, Adam. (1776) 1937. *An Inquiry into the Nature and Causes of the Wealth of Nations*. Modern Library Edition. New York: Random House.

Part 2
Market Failures:
The Post–World War II Narrowing

Paul Samuelson on Public Goods:
The Road to Nihilism

J. Daniel Hammond

This article is an analytical history of Paul Samuelson's writings on the theory of public goods and the role of government. We look first at Samuelson's scholarly work on public goods theory, from "The Pure Theory of Public Expenditure" (1954) to "Pure Theory of Public Expenditure and Taxation" (1969). Then we briefly consider Samuelson's introductory textbook over the same period to look for influence of his scholarly work on public goods on his textbook treatment of public expenditure. This includes the first edition (1948) through the eighth edition (1970) of *Economics: An Introductory Analysis*.

Samuelson and Richard Musgrave are generally considered the fathers of the modern theory of public goods, which since the 1950s has been a staple in the economic analysis of market failure.[1] We focus on Samuelson's scholarly articles and textbook with three questions in mind. How did his theoretical work on public goods condition his views on public policy? How did his mathematical approach to economic analysis affect his ideas on public goods? How did his scholarly work on public goods influence his teaching of basic economic principles through *Economics: An Introductory Analysis*?

Correspondence may be addressed to J. Daniel Hammond, Department of Economics, 209 Kirby Hall, Box 7505, Wake Forest University, Winston-Salem, NC 27109; e-mail: hammond @wfu.edu. I received helpful comments on earlier drafts at the 2014 ASSA and ESHET conferences, in the Wake Forest Economics Workshop, and from an anonymous referee. I wish to thank especially Maxime Desmarais-Tremblay and Claire Hammond.

1. For the legacy of Samuelson, see Pickhardt 2006; for that of Musgrave, see Desmarais-Tremblay 2014.

History of Political Economy 47 (annual suppl.) DOI 10.1215/00182702-2007-3130487

We will find that Samuelson resisted drawing policy implications from his analysis of public goods. If anything, he adjusted his theory of public goods to accommodate public-sector activities that had come to be considered legitimate and necessary in twentieth-century America. Their legitimacy was underpinned by beliefs other than that the services fit the definition of public goods. Ultimately, Samuelson concluded that economic theory has little to contribute to discussion of the appropriate role of government. He referred to this conclusion as nihilistic. This article shows the road that led Samuelson from confidence that economics was on the cusp of great scientific progress at the beginning of his career to what would seem to be the point of despair.

Samuelson's proximate purpose in writing his first article on public goods (1954) was to demonstrate the analytical value of mathematics as a "language" for economic theory.[2] He followed this article a year later with a diagrammatical exposition of the same analysis in order to make it more accessible, and to respond to criticism. But the criticism drew Samuelson into a dialogue in English prose rather than equations or diagrams. This was not because his critics could not understand the mathematics but because they drew implications from his analysis for real-world goods and services such as hospitals and schools. The conclusions did not accord with Samuelson's supposition of appropriate government activities.

One might expect Samuelson to make use in his textbook of an analytical tool that he had a large role in developing. At an intuitive level the theory of public goods is not especially difficult to grasp, and he initially wrote his textbook for students at MIT. But we will find that he did not make use of the theory of public goods in his chapters on public expenditures. External economies and diseconomies make only cameo appearances in the book. In light of the incongruity between the theory and his suppositions about policy mentioned above, the absence of the theory from a book to be used in educating young men and women is less of a puzzle than it seems at first glance.

Paul Samuelson on the Definition and Identification of Public Goods

Samuelson's Scholarly Work

Paul Samuelson and Richard Musgrave are generally credited with developing the modern theory of public goods. Musgrave gets credit for the

2. See Pickhardt 2006, 450–51.

common textbook definition of a public good as a good that is nonrival and nonexcludable.[3] But Samuelson, the economic theorist par excellence, is credited with formalizing the concept in *Foundations of Economic Analysis* (1947) and in two papers on public expenditures in the 1950s.[4] "The Pure Theory of Public Expenditure" (1954) is pure theory in motivation and detail. The article is a mere two and one-half pages long. "Diagrammatic Exposition of a Theory of Public Expenditure" (1955) is what the title indicates, with the aim of making the analysis in the previous article more widely accessible.

"The Pure Theory of Public Expenditure," 1954.   The only context or motivation that Samuelson (1954, 387) gives at the beginning of "The Pure Theory of Public Expenditure" is to say that "except for Sax, Wicksell, Lindahl, Musgrave, and Bowen, economists have rather neglected the theory of optimal public expenditure, spending most of their energy on the theory of taxation."[5] The literature to which he refers is on what was known as the "voluntary exchange theory of public finance." Samuelson's analysis is of optimal public expenditure in the Pareto-efficiency sense that no one can be made better off without making someone else worse off. He assumes two types of goods, private consumption goods and collective consumption goods. The former is rival—one person's consumption is at the cost of another person's consumption. The latter is nonrival—different individuals can consume the same unit of the good simultaneously. The argument is abstract and terse; Samuelson does not give an illustrative example of either type of good. The formal conditions for optimality are from *Foundations of Economic Analysis*, except for the introduction of goods that are nonrival.

Samuelson includes the ethical status of the distribution of goods in his analysis by positing an undefined social welfare function that reflects "ethical preferences" across all possible states of the system. This function is a necessary component of the model. But its determination "is not a 'scientific' task of the economist" except in requiring that if one person becomes better off without anyone else becoming worse off, social welfare improves. The way he demarcates the role of economists with regard to the social welfare function has several interesting implications for economic theory as well as ethics. He claims that "it is not a 'scientific' task

3. See Desmarais-Tremblay 2014.
4. For discussion of the origins and legacy of these two articles by Samuelson, see Pickhardt 2006.
5. On the history of voluntary exchange public finance, including the economists mentioned here, see Johnson, this volume.

of the economist to 'deduce' the form of this function; this can have as many forms as there are possible ethical views" (Samuelson 1954, 387). Thus Samuelson upholds the separation of economics from ethics while acknowledging its dependence on ethics. In addition, the social welfare function is derived not from independent ethical truths but from "ethical views," which are many and perhaps diverse, even contradictory. Lastly, there is an implicit claim that economic theory has more restrictions than ethics with respect to its content. Otherwise no particular economic theory would have any particular truth claim.

Given conditions of production, individual welfare functions, and the social welfare function, there is a "best state of the world," that is, a Pareto-efficient bundle of private consumption goods and collective consumption goods. Samuelson's analytical innovation that has been most acknowledged concerns the collective consumption good, for which individuals' demand curves are added vertically rather than horizontally. This analytical insight, Samuelson had learned, was not wholly new, for it had been developed in the literature on voluntary exchange theories of public finance. Thus his mention at the outset of the work of Sax, Wicksell, Lindahl, Musgrave, and Bowen. His other innovation, which is a step along his way to nihilism, is adding the ethical constraint to the social welfare function. To establish the novelty and importance of the ethical component of the social welfare function, he writes:

> The new element added here is the set (2), which constitutes a pure theory of government expenditure on collective consumption goods. By themselves (1) and (2) define the (s - 1)fold infinity of utility frontier points; only when a set of interpersonal normative conditions equivalent to (3) is supplied are we able to define an unambiguously "best" state.
>
> . . . But what I must emphasize is that there is a different such schedule for each individual at each of the (s − 1)fold infinity of different distributions of relative welfare along the utility frontier. (388)

The policy implication he draws is that laissez-faire reliance on markets and voluntary exchange public finance both lead to suboptimal outcomes by not getting the community to the ethically best point on the utility frontier.

Samuelson remarks that there is no "omniscient calculating machine" on which a planner can solve the maximization problem. He conceives of the market as an "analogue calculating machine." If there are appropriate lump-sum taxes and subsidies, diminishing returns to variable factors and constant returns to scale in production, and convex indifference contours, if competition is maintained, and if all goods are private consumption goods, then with decentralized decisions about what to produce, the market will guide the community to the Paretian "attainable-bliss point." This provides efficiency inclusive of equity. In this highly unlikely set of circumstances, the market will be an effective substitute for the nonexistent "omniscient calculating machine." But there is an additional requirement—that the planner be able to calculate the appropriate tax and subsidy schedules in accord with the ethical constraint. In the model Samuelson has the taxes and subsidies set by the "servant" of the "ethical observer."

The set of necessary conditions includes several margins on which the market might fail to attain the "attainable-bliss point."[6] But Samuelson's focus is on the problems that arise from collective consumption goods. For these, individuals can hide their true valuations, hoping to free ride on others. The free rider problem bedevils equally the market and voluntary public finance. So through neither can the "computational problem" be solved in a decentralized manner. Samuelson (1954, 389) sums up the argument:

> The failure of market catallactics in no way denies the following truth: given sufficient knowledge the optimal decisions can always be found by scanning over all the attainable states of the world and selecting the one which according to the postulated ethical welfare function is best. The solution "exists"; the problem is how to "find" it.

To find it, he suggests that one might "indoctrinate" members of the community to behave like "parametric decentralized bureaucrat[s]," that is, to be honest about their valuations. But we cannot expect people to conform to the indoctrinated rules. So Samuelson leaves us with two "computational" methods that do not work, the market and voluntary-exchange public finance, and with no sense of what a workable alternative might be, if indeed there is one.[7]

"Diagrammatic Exposition of a Theory of Public Expenditure," 1955. A year later Samuelson published "Diagrammatic Exposition of a Theory of Public Expenditure." He offered this diagrammatic presentation and the mathematical model on which it was based (1954) as an alternative to

---

6. "The optimum of all the Pareto optima."

7. On Charles Tiebout's mostly unsuccessful attempt to engage Samuelson on the potential for small communities to overcome the free rider problem, see Singleton, this volume.

the Walrasian model of competitive general equilibrium, which can be formulated "so stringently as to leave no economic role for government" (Samuelson 1955a, 350). His model, like the Walrasian model, is a polar case. But his is a polar case on the side of public expenditure. Referring to the 1954 piece, he writes, "After providing the theory with its needed logically-complete optimal conditions, I went on to demonstrate the fatal inability of any decentralized market or voting mechanism to attain or compute this optimum" (350).

In his 1954 article Samuelson had not identified any real-world or hypothetical nonrival goods. In this piece he identifies a hypothetical private consumption good (bread) and two public consumption goods (a change of name from collective consumption good)—an outdoor circus and national defense. This likely was a response to two critics. Stephen Enke (1955) used Samuelson's 1954 piece to illustrate what he considered the sterility of pure theory—mathematics with symbols but no quantities. "This spinning of theories, with little reference to the real world, can retard progress within economics and bring the profession into disrepute among those who must apply economic theories to problem areas" (Enke 1955, 131). Enke's challenge was on the very point that was Samuelson's initial motivation for writing the 1954 article, the value of mathematics for economics.

One aspect of Samuelson's article in particular that Enke found deficient was that it dealt with polar cases only; all goods in the model are either private consumption goods or collective consumption goods. Most goods and services that governments actually provide do not fit Samuelson's definition of collective consumption goods.

> Now a great many government-provided goods, perhaps most, do not fit this definition, if consumption means enjoyment. Examples are highways, public hospitals and libraries, police and fire protection, and defense against air attack; in each case, for a given public expenditure, I can have better service or more consumption enjoyment if other people will not exercise their rights to those benefits or compete with me for their favorable deployment. Samuelson's collective consumption goods comprise a small class at the opposite extreme from his more numerous private consumption goods. (Enke 1955, 132)

Enke challenged Samuelson to show that his theory could handle the intermediate cases of nonpure private and collective consumption goods. He also raised the question of whether the model could distinguish between the roles of different levels of government—national, state, and local. His closing comment, intended for theorists by way of Samuelson, was that economists have a moral responsibility to provide policy advice rather than indulge in the selfish pleasure of "elegant manipulation of highly abstract models" (133). In response Samuelson (1955a, 350) concedes that "the careful empiricist will recognize that many—though not all—of the realistic cases of government activity can be fruitfully analyzed as some kind of a blend of these two extreme polar cases."

The focus of Julius Margolis's criticism (1955) was Samuelson's separation of the economic problem from the social welfare function. Margolis suggested that by assuming that the "ethical observer" finds the optimal tax and transfer scheme before the economists' work is begun, Samuelson had assumed away the crux of the problem of public expenditures. Margolis claimed that there are not separable "socio-political" and "technical" sectors such that the economist can deal only with the latter. He attributed the separation of the two in Samuelson's model to his being an economic liberal, who considers a private market economy natural and public expenditures departures from the natural. For such a liberal, any move away from the natural market to collective production becomes necessary only by virtue of the technical characteristics inherent in certain goods.

Margolis also made the same point as Enke, that Samuelson's normative model was inadequate as a positive model, for many goods provided by government are not collective consumption goods. Many goods provided by government are divisible and serve private ends. He gave as examples education, hospitals, highways, and even police and judicial services. In some instances government mandates consumption of the good, such as education; in others consumption is optional but free; and in others there is a charge for the good. An adequate positive theory of public expenditure would need to penetrate "the murky waters of political sociology" (Margolis 1955, 348). Here one would find that "existential values" rather than the technical qualities of goods lie behind public expenditure decisions. To see what this would involve, Margolis recommended the work of Edward Banfield, Talcott Parsons, and Edward Shils.

Samuelson's response to Enke's call for policy implications is that there is indeed a policy implication in his analysis. This is that "Wicksell (was right) to worry about the inherent political difficulty of ever getting men to reveal their tastes so as to attain a definable optimum" (Samuelson 1955a, 355). This is a negative policy conclusion about what will not work. But Samuelson does not tell readers what would work. He expresses his desire to "clear myself from Dr. Margolis' understandable suspicion that I am the type of liberal who would insist that all redistributions take place through tax policies and transfer expenditures: much expenditure on education, hospitals, and so on, can be justified by the feasibility consideration that, even if these are not 100 per cent efficient in avoiding avoidable dead-weight loss, they may be better than the attainable imperfect tax alternatives" (356).

In distancing himself from a particular kind of economic liberalism, Samuelson also moves away from where he began, from a normative model of public expenditure to what appears to be a mixture of positive and normative conclusions arrived at from outside the model. He suggests that people vote for paternalistic policies such as education (presumably public education coupled with the requirement that children be sent to school) because they (the people) "do not consider the results from spontaneous market action as optimal" (356). Governments provide some services in sectors subject to increasing returns, and others in "myriad 'generalized external economy and diseconomy' situations, where private pecuniary interest can be expected to deviate from social interests" (356).

As to what Samuelson regarded as the most serious criticism of his analysis, that most functions of government do not fit his definition of public good (i.e., collective consumption good), he responds that he agrees fully, which is why he described his model as a polar case.

> However, to say that a thing is not located at the South Pole does not logically place it at the North Pole. To deny that most public functions fit into my extreme definition of a public good is not to grant that they satisfy the logically equally-extreme category of a private good. . . .
>
> Indeed, I am rash enough to think that in almost every one of the *legitimate* functions of government that critics put forward there is to be found a blending of the extreme antipodal models. One might even venture the tentative suspicion that any function of government not possessing any trace of the defined public good (and no one of the related earlier described characteristics) ought to be carefully scrutinized to see whether it is truly a legitimate function of government. (356; emphasis added)

In responding to Margolis's critique, Samuelson thus broadens his normative "model" to include in-kind transfers, democratically sanctioned paternalistic policies, myriad generalized external economies and diseconomies, and instances of increasing returns. He suggests that future research will show increasing returns and monopolistic competition to be important causes of market failure. Confronted with the difference between the implications of his model of optimal public expenditure and what governments actually spend money on, Samuelson backs away from his model. He also begins to have reservations about the potential of economic theory to contribute to the discussion.

> Economic theory should add what it can to our understanding of governmental activity. I join with critics in hoping that its pretentious claims will not discourage other economic approaches, other contributions from neighboring disciplines, and concrete empirical investigations. (356)

"Social Indifference Curves," 1956.   Samuelson's 1956 paper on social indifference curves provides the next development of his analysis of public expenditure. The paper is ostensibly about whether community indifference curves are possible, a question that he had earlier answered in the negative. He returns to the question here in response to Tibor Scitovsky's work on tariff theory that relied on the curves Samuelson thought that he had proved impossible. Samuelson reconciles the impossibility of Scitovsky community indifference curves with their usefulness in demand theory by deriving what he calls "social welfare contours."

For our purposes, the differences between the two are unimportant. What is important is what Samuelson writes about social groups. He begins with the family and home economics, where there are important consumption externalities. Members of a family have interdependent utility functions based on altruism. Yet economists treat the family as if it were a single individual consumer. Samuelson reasons that if the family can be treated as if it were a single individual, so too can larger social groups in which there are altruistic consumption externalities. "Such problems of home economics are, abstractly conceived, exactly of the same logical character as the general problem of government and social welfare" (Samuelson 1956, 10). Just as transfers are necessary within the family to achieve the ethical optimum, where the marginal social ordinal utility of dollar expenditures or consumption is equal across members of the family, so too are transfers required for larger social groups. The policy insight in this analysis is that for either a family or a nation the transfers must be made just before the final equilibrium is reached or made with foreknowledge of what the equilibrium will be. This requirement is, Samuelson acknowledges, utopian.

Then he comes to the matter of "perfect competition and bliss." He asks whether, assuming that the utopian transfers are made, "perfect competition can be counted on to lead to *the optimum*?" (19). Abraham Wald (1951) proved the uniqueness of the perfectly competitive equilibrium. But Samuelson (1956, 22) proves that this unique equilibrium

> is subject to the possibility that the resulting equilibrium point is one of multiple supply-demand intersections generated by the contrived initial reallocation point. Only one of these multiple points is ethically optimal, but that one could be an unstable intersection point. If so, the market mechanism will not be a good administrative device for reaching the ethical optimum—unless the difficulty is diagnosed and rectified by selection of some other proper initial endowment point.

Samuelson is finding ever-mounting reasons to believe that competitive markets fail and that there are insuperable barriers to finding and arriving at the social optimum. Curiously, however, he concludes the article with the judgment that "the foundation is laid for the 'economics of a good society'" (22).

"Aspects of Public Expenditure Theories," 1958.   In a paper written for the 1955 meeting of the Econometric Society and American Economic Association, Samuelson (1958a, 332–33) presents his vision of the nature of government and public finance by way of imagined history based on his "a priori conceptions of the moment":

> Once upon a time men on this [imagined] planet were all alike and very scarce. Each family hunted and fished its symmetrical acres; and each ended with the same production and real income.
>
> Then men turned to cultivating the soil and domesticating animals. This left even more of the globe vacant, but did not disturb the symmetry of family incomes.
>
> But finally population grew so big that the best free land was all occupied. Now there was a struggle for elbow room. According to the scenario as I choose to write it, the struggle was a gentlemanly one. But men did have to face the fact that recognizing the squatter's rights and respecting *laissez-faire* did result in differences of real incomes among families.
>
> *Optimal transfer expenditure.* Here, then, for the first time, government was introduced on this planet. A comprehensive program of redistributing income so as to achieve a maximum of the community's

social welfare function was introduced. The budget was balanced at a non-zero level: taxes were raised in a non-distorting lump-sum fashion, and transfer expenditure was allocated among families so as to achieve the marginal conditions necessary to maximize the defined social welfare function. . . .

Now why do I describe so bizarre a model? It is to underline this theoretical point: Given a social welfare function, and given the absence of all technological and taste externalities, and given universal constant returns to scale, there would be needed only one type of public policy—redistributive transfers.

There is much that could be said about this fable. For Samuelson, the passage shows that the "economic" problem of efficiency as commonly understood is secondary to an unspecified ethical standard with regard to the distribution of income.

Samuelson's analytical conclusions are not favorable for the prospects of either market allocation of goods and services or public allocation with benefit-based finance. But "the world's work does somehow get done. And to say that the market mechanisms are non-optimal, and that there are difficulties with most political decision processes, does not imply that we can never find new mechanisms of a better sort" (334). He suggests two possible ways to the "bliss point," both of which depend on homogeneity within social groups that would enhance the prospects for people being honest. But he does not develop this idea. Instead he ends the paper on a gloomy note.

Once again in contemplating the dilemmas that most forms of political voting involve, we are reminded of the beautiful and special simplicities of the *laissez-faire* model. But, alas, the difficulties are those of the real world. And it would be quite illogical to conclude from all this that men and technology should be different, should be such as to make the competitive game all-sufficient. That would be as silly as to say that we should all love sawdust because its production is so beautiful. (336)

He suggests that economists' work is not complete and that the next frontier is "exploration of those momentous coalitions of decision-making that are part of the essence of the political process" (336). This seems to suggest that the next step in analysis is to be public choice analysis.

"Public Goods and Subscription TV: Correction of the Record," 1964. Actually, the next step for Samuelson is a curt response to Jora Minasian,

who cited his 1954 and 1958 papers in an evaluation of public goods theory in the context of pricing of television broadcasts. Samuelson (1958a) used television as an example of a mixed good. The marginal cost of adding an additional viewer is zero, that is, television broadcasts are nonrival; yet scrambler technology allows potential viewers to be prevented from viewing, that is, television is excludable. Thus in this piece Samuelson implicitly considers Musgrave's second characteristic of a public good, nonexcludability, for scramble technology has no connection with nonrivalness.[8]

At the time, the Federal Communications Commission was considering whether to allow subscription television programming. Samuelson asks whether scrambler technology turns a public good into a pure private good. His answer is no, for the marginal cost of adding viewers is zero. Efficient pricing at $P = MC$ requires that television be free. This condition of increasing returns puts television in the category of a mixed good, neither a pure public good (despite increasing returns) nor a pure private good (despite excludability).

He suggested that some degree of increasing returns is common to many goods, for example, railroads, water supply, electricity, and post offices, so that user-benefit pricing would be problematic. This poses practical and theoretical problems:

> It is not enough in the decreasing cost case to come closer to marginal cost pricing in the Lerner-Lange manner, making up the deficits by general taxation. As soon as decreasing cost and diversity of product appear, we have the difficult non-local "total conditions" to determine what finite mix of product is optimal. This involves a terrible social computation problem: we must scan the almost infinite number of possible products and select the best configuration; we cannot feel our way to the optimum but must make judgment at a distance to determine the *optimum optimorum*. (Samuelson 1958a, 336)

Minasian argued that the technical characteristics of a good or its production could not be used to determine the optimal allocation system for the good. Minasian's argument turned on the difference between allocation of broadcasts once it has been determined how many and which pro-

---

8. Samuelson argued against nonexcludability as a criterion for something to be considered a public good in two unpublished papers. See "More on Public Goods and Bads: A Road Case" (1959) and "Public Good Theory" (ca. 1970). The former is in box 142 and the latter box 143, Paul A. Samuelson Papers, David M. Rubenstein Rare Book and Manuscript Library, Duke University.

grams will be broadcast, and allocation of resources to programming. He placed the latter problem ahead of the former and suggested that even if the marginal cost of adding viewers to a given program is nil, pricing the program allows for generation of information on the value of different programs.

> A pure theory of public expenditure purporting to identify on economic grounds the goods that are best provided by collective action should have the power to govern choice among alternative institutional arrangements on the basis of their relative merits. The present theory of public goods is incapable of generating the relevant economic information. It consistently rejects a particular system not on the basis of its merit relative to other alternative approaches to a particular problem, but merely because it does not fulfill the conditions of an "ideal" world. Consequently, it cannot be expected to provide and, as the following examples suggest, it does not provide a correct identification of the economic problem. (Minasian 1964, 78–79)

Samuelson (1964, 81) replied that his remarks on public goods and subscription television have "been scandalously misinterpreted." "The reader of this paper [Minasian's] could be pardoned for thinking that I have opposed subscription television. Upon reading my paper, he will be surprised to learn that I expressed no opinion on the merits of commercial television versus subscription television" (81).

Minasian did misinterpret Samuelson, although it is unlikely that he did so for the reason suggested by Samuelson: "Only a bigoted devotee of laissez faire will find the theory of public goods, properly understood, subversive" (83). There are three statements in Minasian's article that misinterpret Samuelson. They are (1) "In a more recent contribution, Professor Samuelson refers to television broadcasting as a pure public good" (Minasian 1964, 71); (2) "Professor Samuelson appears to be opposed to subscription television because it would raise price above marginal cost (which is zero)" (74); and (3) "Professor Samuelson seemed to reject the use of descramblers" (77).

Minasian may have blundered into the first misinterpretation by conflating Samuelson 1954 and 1958a. In Samuelson 1954 there is an unnamed "private consumption good" and an unnamed "common consumption good," the latter having the quality that "each individual's consumption of such a good leads to no subtraction from any other individual's consumption of that good" (387). But in Samuelson 1958a television is identified not as a *pure public good* but as a mixed good. So Minasian was wrong about Samuelson's identification of television with regard to public goods and private goods. But he was right in the sense that television fit the definition of a pure collective consumption good as Samuelson 1954 defined it. Minasian's statements (2) and (3) say that Samuelson *appeared* to oppose subscription television and the use of scramblers, which amount to the same thing. This is not a wholly unreasonable interpretation of Samuelson for the very reason that Samuelson seems in his analysis to be leading up to a statement about the proper allocation and pricing of television and other goods that have some degree of public goodness. But he stops short of doing so. In fact he and Minasian actually agree that, in Minasian's (1964, 78) words, "the *theory* of public goods is of little help in distinguishing those goods that are best provided via community action from those that should be left to individual decisions and preferences."

"Pitfalls in the Analysis of Public Goods," 1967.   James Buchanan (1967) attempted to mediate the dispute between Samuelson and Minasian.[9] He thought that they both muddied the water by commingling theory, made-up examples to illustrate theory, and real-world policy questions. Buchanan's interest was in theory, which he apparently did not think was sufficiently well developed for application to policy. To clarify the theoretical issues, he built a model of television transmission on an island. Stressing that the model was artificial, he began with a signal that comes from afar to a single antenna on the island. He made simple assumptions about cost and considered different ways to allocate the signal to island residents. Buchanan drew the conclusion that free distribution with tax-price financing and a perfectly price-discriminating monopolist could both be Pareto optimal. He likened the public goods problem to Alfred Marshall's theory of joint supply of products.

Buchanan agreed with Samuelson that no set of theoretical tools was fully adequate for evaluating real-world policy questions. But he suggested that Samuelson had succumbed to the temptation of which he accused Minasian, allowing his ideological preferences to guide his argument.

> It is equally unfortunate that Samuelson chose to keep the discussion on the same ground [subscription television]. Finally, it is distressing that Samuelson, who could have had the better of the argument, threw

---

9. For an interesting analysis of Samuelson's influence on Buchanan's work on externalities, see Marciano 2013.

his own advantage away by bringing ideological overtones into what should be a reasoned debate. In so doing, he placed an ideological cloud over the whole theory of public goods, to which he has contributed so much. (Buchanan 1967, 197)

Samuelson's main reaction to Buchanan is that Buchanan's model is unrealistic. This is not unlike Stephen Enke's criticism of Samuelson's "Pure Theory of Public Expenditure."

> Buchanan starts out by playing God, examining the results of "an ideally-operating tax-financed, collective facility" . . .
>   This result satisfies my equations of Pareto-optimality. . . . How did God get there? Buchanan does not tell us. (Samuelson 1967b, 200)

Likewise for Buchanan's "God-like," perfectly price-discriminating monopolist:

> Although that fellow gets referred to in textbooks, he does not exist on land or sea and never will. He is just another name for God. How does he "find out" each man's marginal-utility function? Only by playing a zero-sum game with him. Each man has every incentive not to reveal to his Opponent his marginal utility. Only by fiat of the textbook writer, does the Opponent always win the game's maximum stakes. For him to look into the hearts of 200 million, or 20 thousand, or 2 consumers, and guess right requires miracles. (201)

There are two points to notice about this criticism. The first is that Samuelson's objection seems to be to the idealizations of "pure theory." How his remarks bear on his own analysis he does not say. It would appear that if his criticism applies to Buchanan's analysis, it also applies to his own use of the "servant" of the "ethical observer" to set taxes and subsidies in his 1954 article. The other point about this criticism is that it highlights Samuelson's core conclusion about the public goods problem, that he sees no way in the real world to overcome free riding. If there is no brake that can be applied to free riding, then neither markets nor public allocation with benefit-based taxation will attain social Pareto optimality. Moreover, if people are able to free ride in the tax and subsidy scheme, ability-to-pay financing is unworkable as well.

Samuelson's emphasis on the game-theoretic nature of the problem comes to the fore in his disagreement with Buchanan on the relevance of the theory of joint supply to the public goods problem. Wool and mutton equilibrium, to use Marshall's example of joint supply, has no game theoretic aspect.[10] But with public goods, "as the number of men grows, the problem becomes *more* game-theoretically indeterminate" (Samuelson 1967b, 202n5). This has implications that Samuelson does not acknowledge for his analogy of the nation with the family in "Aspects of Public Expenditure Theories" (1958a). The quantitative difference between the size of a family and that of a nation becomes a qualitative difference as one moves from the small group that is the family to the large group that is the nation.

"Indeterminacy of Governmental Role in Public-Good Theory," 1967. In the same year, Samuelson responds to a piece by Francesco Forte (1967). Forte argued that economists following Samuelson's lead had oversimplified the conditions bearing on decisions about public expenditures. There were considerations other than excludability and rivalness with bearing on the matter of how government should be involved in provision of goods. In some cases, these factors suggest direct public production of the good, and in others, public subsidies to private firms. For example, there might be an advantage in providing national defense directly through government rather than by private firms with public subsidies, because mercenaries would have less loyalty to the nation and because only the government would be large enough to take advantage of the available economies of scale. On the other hand, private but publicly subsidized police may be viable. So Forte concluded that Samuelson had provided a theory of public subsidy, but not of public expenditure. Depending on the circumstances, the subsidy might be to a private firm or to a unit of government.

Samuelson (1967a) writes briefly in reply to Forte that his 1954 and 1955 articles did not imply that private goods should be produced by private enterprises and public goods by government. "Where the consumption externalities intrinsic to a non-private good occur, all that I would insist on is that laissez-faire cannot be counted on to lead to an optimum" (Samuelson 1967a, 47). His analysis has no bearing on the question of what institutional arrangements would approximate optimality by overcoming the game theoretic problems of free riding.

"Pure Theory of Public Expenditure and Taxation," 1969.   Having joined in 1954 a discussion of public expenditure that had a long and rich history of which he was mostly unaware, having used mathematics in which

10. See also his unpublished "Some Difficult Problems in Defining Public Goods" (undated), box 143, Paul A. Samuelson Papers, David M. Rubenstein Rare Book and Manuscript Library, Duke University.

many public finance economists were not proficient, and having provoked criticism that his theory could not account for the bulk of public expenditures, Samuelson seeks in a 1969 paper to set the record straight on his theory of public expenditure and taxation.[11] He wrote this paper for a conference on the public economy and its relation to the private sector. Samuelson thought many of his critics simply did not understand his theory. So he sets out to present his theory in both mathematics and prose, and to situate it in the context of historical and modern literature on public expenditure and taxation. The analysis is to be primarily normative, but with some attention to actual institutions in relation to the optima.

He begins with an ideological classification of economists who had contributed to the literature on taxation. "Conservative" writers favored benefit theories with allocation of the tax burden arising from public expenditures based on benefits received. This form of taxation would mimic the market, where one pays for what one receives. "Radical" writers favored ability-to-pay theories of taxation, with the tax burden designed to be redistributive. Dismissing the notion of a social compact of the sort that might give people rights to their property, Samuelson (1969, 100) favors the utilitarian idea of a social welfare function that "tends to subvert the older notions of 'legitimacy'—that things are done as they are because they have always been so done; that people have a contractual right to no changes." He thinks that the change from a notion of cardinal utility to ordinal utility in the social welfare function resolves the problem of the "crude and materialistic calculus of hedonism" in the older utilitarian formulations. It is not entirely clear what he considers crude—the calculus of hedonism, or hedonism.

The two different theories of taxation reflect different ideas of justice:

On the one hand, a just or equitable society is one in which incomes are properly allocated to produce the greatest bliss for the whole universe—even if that means sacrificing something of one man's well-being in a good cause of adding more to the rest of mankind's well-being. Against this is the notion that each man, by virtue of being a man, has an inviolable core of rights that cannot be infringed even to secure some net increment to the social good, or at least cannot be infringed in his case unless all others (who are somehow comparable!) are being similarly treated. (100–101)

11. He returns to his 1954 title, "The Pure Theory of Public Expenditure," dropping "the" and adding "taxation."

In a footnote Samuelson suggests that this second theory of justice will become more important for libertarians the farther the actual economy moves away from Victorian capitalism, "putting the burden of proof upon any departure from their defined condition of inviolable natural rights and individual liberties (inclusive of property rights)" (101n2).

Samuelson reiterates two themes of his earlier papers. The first is that voluntary tax payments according to benefits received is not feasible. The second is that for optimality, allocation of benefits from public expenditures and of redistribution via ability-to-pay taxation must be solved simultaneously. He also clarifies that in his model a public good might enter one person's indifference function positively, another person's negatively, and another person's not at all. There is no requirement that the benefits from a public good be the same for all. All that is required is that the consumption externality be nonzero for at least one person. "A public good—call it x or x_2 or x_{n+m}—is simply one with the property of involving a 'consumption externality,' in the sense of entering into two or more persons' preference functions simultaneously" (102).

Then he presents the mathematics of his "pseudo-demand" analysis, which is the demand that would be used by an "omniscient planner" with knowledge of every individual's indifference function. He does not deal with the matter of what kind of exclusion devices might actually be used by the omniscient planner to reveal indifference functions for goods with consumption externalities, "since this is all merely a computing algorithm, which an electronic computer could use, dispensing with the dramatic device of a referee and market terminology" (103).

At this point in his contribution to the literature on public goods, Musgrave's *Theory of Public Finance* (1959) contained the analysis that Samuelson was most concerned to compare and contrast with his own.[12] The points of comparison with Musgrave are technical matters having to do with the general equilibrium system and its component social production-possibility frontier, individual preference functions for public and private goods, and Bergsonian social welfare functions.[13] But he is also concerned to convey in no uncertain terms his belief that his analysis, which he thinks others are "groping toward," reveals that the search for an attainable social Pareto optimal allocation is at a dead end. As he puts it in the heading for section 4 of the paper, the analysis is an "affirmation of doubts."

12. He points to Leif Johansen's *Public Economics* (1965) as the analysis that indicates the author's fullest understanding of his own and as what is closest to his in content.

13. See Bergson 1938.

It is striking how Wicksell and Lindahl, and even Musgrave and Johansen (and now Dorfman's name can perhaps be added), after getting a glimpse of the pseudo-equilibrium descend to the swampland of mathematical politics, ending up with inconclusive behavior patterns by legislatures, factions and parties, running inevitably afoul of Arrow's Impossibility Theorem. Game theory, except in trivial cases, propounds paradoxes rather than solves problems. (Samuelson 1969, 106)

Despite the best attempts to find a voting mechanism that would lead to Pareto optimality, there is no way around the prisoner's dilemma inherent in the distributional consequences of politics. Samuelson affirms that "Pareto-optimality is a definition not an inevitable destination" (107).

Although Samuelson's first paper on the public expenditure problem in 1954 was conceived as a demonstration of the usefulness of mathematics in economics, he must have thought that he had stepped into a "swampland" of English prose. For much of the discussion after 1954 concerned what, in "the pure theory of public expenditure," $X_{n+1}, \ldots X_{n+m}$ "collective consumption goods" actually were. Samuelson expresses regret that his analysis was in terms of polar cases of pure collective consumption and private consumption goods, for it has become clear that no actual goods are at either pole. He had tried to resolve this problem of relating the pure theory to the world of actual goods and actual public expenditures by suggesting that actual goods fell between the two poles as a mixture of the two types. But this resolution seemed not to lend itself to analysis, so in 1969 he sought to clarify the definition of a public good in such a way that provides a better fit between theory and reality. This is that a public good enters two or more people's utility function. The definition does not require that it affect everyone's utility. Therefore virtually every good is a public good. The private good pole has become a "knife edge," with everything that does not balance on the edge falling into the public good category. The implication Samuelson (1969, 109) draws is rather ominous:

This does, however, lead to an uncomfortable situation. If experts remain nihilistic about algorithms to allocate public goods, and if all but a knife-edge of reality falls in that domain, nihilism about most of economics, rather than merely public finance, seems to be implied.

He makes a few suggestions of possible ways to avoid his "nihilist" conclusion, but without evidence of much hope for their prospects.[14]

---

14. I first became aware of Samuelson's use of the term *nihilism* in reference to welfare theory through my student Joshua Binney's (2011) senior honors thesis.

Economics: An Introductory Analysis

With Samuelson's first article on public goods published in 1954, it is not surprising that the concept does not appear in the first edition (1948) or the second (1951) of his textbook. Neither edition has index entries for "collective consumption good" or "public consumption good," the terms he uses in the 1954 and 1955 articles. Nor does the 1955 third edition. The first three editions also have no index entries for "market failure."

The first edition does use the term "collective consumption" as a synonym for goods produced or financed by government, but not in the technical sense in which he used the term in "The Pure Theory of Public Expenditure." In a discussion of "socialism and the New Deal," he writes:

> The increase in government expenditure means that as a nation we are consuming more of our national product *collectively* rather than individually through private money purchases. Rather than pay to ride on the public roads as we do to ride on railroads, we pay for such valuable services by taxes.
>
> But note that such collectively consumed goods and services are still *largely produced by free private enterprise.* (Samuelson 1948, 158–59)

The third edition has three index entries for "external economies and diseconomies." All three are to footnotes, and only the third involves welfare economics. The first two, in chapters on demand and supply, refer to Alfred Marshall's discussion of external economies because of reductions in factor prices or increases in productivity that result from an industry's expansion. The third footnote is in an appendix on general equilibrium and welfare economics to the chapter "Profits and Incentives." This footnote is in a discussion with the heading "Review of Commodity and Factor Pricing: General Equilibrium and Parable of Ideal Welfare Pricing," and within that in a subsection titled "Welfare Economics in a Free Enterprise Economy." His use of the word *parable* in the section title suggests that he thinks ideal welfare pricing has little direct applicability to the actual American economy. Samuelson lists criticisms of the US economy by "friendly and unfriendly" critics "from various ethical viewpoints." The first is that "the existing distribution of property, income, education, and economic opportunity is the result of past history and does not necessarily represent a perfect optimum according to the ethical philosophies of Christianity, Buddhism, paganism, the American creed, or other ideologies" (Samuelson 1955b, 608). The second criticism is the prevalence of monopoly in the American economy and "the limited appearance of perfect competition" (609). The third object of criticism is the waste from unemployment and the business cycle. And the footnote adds a fourth criticism, "that individual firms, in making their decisions, never take into account the possible effects of their production decisions on other firms or industries" (609n1). This creates external diseconomies and economies, as when people or firms digging oil wells do not take account of the fact that they extract oil from a common pool. Samuelson gives A. C. Pigou's *Economics of Welfare* as a reference. He also says that with perfect competition there is insufficient incentive for invention because would-be inventors know that they could not fully capture the return from their innovations.

So the third edition of *Economics: An Introductory Analysis* makes use of welfare theory only in a single footnote, and this in the context of critiques of the American economic system rather than public policy. The two chapters of the third edition on the economic role of government— "Expenditure, Regulation, and Finance" and "Federal Taxation and Local Finance" (chapters 6 and 7)—are descriptive rather than analytical.

The fourth edition (1958b) is little different from the third. There are the same two descriptive chapters on the role of government in expenditures, regulation, and finance. This edition has two index entries for "external economies and diseconomies." One is repeated from the third edition and has to do with declining cost industries. The second is in a new discussion of the economics of technology and concerns external economies in scientific knowledge from the development of nuclear power. The fourth edition has three index entries for "collective consumption," all in chapter 6, "The Economic Role of Government: Expenditure, Regulation, and Finance." The context for all three is descriptive rather than analytical. So they do not concern externalities or public goods. The first uses collective consumption as a synonym for government expenditures as in the first edition. The second use of the term is in making the distinction between government expenditures and transfer payments. The third is in the context of explaining how taxes redirect resources from "the community's private consumption activities and shifting them to its collective governmental activities" (122).

An additional use of the term that is not indexed, and does involve externalities but only indirectly in a reference to "more advanced economics texts," is in chapter 3, "Functioning of a 'Mixed' Capitalistic Enterprise System." In a section under the heading "The Economic Role of Government," Samuelson writes:

More than this, government provides certain indispensable *collective* services without which community life would not be thinkable, and which by their nature cannot appropriately be left to private enterprises. Government came into existence once people realized, "Everybody's business is nobody's business." Obvious examples are the maintenance of national defense, of internal law and order, and the administration of justice. (44)

A footnote gives the "famous example" of lighthouses. "These save lives and cargoes. But lighthouse keepers can't reach out to collect fees from skippers. 'So,' says the more advanced economics texts, 'we have here a divergence between *private* advantage and money cost (as seen by a man crazy enough to try to make his fortune running a lighthouse business) and true *social* advantage and cost . . . ' Naturally, a beginning text will only mention such issues" (44n1).

Conclusion

Our overall conclusion is that after two decades of work on the theory of public expenditure, Paul Samuelson was left with doubts about the nature and purpose of economics and by implication of prospects for scientific progress in the discipline. This conclusion is ironic because it is drawn from a survey of the writings of the preeminent economist in the period in which economics and its practitioners were coming into their greatest prestige. The first Nobel Prize in Economic Sciences was awarded in 1969, the publication year of the last article covered here. The next year, 1970, Samuelson received the prize, "for the scientific work through which he has developed static and dynamic economic theory and actively contributed to raising the level of analysis in economic science."

In the modern era, science is thought to deal with observables. Samuelson expressed in his textbook the belief that economics was a science and that theory is properly the handmaiden of observable facts. He wrote in the first edition of *Economics*:

Properly understood, therefore, theory and observation, deduction and induction cannot be in conflict. Like eggs, there are only two kinds of theories: good ones and bad ones. And the test of a theory's goodness is its usefulness in illuminating observational reality. Its logical elegance and fine-spun beauty are irrelevant. Consequently, when a student says, "That's all right in theory but not in practice," he really means "That's not all right in theory," or else he is talking nonsense. (Samuelson 1948, 8)

In the introduction to *Foundations* Samuelson ([1947] 1983, 4) invited readers to envision a unified (foundational) economic theory that would overcome the barrenness and "unmistakable signs of decadence which were clearly present in economic thought prior to 1930." The new methods on display in *Foundations* would yield *meaningful theorems*, that is, hypotheses about empirical data that "could conceivably be refuted, if only under ideal conditions" (4).

When he wrote his first article on the theory of public expenditure he was confident that mathematics was the language of economic theory. He famously argued at the 1951 American Economic Association conference that mathematics is a language and thus fundamentally no different from English. Use of mathematics is neither necessary nor sufficient for success as an economic theorist. However, theorists who use mathematics are more likely to be successful than those who do not. In short, mathematics facilitates the development of good theory (1952). His first article on the public goods problem (1954) was intended to demonstrate the usefulness of mathematics for economic analysis. We have seen, however, that in selecting the theory of public expenditure as his vehicle for this demonstration, he was drawn into a discussion of the appropriate roles of government. Through the ensuing dialogue, English prose supplanted mathematics. Ultimately, terms such as "collective consumption goods" refer to goods and services such as education or roads, not to Greek letters.

Samuelson's (1952) acknowledgment that mathematics is not *sufficient* for good economic analysis, along with his statement to readers of his textbook that economics is an empirical science, was a de facto acknowledgment of Stephen Enke's (1955, 131) point that "spinning of theories, with little reference to the real world, can retard progress in economics and bring the profession into disrepute among those who must apply economic theories to problem areas." Most economists who have written on the public goods problem have seen this literature either as a normative theory of the appropriate division of labor between the public and private sectors or as a positive theory of the functioning of government. Leif Johansen (1965, 124), whose work Samuelson saw as compatible with his own, put it this way:

In the first place the attempt may be made to establish a theory as to how public expenditure is in fact determined in an economic set-up such as, e.g., the contemporary Norwegian one. In the second place it would be possible to aim at formulating a more normative theory as to how one might achieve an optimal determination of the level of public expenditure.

When Enke pointed out that many services provided by governments did not fit Samuelson's definition of nonrival collective consumption goods, Samuelson became trapped in a no-man's land between normative theories of public expenditure and the positive theory that became known as "public choice." He did not want to give up "legitimate" functions of government that failed to fit the normative theory. But he also did not choose to descend into what Julius Margolis referred to as "the murky waters of political sociology." This led to Samuelson's conclusion that economic theory has nothing to say about the appropriate roles of government.

Michael Pickhardt (2006) pointed out that Samuelson did no additional work on public goods theory after 1969. We might also note that what he wrote between 1955 and 1969 was concerned not with new analysis but with the interpretation and implications of his 1954–55 analysis. The mathematics of "The Pure Theory of Public Expenditure" translated nicely into the diagrams of "Diagrammatic Exposition of a Theory of Public Expenditure." But neither translated well into English-language descriptions of either actual or ideal, that is, Pareto-optimal, government activities. The question arises of why Samuelson insisted on Pareto optimality rather than consider Pareto improvements. This is the way that many economists think of using economic theory in public policy analysis. We can only speculate here, but perhaps the all-or-nothing dichotomy was endemic to the abstract mathematical approach that he used.

An implicit pair of twofold hierarchies concerning the purpose and potential for economic analysis is evident in Samuelson's textbook and scholarly work on public goods. The first, from his textbook, is that the theorems of welfare economics are applicable only after the problem of full employment has been resolved. This is the "neoclassical synthesis." "If modern economics does its task so well that unemployment and inflation are substantially banished from democratic societies, then its importance will wither away and the traditional economics (whose concern is wise allocation of fully employed resources) will really come into its own—almost for the first time" (Samuelson 1958b, 12). The second hierarchy is that nonscientific ethics has priority over scientific economics through the social welfare function. Just as the principles of traditional economics come into play only once noninflationary full employment is attained, the *optimum optimorum* can be identified only once income is distributed equitably. The irony here is that what is most important, the ethical optimum, is least subject to rigorous analysis. Ethics trumps efficiency; yet ethics is not scientific, so a modern social scientist has little to say about its substance.[15] Moreover, from the following statement in "Diagrammatic Exposition of a Theory of Public Expenditure," it would appear that ethics may be impervious to rational analysis. "Economics cannot deduce a social welfare function; what it can do is neutrally interpret any arbitrarily specified welfare function" (Samuelson 1955a, 353). One simply presumes that society's ethical standard is equality of the marginal "social welfare significance" of every good across all persons. "Social welfare significance" is an empty box.

In *Foundations* Samuelson ([1947] 1983, 4) looked back over the history of economics and imagined an economist who

> has consoled himself for his barren results with the thought that he was forging tools which would eventually yield fruit. The promise is always in the future; we are like highly trained athletes who never run a race, and in consequence grow stale. It is still too early to determine whether the innovations in thought of the last decade will have stemmed the unmistakable signs of decadence which were clearly present in economic thought prior to 1930.[16]

Put this alongside Samuelson's (1969, 109) statement two decades after *Foundations* was published—"If experts remain nihilistic about algorithms to allocate public goods, and if all but a knife-edge of reality falls in that domain, nihilism about most of economics, rather than merely public finance, seems to be implied." The optimism, if not hubris, of the young man has given way to hopelessness about the social utility of economics. Samuelson affirmed this conclusion in an unpublished 1974 piece:

> From the beginning I have earned the reputation for corrosive nihilism concerning the existence of any voting device or algorithm that would achieve the optimality state or states defined by the general theory of public goods. This was not out of desire to be perverse. My heart would love to be able to believe that the emperor wears gorgeous clothes. But my reason, adult-like, requires me to insist that he is naked when he really is naked. (3)

The project of mathematizing and formalizing economics had not brought progress, unless one counts arriving at nihilism as progress.

15. One could object that ethics can be scientific, but it is clear that Samuelson did not have scientific ethics in mind.

16. Samuelson wrote *Foundations* between 1937 and 1940. See Backhouse 2014.

References

Backhouse, Roger E. 2014. "How Paul A. Samuelson's *Foundations of Economic Analysis* Came to Be." papers.ssrn.com/sol3/papers.cfm?abstract_id=2510383.

Bergson, Abram. 1938. "A Reformulation of Certain Aspects of Welfare Economics." *Quarterly Journal of Economics* 52 (February): 310–34.

Binney, Joshua D. 2011. "When Markets Fail: The Pigouvian Margins, the Coase Theorem, and the Ratification of Government Intervention." Honors thesis, Wake Forest University.

Buchanan, James M. 1967. "Public Goods in Theory and Practice: A Note on the Minasian-Samuelson Discussion." *Journal of Law and Economics* 10 (October): 193–97.

Desmarais-Tremblay, Maxime. 2014. "On the Definition of Public Goods." CES Working Paper 4, Université Paris 1.

Enke, Stephen. 1955. "More on the Misuse of Mathematics in Economics: A Rejoinder." *Review of Economics and Statistics* 37 (2): 131–33.

Forte, Francesco. 1967. "Should 'Public Goods' Be Public?" *Papers on Non-market Decision Making* 3 (1): 39–46.

Johansen, Leif. 1965. *Public Economics.* Amsterdam: North-Holland.

Marciano, Alain. 2013. "Why Market Failures Are Not a Problem: James Buchanan on Market Imperfections, Voluntary Cooperation, and Externalities." *History of Political Economy* 45 (2): 223–54.

Margolis, Julius. 1955. "A Comment on the Pure Theory of Public Expenditure." *Review of Economics and Statistics* 37 (4): 347–49.

Minasian, Jora R. 1964. "Television Pricing and the Theory of Public Goods." *Journal of Law and Economics* 7 (October): 71–80.

Musgrave, Richard. 1959. *The Theory of Public Finance: A Study in Public Economy.* New York: McGraw-Hill.

Pickhardt, Michael. 2006. "Fifty Years after Samuelson's 'The Pure Theory of Public Expenditure': What Are We Left With?" *Journal of the History of Economic Thought* 28 (December): 439–60.

Samuelson, Paul A. (1947) 1983. *Foundations of Economic Analysis.* Cambridge, Mass.: Harvard University Press.

———. 1948. *Economics: An Introductory Analysis.* New York: McGraw-Hill.

———. 1951. *Economics: An Introductory Analysis.* 2nd ed. New York: McGraw-Hill.

———. 1952. "Economic Theory and Mathematics: An Appraisal." *American Economic Review* 42 (May): 56–66.

———. 1954. "The Pure Theory of Public Expenditure." *Review of Economics and Statistics* 36 (4): 387–89.

———. 1955a. "Diagrammatic Exposition of a Theory of Public Expenditure." *Review of Economics and Statistics* 37 (4): 350–56.

———. 1955b. *Economics: An Introductory Analysis.* 3rd ed. New York: McGraw-Hill.

———. 1956. "Social Indifference Curves." *Quarterly Journal of Economics* 70 (1): 1–22.

———. 1958a. "Aspects of Public Expenditure Theories." *Review of Economics and Statistics* 40 (4): 332–38.

———. 1958b. *Economics: An Introductory Analysis.* 4th ed. New York: McGraw-Hill.

———. 1964. "Public Goods and Subscription TV: Correction of the Record." *Journal of Law and Economics* 7 (October): 81–83.

———. 1967a. "Indeterminacy of Governmental Role in Public-Good Theory." *Papers on Non-market Decision Making* 3 (1): 47.

———. 1967b. "Pitfalls in the Analysis of Public Goods." *Journal of Law and Economics* 10 (October): 199–204.

———. 1969. "Pure Theory of Public Expenditure and Taxation." In *Public Economics: An Analysis of Public Production and Consumption and Their Relations to the Private Sectors*, edited by J. Margolis and H. Guitton, 98–123. London: Macmillan.

———. 1970. *Economics: An Introductory Analysis.* 8th ed. New York: McGraw-Hill.

———. 1974. "Public Goods Twenty Years Later." June. Box 143, Paul A. Samuelson Papers, David M. Rubenstein Rare Book and Manuscript Library, Duke University.

Wald, Abraham. 1951. "On Some Systems of Equations of Mathematical Economics." *Econometrica* 19 (October): 368–403.

Public Goods, Market Failure, and Voluntary Exchange

Marianne Johnson

The growth of the federal government throughout the first half of the twentieth century sparked interest in classifying and studying governmental expenditures, which had been all but ignored in English-language public finance. By the early 1950s, a fundamental discussion was under way about the nature, definition, and characteristics of public goods, and the related concepts of social goods, pure or impure collective goods, collective wants, merit goods, or social wants. While externalities fit neatly into neoclassical economics, the nature of the market failure associated with public goods was harder to identify, and solutions proved problematic. An interesting thread in the story of public goods relates to the application of theories of voluntary exchange, the idea that the revenue-expenditure process should be determined by the same fundamental laws and procedures that govern revenue, expenditures, and prices in the private aspects of the economy. In this way, voluntary exchange carried over important democratic features of the market to the political arena.

Voluntary exchange theory was briefly canvassed by Paul Samuelson in his classic contributions to public goods (1954, 1955). It earned the scorn of Richard Musgrave (1941, 324), who characterized it as a "fictitious

Correspondence may be addressed to Marianne Johnson, Department of Economics, Sage 2414, 800 Algoma Boulevard, University of Wisconsin–Oshkosh, Oshkosh, WI 54901; e-mail: johnsonm@uwosh.edu. I would like to thank Steven Medema, Manuela Mosca, and Richard Wagner for their helpful insights and suggestions.

History of Political Economy 47 (annual suppl.) DOI 10.1215/00182702-3130499

model" that failed as a scientific theory because it could not accurately explain the revenue-expenditure process. James M. Buchanan championed voluntary exchange as a democratic alternative to the Pigouvian "government-as-solution" for market failures that ruled orthodox public finance. Yet, despite such high-profile treatment, histories of public goods largely relegated voluntary exchange to the sidelines (Cornes and Sandler 1999; Desmarais-Tremblay 2013; Pickhardt 2006; Sturn 2010; the exception is Head 1974). Similarly, voluntary exchange receives short shrift in histories of public choice, passed over for political efficiency, unanimity, and government failure (Backhaus and Wagner 2005; Brennan 2004; Medema 2005, 2011; Wagner 2004). That voluntary exchange as a theory has faded out of the public finance literature belies the role it served as the springboard for launching the modern public goods debate.

The debate over voluntary exchange goes well beyond its theoretical mechanics or questions of the theory's correctness. Rather, discussions of voluntary exchange reveal how the larger context of the postwar period shaped thinking in public economics. Voluntary exchange was employed in a fundamental discussion about how to delineate the appropriate boundaries of public economics inquiry and the economic role of government. Interwoven into this story is a related discussion about democracy and how to model individual-government decision making. How economists perceived the market failure engendered by public goods and the potential of voluntary exchange to provide a solution was closely tied to precepts of individual behavior, theories of government, and beliefs as to how government functioned and should thus be modeled.

Origins of Voluntary Exchange Theories

The basic premise of voluntary exchange derives from the much older benefit principle of taxation, which suggests that people should pay taxes based on the benefits they receive from government-provided goods and services. The benefit approach is distinguished from ability-to-pay, which suggests setting taxes based on faculty or concepts of justice or fairness, which results in the wealthy paying relatively more in taxes. While there are a variety of origins and justifications for ability-to-pay, in all cases, taxes are divorced from expenditures and considerations of who benefits from government-provided goods and services (Musgrave 1959, 90–96). Ability-to-pay historically dominated English-language public finance, from J. S. Mill through A. C. Pigou. In contrast, the benefit principle was more closely associated with the German and Italian traditions in public finance.

The idea of framing individual interactions with government as a series of voluntary exchanges where individuals weigh the benefits received against the cost (tax price) originated in the 1880s Continental public finance literature, as practitioners attempted to extend marginal utility analysis to problems of public finance. Driven by the changing political landscape of Europe in the 1880s and greater demand for responsive government, voluntary exchange emerged as a competitor to models that represented government as monolithic decision maker. In voluntary exchange models, choices about government-provided goods and how to pay for them are made within a political system that organizes individual preferences into a collective decision. Voluntary exchange was closely connected with the emerging democratic movements and extension of the franchise in late nineteenth-century Europe. Early variations can be found in Emil Sax (1887), Antonio de Viti de Marco (1888), Knut Wicksell (1896), and Erik Lindahl (1919).[1]

One leader of the *scienza delle finanze* tradition, de Viti (1936), provided an early argument that state activity in a democratic society could be modeled using a contractual framework. Much like individuals demand private goods, they also demand collective goods. For de Viti, collective goods or needs constituted a broad category of goods and services that arise out of the nature of communal living.[2] These may be supplied by the market, particularly if the good is demanded by only a subset of the population. For collective goods demanded generally, individual decisions should be made analogously to decisions about private goods, prioritizing production at least-cost. Taxes should be understood as prices for collective goods, voluntarily paid, with an equilibrium resulting through a series of adjustments to tax prices and the quantities of the public good provided. De Viti argued that in a modern democratic state, expenditures and

---

1. Voluntary exchange can be difficult to track, as it went by different names and descriptions prior to Musgrave 1939. Colm ([1936] 1955) referred to the "monoistic theory" of the state to describe the idea of voluntary exchange, and Seligman (2001, 96) called it a "contractual theory of the state."

2. De Viti (1936, 45) accepted that at times, the state may provide for individual wants while private companies provide collective wants. However, a number of "public services . . . are on the way to assuming a permanent place in the business of the State." De Viti's collective goods examples centered on health and hygiene—goods that were not divisible and could not be easily priced on a use basis. For a more detailed discussion of de Viti's position on collective goods, see Eusepi and Wagner 2013.

taxes must have coequal importance in the decision process; in exchange for tax payments, individuals require the opportunity to evaluate what they receive in benefits.[3]

The theme of democratic decision making carried over into Wicksell's ([1896] 1967, 72) analysis of voluntary exchange, which he viewed as "nothing more than the benefit principle" extended and expanded, "apply[ing] the modern concept of marginal utility and subjective value to public services and to individuals' contributions for these services."[4] Though conceptually appealing, the benefit principle seemed impractical for funding most government services, as Wicksell recognized; his innovation was coupling the decision to provide the service with a tax plan and voting scheme, thereby allowing individuals to determine subjectively for themselves whether the service was worth the cost. A proposal would pass if unanimously supported, unanimity guaranteeing the voluntariness of the exchange. Wicksell believed that shifting from a political system that relied on coercion, in which many individuals felt that they did not receive benefits comparable with what they paid in costs, to a system in which exchanges with government were voluntary, was a hallmark of democracy and would actually lead to an expanded role for the state (91). Such a system would guarantee that "justice would thereby have been done at least to the extent that each man received his money's worth" (75).

Lindahl (1919) followed Wicksell's approach with a more mathematically sophisticated version of his own,[5] also emphasizing freely formed governments, protection of minority interests, and the sharing of political power. However, the variants produced by the Scandinavians and the Italians did not generate much interest in the English-language literature. A. C. Pigou's field-defining *A Study in Public Finance* (1928) does not mention

3. See Kayaalp 2004, Medema 2005, and Eusepi and Wagner 2013.

4. Wicksell likely came across the basic idea in Sax or Ugo Mazzola, for there is no evidence he read de Viti's Italian treatise prior to the publication of *Finanztheortische Untersuchungen* (1896). It is also not clear that he read Mazzola; rather, it seems Wicksell read German reviews of Mazzola's works.

5. Kayaalp (2004, 22–23) classifies Wicksell as a voluntary exchange model, though he views Lindahl's modification as more complicated, sharing features with both voluntary exchange and ability-to-pay. Musgrave (1986, 94), though originally classifying Wicksell's approach as voluntary exchange (1939), changed his mind and concluded that "[Wicksell] scornfully rejected as unrealistic the assumption, first advanced by Mazzola, that the political process of public provision and its finance through taxation functions in analogy to voluntary exchange in the market." This pivot is likely attributable to the long-running debate that Musgrave engaged in with Buchanan over the correct interpretation of Wicksell, as well as the influence of Samuelson's vision of public goods (on the latter, see Desmarais-Tremblay 2013).

voluntary exchange, nor does C. F. Bastable's *Public Finance* (1903). Some of this has been attributed to the language barrier (Eusepi and Wagner 2013), though more commonly cited is the fundamental incompatibility between voluntary exchange theories and the Anglo-Saxon approach to public finance (Backhaus and Wagner 2005; Buchanan 2007; Kayaalp 2004). The notable exception was a London School of Economics scholar, F. C. Benham (1934b), who published a laudatory review of de Viti's *Principii di economia finanziaria* in *Economica*. Widely read in the Continental public finance literature, Benham (1934b, 366) was perhaps the first to recognize the link between de Viti's work and Wicksell's conceptualization. Yet, despite finding the democratic features of voluntary exchange appealing, Benham concluded that such theories were fundamentally unworkable—both in their ability to determine appropriate expenditure levels and in collecting the taxes without compulsion. "The economist must leave these questions to the political scientist" (Benham 1934a, 455).

Voluntary exchange did not fare better with the Americans. In his famously acerbic review of de Viti's *First Principles of Public Finance* (1936), Henry Simons (1937, 714) had nothing good to say and would accede only that voluntary exchange was a "vaguely analogical application" of price theory.[6] Gerhard Colm ([1936] 1955, 32), despite coming out of the German cameralist tradition, claimed that "every theory which tries to explain the administrative and the market economy by the same principles, encounters failure." Harold Groves allocated less than a paragraph to voluntary exchange in the appendix to his seven-hundred-page textbook, *Financing Government* (1939). Arguing his case for a rethinking of public finance theory, the Canadian economist Stewart Bates (1937, 173) appreciated the democratic appeal of voluntary exchange, but rejected it on a practical level because individuals are "not free to take a little less government service and a little more private service, nor, as individuals, can they take a little less defense and a little more education."

---

6. Some have wondered why such a thoughtful practitioner of public finance could find no use for de Viti's treatise. In an interview, Buchanan speculated that "of course my prejudices come as a result of my own thinking about it, that is: Benham was right and Simons was totally wrong. But why? I thought about that yesterday, when you were coming down to talk to me. Why did Simons, who was one of my professors, a very very very bright man, why should he have reacted that way? He called it 'a monument of confusion.' I think the mindset of the American and English economists were just so locked in to studying markets and no attention paid whatsoever to the organization of the collective sector, that it just didn't make much sense to him; it's the only way I can figure, because he was very sharp, very bright, but he didn't get into that category at all. I never knew Benham, but certainly in that review he understood the impact of the book" (quoted in Mosca 2011, 10).

E. R. A. Seligman was perhaps the only one to recognize the issue for what it was. Though attributing the origins of "contractual theory" to Nassau Senior and Jean-Jacques Rousseau in his course lecture notes from 1927, Seligman (2001) summarized the approach as one representing a quid pro quo between individuals and government. As the intellectual parent and architect of the US progressive income tax, Seligman, however, cleaved to ability-to-pay, viewing its embrace as politically and socially necessary to guarantee passage of the federal income tax. Seligman represented income tax payments as contributions to the family, made for the good of all, rather than for selfish benefit, as portrayed in voluntary exchange theories. What Seligman (2001, 41–42) did recognize was, when comparing a patriarchal theory of the state with a contractually (voluntarily) based theory, "as one magnifies the state, the other minimizes the state, [making] it equal with the individual."

Musgrave and Voluntary Exchange

By the eve of the Second World War, voluntary exchange theory had barely managed to become a footnote in the English-language literature, and it looked as if Simons (1938, 3) was right to relegate it to "the history of doctrine." Musgrave's analysis was to be the death knell. Musgrave argued that voluntary exchange and the benefit principle "differ distinctly." In early conceptualizations, the benefit principle was put forward as an ethical standard—taxation according to benefit; whereas voluntary exchange theory made taxation according to benefit a condition of equilibrium (Musgrave 1939, 212). These theories all postulated taxes as voluntary purchase payments for individual shares of a good provided by the government and "explain the revenue-expenditure process as a phenomenon of economic value and price, determined by fundamentally the same 'laws' that govern market price in a private economy" (214).

Musgrave's interest in public finance originated during his undergraduate studies in his native Germany, a combination of the deep German tradition of *Finanzwissenshaft*, the influence of notable and active German scholars such as Wagner, Colm, and Otto Pfleiderer, and the economic challenges of the Weimar Republic (Sinn 2009).[7] In his dissertation,

7. Musgrave completed his undergraduate degree in Germany, coming to the United States in 1933 on a one-year academic exchange. After a year at Rochester, he moved to Harvard in 1934, receiving his MA in 1936 and his PhD in 1937. His dissertation, "The Theory of Public Finance and the Concept of 'Burden of Taxation,'" was completed under the supervision of H. H. Burbank.

Musgrave drew on the German literature, though he adopted a distinctly Anglo-Saxon view of the central problems of public finance. This evolved into his first paper: working from Lindahl's model, Musgrave (1939) argued that voluntary exchange failed on two levels. First, it could not provide a realistic explanation of the actual revenue-expenditure process, because the underlying assumption of competitively determined prices for government-provided goods was flawed. The political process would yield at best an imperfectly competitive outcome, and compulsion would still be necessary in the revenue collection process (Musgrave 1939, 220, 231–32). For the same reason, voluntary exchange theory also failed as a solution to the problem of guaranteeing justice in taxation. Offering by far the most technical consideration of a theory of voluntary exchange, Musgrave concluded that "in view of the unrealistic nature of the voluntary exchange assumption [tax prices as voluntary payments], the theory—quite apart from the internal logic of its argument—appears to be of little practical significance" (220).

Voluntary exchange was, at best, an analogy (215; see also Musgrave 1941, 319). Whereas a theory indicates an accepted valid explanation of some phenomenon demonstrated through repeated testing, analogies fall short of a scientific standard, merely indicating a partial similarity that could serve as the basis of a comparison.[8] Yet Musgrave even disputed whether voluntary exchange could serve as an accurate analogy, arguing that the initial premise failed to hold. Collective or public goods do "not fit into this pattern" of decisions made in the market for private goods because the "essential condition of *voluntary* choice is not fulfilled where collective wants are concerned" (Musgrave 1941, 319, 320). Musgrave ultimately dismissed all such discussion, claiming that "the actual functioning of this process is an empirical problem in sociology. The question of how it *should* function is a matter of political philosophy" (322).[9]

Benham (1934a), Bates (1937), Alfred Neal (1940), and Musgrave all dispatch voluntary exchange theory as being "altogether unrealistic" (Musgrave 1941, 322), obscuring the necessity of compulsion in the revenue collection process. They did, however, recognize the intellectual appeal of a theory built around the premise of democratic decision mak-

8. The characterization of voluntary exchange as an analogy is evident throughout the literature; see Margolis 1955, 347; Samuelson 1955, 355; and McGuire and Aaron 1969, 38.

9. Others agreed: Neal (1940, 249) concluded that "we must therefore agree with Musgrave and reject the voluntary exchange theory as being decidedly too limited to be of much use as a practical tool of analysis in matters of public finance or public planning."

ing. In contrast, Buchanan was to make voluntary exchange a central feature of his vision for modeling government-individual interactions.[10]

From Footnote to Foundation

Buchanan's earliest work considered problems of fiscal federalism. In these, Buchanan sought to counter the increased centralization of tax policy goals and design, arguing that the same objectives could be achieved in a more federalist system. Without strategies to equalize fiscal burdens across states, Buchanan (1950, 599) was concerned that large-scale centralization of political power was inevitable. This was related to a deeper and more philosophical issue. Buchanan (2007, 83) was highly dissatisfied with the standard approach to public finance that "implicitly postulated [government] to be exogenous to the economy . . . a monolithic and benevolent decision maker." From the start, Buchanan was angling to remake public finance in two significant ways. First, building on the Chicago price theory paradigm, Buchanan wanted a mechanism by which the voluntary features of exchange in the market could be applied to individuals' exchanges with government. In this, Buchanan followed Frank Knight's (1924) model of congested toll roads more so than Simons's work on federal income taxation. Second, Buchanan wanted to expand the scope of public economics. While others relegated governmental decision making to political science, sociology, or philosophy, Buchanan was quite ready to claim this as ground for public finance proper. These two tasks occupied much of his focus prior to the 1960s—and both leveraged voluntary exchange as part of the basic argument (Johnson 2014).

The evolving role played by voluntary exchange in Buchanan's thinking can be traced from his earliest publications. Initially, voluntary exchange offered an attractive alternative to orthodox public finance, one that comported well with Buchanan's precepts on individual choice and democracy. Heavily influenced by Knight and Simons at Chicago, Buchanan (1948, 6–7) started with the premise that either you believe that an economic problem can "best be solved by a competitive free enterprise system operating within the limits of defined 'rules of the game'" or you

10. This distinction was also noticed by Head (1974, 152), who stated that "from the outset, a characteristic of the modern development has been the emphatic rejection of what was described by Musgrave as the 'voluntary exchange theory' of the public goods pioneers, notably Lindahl. By contrast, the most striking feature of Buchanan's exposition is that the theory of public goods is developed explicitly as a voluntary exchange theory of the public economy."

accept the basic tenet "asserting that a freely competitive system is not the ultimate means and that instead greater political direction of economic life is required for the optimum solution of the economic problem." From this followed two ways of thinking about government: individualistic models and organistic models. In the latter, government is an exogenous entity, and decisions are made based on some predetermined concept of social welfare. Individualist models of government start from the premise that individuals are the appropriate decision-making units and the features of exchange in the market should be applied to individual exchanges with government (Buchanan 1949, 496). This was an ethical choice.

Rejecting organistic models of the state, claiming that "vague and general terms, such as 'social utility' and 'social welfare,' are of little use in the discussion of policy problems," Buchanan (1949, 498) carefully distinguished between policies approved through the fiscal mechanism, which would be subject to the political caprices of the current government, and policies approved under voluntary exchange. From here, Buchanan laid out his case for coevaluating taxes and expenditures (benefits) at the individual level, a call that becomes the leitmotif of his early work. In this approach, individuals explicitly evaluate pairs of expenditure-tax proposals, since "both the level of tax burden and the range of publicly provided services must be included" (Buchanan 1950, 586). Rational individuals will choose to engage in trade with government when they receive more in benefit than is paid in costs. Buchanan argued that operating from a premise of quid pro quo was an ethical choice that should not be conflated with the practicality of apportioning the tax burden. Buchanan's approach was revolutionary in English-language public finance. Pigouvian economics had always worried solely about the distribution of the tax burden, not the distribution of benefits from the corresponding expenditures. When considerations of benefits are included, individualistic models become compelling. At this point, however, Buchanan (1949) does not extend the criterion of Pareto efficiency to voluntary exchange outcomes—that comes later.

To understand Buchanan's position on voluntary exchange it is necessary to consider the precepts under which he operated and how they differed from those typically adopted in mainstream public finance and perhaps best represented by Musgrave.[11] Buchanan (2007, 5) tells us, "I had

---

11. Musgrave opted for an organistic model in his planning approach and did not give much consideration to how individual wants are transformed into social wants for making decisions. Vaguely, Musgrave assumed some sort of democratic process would be involved, coupled with some element of compulsion. This sort of hand waving was anathema to Buchanan. Generally, Musgrave had a highly positive view of government and what it could accomplish (Buchanan and Musgrave 1999).

always been antistate, antigovernment, antiestablishment," which in turn shaped his approach to government policymaking. "We are democrats here not autocrats," he told his 1963 public finance class before assigning them an essay on "the problem of fiscal dimension" (quoted in Wagner 2014, 5). Buchanan combined this with a fundamental philosophical (sociological) orientation to exchange rather than conflict. This manifested in his being a "zealous advocate of the market order" (Buchanan 2007, 5) following Frank Knight as well as adopting Wicksell's optimistic unanimity rule. "Buchanan's constitutional economics starts from the presumption that people want to live together in harmony" (Wagner 2014, 22).[12]

To illustrate the applicability of voluntary exchange, Buchanan authored a series of papers that demonstrated how the theory could be applied to a number of public goods–type problems, from marginal-cost pricing of government services to highway construction (Buchanan 1951, 1952a, 1952b).[13] In doing so, Buchanan exposed several glaring deficiencies that plagued contemporary public finance: modeling government decision making, explaining decisions about expenditures, and evaluating government actions. By 1952, Buchanan started to leverage voluntary exchange combined with a unanimity rule to establish a positive criterion for evaluating government policy. Only unanimity could ensure that all expenditures undertaken were "genuinely beneficial" at the level of the individual (Buchanan 1952b, 601). Hence voluntary exchange could solve the problem of government-provided goods while generating the political equivalent of Pareto efficiency in the market. Imposing a reverse chronological reading of his own work, Buchanan (2007, 5–6) retrospectively emphasizes the unanimity–Pareto efficiency congruence:

> Wicksell laid out a set of ideas that seemed to correspond precisely with those that I had already had in my head, ideas that I could not have expressed and would not have dared to express in the public-finance mindset of the time. Wicksell told us that if economists really want to apply the test of efficiency to the public sector, only the rule of

12. "The difference resides in whether the analytical point of departure is grounded in concord or discord among the members of society. . . . Buchanan's distinction between choice of rules and choice of strategies within rules is based on some point of agreement from which social life subsequently proceeds" (Wagner 2014, 20).

13. I freely admit that the use of the term *public good* prior to the 1960s is problematic and thank Hammond (this volume) for pointing this out. The concept did not acquire an analytical definition until well after the Musgrave-Buchanan discussion commenced. Economists in the 1940s and early 1950s had not reached a consensus on the terms and employed different terms with different meanings. Certainly, they were not only thinking about goods that fit Musgrave's definition rather than simply thinking of services provided by government.

> unanimity for collective choice offers the procedural guarantee. . . .
> Economists should . . . cease and desist proffering advice to nonexistent
> and benevolent despots.[14]

In actuality, Buchanan does not make the argument that unanimity is
equivalent to Pareto efficiency until his paper on marginal cost pricing
(1951), perhaps the sixth or seventh paper he published.[15] Rather, Buchanan
initially employed voluntary exchange as an operational theory of expenditure-tax decision making, setting it up as a competitor to orthodox public finance models.

The flurry of articles employing voluntary exchange in Buchanan's
early career quickly became less a method of product differentiation and
more a fundamental building block for his approach to public finance. As
public choice emerged as a distinct enterprise in the 1960s, the solutions
for public goods and externalities were rooted in the conceptual aspects of
voluntary exchange (Buchanan and Tullock 1962; Buchanan 1968). The
ethical premise of voluntary exchange and quid pro quo was paired with a
corresponding emphasis on democratic processes and decision making,
echoing de Viti and Wicksell. Buchanan argued that voluntary exchange,
coupled with the unanimity rule, worked because it made explicit each
individual's costs and benefits from a particular expenditure-tax proposal.
While in the private market unanimity is implicit and is not imposed (but
rather is a characteristic of free trade), explicit unanimity in the collective
decision-making process regarding government-provided goods could
achieve the same efficiency (Buchanan 1968, 83). Buchanan concluded
that voluntary exchange "serves much the same function here as the economist's assumption of perfect competition in the theory of private-goods
demand and supply" (97). The features of the competitive market—individualism, voluntarism, and quid pro quo—became more pronounced
over time in the public choice literature. Its "central organizing principle"
derived directly from the Wicksellian tradition of voluntary interactions
(Wagner 1997; see also Eusepi and Wagner 2013).

Buchanan defined direct individual participation in the revenue-expenditure process as a hallmark of democracy that needed to be included in the
modeling process. This made him heir apparent to the continental public

---

14. On the origin, motivations, and accuracy of the Wicksell discovery story, see Johnson
2014.

15. Buchanan turned out a wealth of work between 1949 and 1952. Considering publication
lags and unknown acceptance dates, it is difficult to place the papers in an exact chronological
order from the perspective of when they were written.

finance tradition, simultaneously placing him outside mainstream public economics (Backhaus and Wagner 2005). Buchanan's position ran counter to majority-rule democracy, with most decisions made at parliamentary or congressional levels, of which Buchanan and many others, including Duncan Black and Mancur Olsen, viewed as an inefficient or even highly problematic way to translate individual preferences into group action.

Thus there is a distinct trajectory in Buchanan's use of voluntary exchange that runs from treating it as an ethical precept to establishing it as a (mostly) positive theory of public choice. For Buchanan, voluntary exchange was clearly superior to the ambiguous ability-to-pay, which failed as a positive theory, unable to identify deterministic policy conclusions (Buchanan 1960).[16] The concept of voluntary exchange is more difficult because it blurs the distinction. As a positive matter, there are voluntary exchanges. As a normative matter, "voluntary" is associated with good in democratic, individualistic societies. With regard to Buchanan, it is clear that as a normative matter he was interested in seeing the domain of voluntary action expanded. As a positive matter, he thought that voluntary interaction could generate a greater volume of public provision than most economists appreciated. However, many in public finance did not accept either the precepts or any claim to explanatory value.[17] This rift became more pronounced in the discussion launched by Samuelson's classic articles on public goods.

Midcentury Moderns

The Musgrave-Buchanan discussion over the relevancy and usefulness of voluntary exchange preceded the modern public goods debate; in doing so, it brought several issues to the fore, including the need to understand the pricing, extent, and evaluation of public goods provision. By the early 1950s, however, economists were no closer to reaching a consensus on the nature, definition, and characteristics of government-provided goods than they had been a half-century earlier. M. H. Hunter's (1930, 46–47) decades-old complaint of failed classifications and lack of scientific exactness in

16. The "principle [of ability-to-pay] owes its popularity to its very ambiguity; it can be used to criticize, or alternatively support, almost an infinite number of distributions of the tax load" (Buchanan 1960, 47).

17. Murray Rothbard (2010, 295) argued that "it is important to emphasize that this book [*Prices, Income, and Public Policy* (1959)] brings home as few have done to me how much can go wrong if one's philosophical approach—one's epistemology—is all wrong. At the root of all the troubles of the book lies the weak, confused, and inconsistent positivism."

definitions still held true. It was not until Musgrave 1969 that the nonrival and nonexcludable criteria for public goods were first clearly articulated; this has since become the textbook definition (Desmarais-Tremblay 2013; Pickhardt 2006). The two central features employed in the 1940s and early 1950s centered on the Continental European contribution of jointness, lumpiness, or indivisibility combined with the generally accepted difficulty of exclusion, which generates free riding.[18]

Prior to Samuelson's contributions (1954, 1955), little attention was given to the problem of public goods in mainstream economics journals. Samuelson (1954, 388) dramatically reframed the debate, claiming to take his inspiration from the "voluntary exchange theories of public finance of the Sax-Wicksell-Lindahl-Musgrave type." In Samuelson's model, the optimum value of pure public goods expenditure was determined by an outside observer who has information on the preferences and incomes of all individuals in the economy. This was necessary, since approaches that relied on benefit taxation could not solve the fundamental problem of free riding or eliminate incentives for individuals to misrepresent the benefits they would receive from the provision of a public good. Hence Samuelson's (1955, 355) method was not a revival of the voluntary exchange theory but an illustration as to why that approach could not work. Samuelson (1954, 388) concluded that "no decentralized pricing system can serve to determine optimally these levels of collective consumption" and no public body could determine the optimal levels. Additional details can be found in Hammond, this volume.

For Samuelson, the public goods tradition arising in the Italian and Scandinavian literatures defined the problem correctly, but not the solution. Voluntary exchange theories suffered from the "fatal inability of any decentralized market or voting mechanism to attain or compute this [public goods] optimum" (Samuelson 1955, 350). In fact, "much of what goes by the name of the 'voluntary exchange theory of public finance' seems pure obfuscation" (355). This statement raises two interesting questions: To which theories was Samuelson referring, and what were they obfuscating? In answer to the first, there were not many candidates—either Samuelson was referring to the original voluntary exchange theories by de Viti,

18. This presumption was common in the literature (e.g., Bowen 1943): utility maximizing agents would not voluntarily contribute to public goods because their nature implies that a single agent's contribution would not affect the total level of public good provided. This problem is compounded by the fact that agents who do not contribute cannot be prevented from consuming the public good (nonexcludability).

Wicksell, and others, or he was referring to Buchanan. By 1954, Buchanan had published five articles that prominently employed voluntary exchange theory, and was the only active proponent of the theory.[19]

Even if Samuelson had previously been unaware of Buchanan's position, the two exchanged a series of letters on public goods during the early months of 1955. The exchange illustrated Samuelson's impatience with what he saw as Buchanan's reliance on artificial preference revelation schemes and his hyperindividualistic focus (Samuelson's letters to Buchanan, quoted in Marciano 2013, 238–39).[20] Returning to the argument a decade later, Samuelson (1969, 107n, 504) rejected the voluntariness of voluntary exchange, stating that "Wicksell deserves credit for exposing the nonsense of voluntarism in pseudo-tax and other formulations," and "it pays no one to behave according to the voluntary exchange theory." Buchanan, however, was generally convinced that his viewpoint could be reconciled with Samuelson's public goods solution at least in the case of a pure public good (Buchanan 1962; see also Marciano 2013). This comes out not only in his work but also in that of his students (e.g., Johnson and Pauley 1969).

All of this suggests a speculative answer to the second question. Voluntary exchange theories obfuscated the necessity of government-based solutions for public goods. Government was necessary because individuals would not voluntarily reveal their true preferences under any circumstances. The failure to come to a meeting of the minds[21] on the issue of revealed preferences and individual-market incentives served as a challenge for Buchanan to articulate his own theory of public goods and as the impetus for *The Demand and Supply of Public Goods* (1968) and the emergence of public choice (Wagner 2014; Brennan 1998). The split was less about the mechanics of the solutions than the underlying precepts about the nature of government and government-individual interactions.

---

19. Regarding voluntary exchange, Buchanan stated, "There weren't any current people working in that area . . . you didn't have anyone who was sort of carrying it forward at that time" (quoted in Mosca 2011).

20. Marciano (2013, 241) argues that there is no evidence that Samuelson was referring to Buchanan in this "cutting" statement.

21. See Marciano 2013, 238–41, in particular, Buchanan's letter to H. P. B. Jenkins that "the little debate I started with Samuelson faded away after a few interesting exchanges. I suppose he came to the conclusion that I could not speak his language and he never seemed to understand mine" (quoted in Marciano 2013, 241). Samuelson felt the same, responding to Buchanan that "your interpretation of my writings differs considerably from my own" (quoted in Marciano 2013, 242).

Which is less realistic: Samuelson's omniscient monolithic decision maker, Musgrave's benevolent policy director, or Buchanan's voluntary taxpayer? And what do policy directors and monolithic decision makers imply for a democratic country with a market-based economy? While Buchanan may have viewed the appeal of voluntary exchange as largely conceptual, he was not willing to cede that it was less feasible or policy relevant than the options proposed by more orthodox practitioners of public finance. This is particularly true when it came to strategies to mitigate market failures.

Samuelson's public goods solution spurred an outpouring of related work, though very little addressed voluntary exchange. Notable exceptions were Leif Johansen (1963), Martin McGuire and Henry Aaron (1969), and Duncan Foley (1970), all of whom attempted to update Lindahl's model to generate something akin to the Samuelsonian equilibrium. Johansen (1963) did not believe that the theories could be reconciled.[22] Sympathetic to Musgrave's position, McGuire and Aaron (1969, 38l) proceeded in their analysis "as if the voluntary exchange analogy were applicable" despite rejecting the initial premise, arguing that "voluntary exchange is impossible in practice." They conclude that the benefit principle, which relies on the underlying assumption that taxes can be understood as the price paid by individuals for publicly provided goods through voluntary exchange with government, was already discredited by the fundamental lack of incentive for people to reveal their true preferences. The authors could find no equivalent mechanism in the private market for public goods, excepting "highly imperfect processes of voting and pressure groups" (38).

Voluntary Exchange, Public Goods, and Market Failure

Despite disagreements over the definition of public goods, it was generally agreed that the source of market failure was different for public goods than for externalities. In the former case, the market failure arose from the combination of the very features that defined a public good—nonrivalry and

---

22. "I have not meant by these notes to take a stand in the contest between the Lindahl theory and other approaches to a theory of public expenditures. I would agree with many criticisms against the Lindahl theory that are raised by Musgrave. . . . Furthermore, I am very much in doubt about the very basis of Lindahl's theory (as well as Samuelson's . . .) viz. the treatment of public goods entirely in terms of individualistic preference scales. Since no one has offered an obviously better theory, however, I think the Lindahl theory still deserves interest" (Johansen 1963, 358).

nonexcludability—rather than from the mispricing that characterizes externalities (Bowen 1943; Colm [1936] 1955; Head 1974; Musgrave 1939; Samuelson 1954). Most believed that the market failure engendered by public goods necessitated a wholesale government solution to the problem; the marginal adjustments that could be used to correct for externalities would be insufficient to generate an efficient outcome. In the case of public goods, there were "no decentralized organizational rearrangements, no private bookkeeping devices" that could eliminate the problem as with externalities. Rather "there is failure by existence" (Bator 1958, 371).

In many ways, the Buchanan-Musgrave-Samuelson argument over the relevancy of voluntary exchange was really about the nature and use of government to resolve market failure. While Samuelson (1954, 1955) provided a clever solution to efficiently provide public goods, in reality it was no more feasible than the voluntary exchange theories he derided. Coming out of a tax-engineering tradition, reconstructing economies and tax systems after the Second World War, Musgrave argued that the real choice came down to accepting imperfect (inefficient) solutions for collective wants or forgoing the benefits of government services. Musgrave accepted an activist state as a factual representation of reality, with government provision of public goods necessary for a civil and well-functioning society. With that comes an inescapable fact: "It is obvious that a social system cannot function without some degree of compulsion" (Musgrave 1941, 320). Rather than an institution to be minimized, government ought to be used to maximize social welfare (Buchanan and Musgrave 1999, 31). Samuelson agreed, generally preferring to err on the side of an overactive government rather than a passive one (Maas 2014). For both, a theory of government was unnecessary to operationalize policy.

Public choice scholars did not reject the concept of market failure per se; indeed, Buchanan (1962, 1965) made notable contributions to the market failure literature on externalities, but proclaimed that "market failure on its own meant nothing" (quoted in Brennan 1998, x). The presumption that market failure required a government response was flawed because government should be subject to the same evaluative criteria as the market. Buchanan thus sought to undermine the premise of orthodox public finance advanced by Pigouvians that government could succeed where markets failed. He argued that it is not necessarily the case that "externalities are either reduced or eliminated by the shift of activity from market to political organization" (Buchanan 1962, 17). Buchanan particularly objected to political actions that place restraints on private behavior as a way to mitigate externalities as well as "complex gimmicks and gadgets" where economists eschew real-world applicability, since their task is "not that of the politician" (18).[23]

The extent to which externalities and public goods were coming to be seen as ubiquitous in the public finance literature implied that markets never worked—a frightening presumption. For Buchanan (1962, 19), the theoretical desirability of a government solution was often at odds with the practical ability of the government to actually achieve a more efficient outcome. Rather, Buchanan argued that the polar case of a pure public good was a fiction—or at best, a useful but unrealistic theoretical construction. Most public goods should be categorized as "impure" or congestible, sharing their important features with externalities. Additionally, many public goods were localized or took a form where exclusion was theoretically possible, as in the case of a toll road or public swimming pool: "In absence of the large-number problem, efficient outcomes will tend to emerge from voluntary exchange processes" (Buchanan 1968, 187). Free riding should not be seen as rational or endemic. Under the right rules, no individual would have an incentive to vote against a plan that yielded positive net benefits; doing so would risk the plan being rejected and replaced with an alternative that possibly yielded fewer or zero net benefits. Consequently, an agent would vote against a proposal only if the benefits are truly negative (92). If externalities and impure or congestible public goods were really a problem, someone would propose an acceptable solution to the group. If no agreement could be made, this suggested the problem did not really exist at the level of individual preferences. Buchanan (1962) was hesitant to accept that any compulsion must be necessary—rather, institutions needed to be redesigned to better guarantee democratic decision making, and economists should give thought to how to do this.

By the mid-1960s, Buchanan had staked out a position on public goods in direct opposition to those provided by Musgrave and Samuelson. In a series of publications, Buchanan (1962, 1965, and 1968) argued that (1) public goods were in fact a subcase of externalities and that impure public goods were much more the reality than Samuelson's polar case. (2) It was not evident that public goods always constituted a case of market failure that demanded government intervention; rather, (3) changes in institu-

---

23. Though, to be fair, Samuelson may not have been concerned with the same problem as Pigou, mitigating externalities.

tional arrangements, the formation of clubs, and clarifications of property rights could mitigate the problems engendered by impure public goods in a more democratically consistent way.

Voluntary Exchange and Democracy

The originators of voluntary exchange theory were highly sensitive to the democratic implications of their theories; in fact, this was much of the appeal. Wicksell ([1896] 1967, 84, 87) rejected the "outdated political philosophy of absolutism" as well as a "philosophy of enlightened and benevolent despotism" for voluntary exchange and "progress toward parliamentary and democratic forms of public life." The democratic features of voluntary exchange were also widely recognized in the second wave of evaluation that began at the end of the 1930s. Neal (1940) objected to Musgrave's (1939) planning approach as "subverting democracy." Though unrealistic, voluntary exchange at least had the advantage of adhering to democratic decision making. Similarly, Benham (1934a, 450) claimed that the ideas behind voluntary exchange were "implicitly accepted by all who prefer democracy to other systems of government." Bates (1937, 173) found voluntary exchange "a useful reminder that in the long run the state expenditures and taxes must reflect the preference scales of the citizens."

Yet, though recognized as a desirable feature, modeling collective decisions in a consciously democratic framework was at odds with the methodological traditions of Pigouvian public finance, where government was treated as an exogenous entity (Aslanbeigui and Oakes, this volume). Generally, this issue was subsumed by the debates over defining government-provided goods and constructing efficient solutions and received only marginal attention in mainstream public finance. Buchanan brought the issue to the fore, complaining that Samuelson's solution for public goods lacked important democratic features, including a method of soliciting input from individual voters. "Such a principle is not only politically unimaginable in modern democracy; it is also conceptually impossible" (Buchanan 1962, 27).[24]

---

24. Part of the argument hinged on differing views of democracy. Voluntary exchange, like market transactions, allowed individuals to freely choose to consume or not, but did not offer any remedy for those without the resources to engage in trade. Musgrave had a more inclusive view of democracy, where everyone was involved in the decision making, but there were no guarantees that policies would be Pareto improving. Which approach was preferred hinged on authorial precepts as well as views on what constituted positive (versus normative) knowledge.

At the root of the voluntary exchange debate was a battle over larger issues. The first half of the twentieth century witnessed enormous growth in federal government expenditures, the rise of the welfare state, and ascendency of the Keynesian vision of public finance as a way to manage employment. Yet, by the 1950s, the shadow of US-Soviet relations began to loom large over the social sciences; in economics it manifested in a presumption for free market efficiency and government nonintervention, with the charge led by Chicago school economists. For them, the phrase "market failure" was heavily loaded and carried with it an implied necessity for rectification. Buchanan argued that market failure was not as ubiquitous as suggested, nor was there a guarantee that government action could mitigate the problem. Better was the claim that voluntary coordination could resolve externality and public goods problems. It is no surprise that the public choice and law and economics movements originated in Chicago (Medema 2011).

By the 1970s, control of the narrative on market failure shifted profoundly. Previously, attention in economics and political science focused on how well-conceived government intervention could rectify market failures. Thanks to the government-failure literature of Buchanan and Ronald Coase, this presumption shifted to a null hypothesis that market failure is better left to market resolutions (Moss 2010, 5). Even if markets failed, it was unlikely that government intervention could do better. This represented a profound shift in the practice of public economics, separating public choice from the dominant Pigouvianism and erecting a challenge to mainstream public finance to prove government-organized solutions could meet the neoclassical criterion of Pareto efficiency. The Tiebout hypothesis provides a variation on this theme (Singleton, this volume).

Thus, the split over the relevancy of voluntary exchange touches on deeply fundamental questions in public economics about the nature and extent of market failure, the ability of government to rectify market failure, and the role for government in the economy. At the most basic level, it is impracticable to adjudicate the voluntary exchange debate, since the positions taken rely on different antecedent assumptions as to the nature of individuals and government. In contrast to early advocates of voluntary exchange who thought the approach would enlarge the role of the state, Buchanan and other modern supporters positioned voluntary exchange as a way to minimize the state's role, in which they have little faith, and maximize the role of the individual, who is assumed to make rational and socialized decisions (Buchanan 1968). Free riding is seen as a pathological case rather than the norm; instead, people are presumed to be inclined to voluntary cooperation. In contrast, economists who dismiss voluntary exchange as unrealistic tend to magnify a role for the state and view individual actions with suspicion; for them, free riding is a rational, omnipresent response (Musgrave 1941; Samuelson 1954, 1955). These differences quickly become ideological (Buchanan and Musgrave 1999; see also Marciano 2013 for a similar discussion). In fact, the differing views of individuals and government in the public choice and public finance literatures has been a widely canvassed topic, with the points of disagreement being generally agreed on by representatives of both groups (Buchanan and Musgrave 1999; Desmarais-Tremblay 2013; Johnson 2004; and Marciano 2013).

How individual-government interactions are modeled says a lot about how economists think and what sorts of policies they are willing to accept; these views are often rooted in deeper precepts. Thus we see a story that positions free markets and voluntary exchange as democratic processes, on the one side, arrayed against social management and compulsion, on the other. Yet it goes even deeper. Musgrave would certainly prefer democratic government to any alternative, as would Samuelson, but they are largely satisfied by what they saw as the outcomes of majority-rule democracy and significant bureaucratic (expert) decision making (Buchanan and Musgrave 1999, 227–28; Maas 2014). Implicit in Musgrave's worldview is that not everyone will be happy with every outcome, and hence some level of coercion is always necessary. Samuelson is less worried about coercion than the implications of decisions being made by nonexperts, preferring a world of government technocrats to a situation where individuals who can hold policies and decisions hostage by unanimity requirements. In contrast, Buchanan's democracy is individualistic in the extreme, and much of his energy went to considering constitutional reform, supermajorities, and unanimity voting rules that guarantee Pareto-efficient outcomes.

Conclusions

Excepting Musgrave 1939 and its companion counterpoint in Buchanan 1949, voluntary exchange theory occupies a small space in the history of recent economic thought, with fewer than fifty mentions in books and articles in the English-language literature prior to 1970. Yet the midcentury debate over the relevancy of voluntary exchange, its precepts, and its antecedent assumptions served as the springboard to launch the modern debate over public goods. Positions taken on voluntary exchange shed light on the larger discussions roiling public economics in the postwar period, a time when the field was struggling to define the appropriate scope for inquiry and the economic role of government.

Simons (1938, 3) once pointed out that "taxation according to benefit, as a slogan, has an interesting history, which illustrates what a variety of uses and masters a good phrase may serve." Voluntary exchange is much the same. The language of economic storytelling is important. Different schools of thought elevate certain terms and certain representations of reality over others. Hence the argument over the relevancy of voluntary exchange is in many ways less about the theory and more about how individuals and government are to be represented. The fundamental disagreement over the applicability of voluntary exchange theory and its realism or relevance to public economics hinges on precepts about the nature of individuals and of government.

It should be clear at this point that the treatment of voluntary exchange theories had as much to do with the larger political-social-economic context of the postwar period as it did the internal mechanics, realism, or functionality of the theory. While critics of voluntary exchange did much to impugn its mechanics and practicality, they did little to negate its philosophical appeal. Voluntary exchange, by its nature, was a democratic solution to the market failure engendered by public goods. Hence its resurrection by Buchanan in the public economics literature was a logical outcome of the growth of neoliberalism and free market economics in the postwar period. Its contribution to sparking the public goods debate in the 1950s brought out into the open questions about how to model individual-government decision making, the appropriate scope for public economics inquiry, and the economic role of government.

References

Backhaus, Jürgen G., and Richard E. Wagner. 2005. "From Continental Public Finance to Public Choice: Mapping Continuity." In *The Role of Government in the History of Economic Thought*, edited by Steven G. Medema and Peter Boettke. *History of Political Economy* 37 (supplement): 314–32.

Bastable, C. F. 1903. *Public Finance*. London: Macmillan.

Bates, Stewart. 1937. "Classificatory Note on the Theory of Public Finance." *Canadian Journal of Economics and Political Science* 3 (2): 163–80.

Bator, Francis M. 1958. "The Anatomy of Market Failure." *Quarterly Journal of Economics* 73 (3): 351–79.

Benham, F. C. 1934a. "Pure Theory of Public Finance." *Economica* 1 (4): 436–58.

————. 1934b. Review of *Principii di economia finanziaria*, by Antonio de Viti de Marco. *Economica* 1 (3): 364–67.

Bowen, Howard R. 1943. "The Interpretation of Voting in the Allocation of Economic Resources." *Quarterly Journal of Economics* 58 (1): 27–48.

Brennan, Geoffrey. 1998. Foreword to *The Demand and Supply of Public Goods*, by James M. Buchanan. Indianapolis, Ind.: Liberty Fund.

————. 2004. "Life in the Putty-Knife Factory." *American Journal of Economics and Sociology* 63 (1): 75–104.

Buchanan, James M. 1948. "Fiscal Equity in a Federal State." PhD diss., University of Chicago.

————. 1949. "The Pure Theory of Government Finance: A Suggested Approach." *Journal of Political Economy* 57 (6): 496–505.

————. 1950. "Federalism and Fiscal Equity." *American Economic Review* 40 (4): 583–99.

————. 1951. "Knut Wicksell on Marginal Cost Pricing." *Southern Economic Journal* 18 (2): 173–78.

————. 1952a. "Federal Grants and Resource Allocation." *Journal of Political Economy* 60 (3): 208–17.

————. 1952b. "Wicksell on Fiscal Reform: Comment." *American Economic Review* 42 (4): 599–602.

————. 1960. "Social Choice, Democracy, and Free Markets." *Journal of Political Economy* 62 (2): 114–23.

————. 1962. "Politics, Policy, and the Pigouvian Margins." *Economica* 29 (February): 17–28.

————. 1965. "An Economic Theory of Clubs." *Economica* 32 (125): 1–14.

————. 1968. *The Demand and Supply of Public Goods*. Chicago: Rand McNally.

————. 2007. *Economics from the Outside*. College Station: Texas A&M University Press.

Buchanan, James M., and Richard A. Musgrave. 1999. *Public Finance and Public Choice: Two Contrasting Visions of the State*. Cambridge, Mass.: MIT Press.

Buchanan, James M., and Gordon Tullock. 1962. *The Calculus of Consent: The Logical Foundations of Constitutional Democracy*. Ann Arbor: University of Michigan Press.

Colm, Gerhard. (1936) 1955. "The Theory of Public Expenditure." In *Essays in Public Finance and Fiscal Policy*, 27–43. New York: Oxford University Press.

Cornes, Richard, and Todd Sandler. 1999. *The Theory of Externalities, Public Goods, and Club Goods*. New York: Cambridge University Press.

De Viti de Marco, Antonio. 1888. *Il carattere teorico dell'economia finazaris*. Rome: Loreto Pasqualucci.

————. 1936. *First Principles of Public Finance*. Translated by E. Pavio Marget. New York: Harcourt Brace.

Desmarais-Tremblay, Maxime. 2013. "On the Definition of Public Goods: Assessing Richard A. Musgrave's Contribution." Centre d'économie de la Sorbonne Working Paper 2014.04, Université Panthéon-Sorbonne (Paris 1).

Eusepi, Guiseppe, and Richard E. Wagner. 2013. "Tax Prices in a Democratic Polity: The Continuing Relevance of Antonio de Viti de Marco." *History of Political Economy* 45 (1): 99–121.

Foley, Duncan K. 1970. "Lindahl's Solution and the Core of an Economy with Public Goods." *Econometrica* 38 (1): 66–72.

Groves, Harold. 1939. *Financing Government*. New York: Henry Holt.

Head, John G. 1974. *Public Goods and Public Welfare*. Durham, N.C.: Duke University Press.

Hunter, M. H. 1930. "The Problem of Classification: Public Expenditures and Public Revenues." *American Economic Review* 20 (1): 46–53.

Johansen, Leif. 1963. "Some Notes on the Lindahl Theory of Determination of Public Expenditures." *International Economic Review* 4 (3): 346–58.

Johnson, David B., and Mark V. Pauley. 1969. "Excess Burden and the Voluntary Theory of Public Finance." *Economica* 36 (143): 269–76.

Johnson, Marianne. 2004. "Wicksell's Unanimity Rule: Buchanan's Dominance Considered." *American Journal of Economics and Sociology* 64 (4): 1049–72.

———. 2014. "James M. Buchanan, Chicago, and Post War Public Finance." *Journal of the History of Economic Thought* 36 (4): 479–97.

Kayaalp, Orhan. 2004. *The National Element in the Development of Fiscal Theory*. New York: Palgrave Macmillan.

Knight, Frank. 1924. "Some Fallacies in the Interpretation of Social Cost." *Quarterly Journal of Economics* 38 (4): 582–606.

Lindahl, Erik. 1919. *Die Gerechtigkeit Besteuerung*. Lund: Gleerup.

Maas, Harro. 2014. "Making Things Technical: Samuelson at MIT." In *MIT and the Transformation of American Economics*, edited by E. Roy Weintraub. *History of Political Economy* 46 (supplement): 272–94.

Marciano, Alain. 2013. "Why Market Failures Are Not a Problem: James Buchanan on Market Imperfections, Voluntary Cooperation, and Externalities." *History of Political Economy* 45 (2): 223–54.

Margolis, J. A. 1955. "Comment on the Pure Theory of Expenditure." *Review of Economics and Statistics* 37 (4): 347–49.

McGuire, Martin C., and Henry Aaron. 1969. "Efficiency and Equity in the Optimal Supply of a Public Good." *Review of Economics and Statistics* 51 (1): 31–39.

Medema, Steven G. 2005. "'Marginalizing' Government: From *la Scienza delle Finanze* to Wicksell." *History of Political Economy* 37 (1): 1–25.

———. 2011. "Public Choice and the Notion of Creative Communities." *History of Political Economy* 43 (1): 225–46.

Mosca, Manuela. 2011. *Una storia degna di memoria*. In *Antonio de Viti de Marco: Una storia degna di memoria*, edited by Manuela Mosca, 7–14. Milan: Bruno Mondadori.

Moss, David. 2010. "Reversing the Null: Regulation, Deregulation, and the Power of Ideas." Harvard Business School Working Paper 10-080.

Musgrave, Richard A. 1939. "The Voluntary Exchange Theory of Public Economy." *Quarterly Journal of Economics* 53 (2): 213–37.

———. 1941. "The Planning Approach in Public Economy: A Reply." *Quarterly Journal of Economics* 55 (2): 319–24.

———. 1959. *The Theory of Public Finance*. New York: McGraw Hill Book.

———. 1969. "Provision for Social Goods." In *Public Economics: An Analysis of Public Production and Consumption and Their Relations to the Private Sector*, edited by J. Margolis and H. Gutton, 124–44. New York: St. Martin's Press.

———. 1986. *Public Finance in a Democratic Society: Collected Papers*. Vol. 2. New York: New York University Press.

Neal, Alfred C. 1940. "The 'Planning Approach' in Public Economy." *Quarterly Journal of Economics* 54 (2): 246–54.

Pickhardt, Michael. 2006. "Fifty Years after Samuelson's 'The Pure Theory of Public Expenditure': What Are We Left With?" *Journal of the History of Economic Thought* 28 (4): 439–60.

Pigou, A. C. (1928) 1960. *A Study in Public Finance*. New York: St. Martin's Press.

Rothbard, Murray. 2010. "Untitled Letter Critical of Chicago School Economics." In *Strictly Confidential: The Private Volker Fund Memos of Murray N. Rothbard*, edited by David Gordon. Auburn, Ala.: Ludwig Von Mises Institute.

Samuelson, Paul. 1954. "Pure Theory of Public Expenditure." *Review of Economics and Statistics* 36 (November): 387–89.

———. 1955. "Diagrammatic Exposition of a Theory of Public Expenditures." *Review of Economics and Statistics* 37 (November): 350–56.

———. 1969. "Pure Theory of Public Expenditure and Taxation." In *Public Economics: An Analysis of Public Production and Consumption and Their Relations to the Private Sector*, edited by J. Margolis and H. Gutton, 98–123. New York: St. Martin's Press.

Sax, Emil. 1887. *Grundlegung der Theoretischen Staatswissenschaft*. Vienna: Holder.

Seligman, E. R. A. 2001. "Edwin Seligman's Lectures on Public Finance, 1927–1928." In *Research in the History of Economic Thought and Methodology*, edited by W. J. Samuels, M. Johnson, and L. Fiorito. Vol. 19C.

Simons, Henry C. 1937. Review of *First Principles of Public Finance*, by Antonio de Viti de Marco. *Journal of Political Economy* 45 (5): 712–17.

———. 1938. *Personal Income Taxation: The Definition of Income as a Problem of Fiscal Policy*. Chicago: University of Chicago Press.

Sinn, Hans-Werner. 2009. "Please Bring Me the New York Times: On the European Roots of Richard Abel Musgrave." *International Tax and Public Finance* 16 (1): 124–35.

Sturn, Richard. 2010. "'Public Goods' before Samuelson: Interwar *Finanzwissenschaft* and Musgrave's Synthesis." *European Journal for the History of Economic Thought* 17 (2): 279–312.

Wagner, Richard. 1997. "Choice, Exchange, and Public Finance." *American Economic Review Papers and Proceedings* 87 (2): 160–63.

———. 2004. "Public Choice as an Academic Enterprise: Charlottesville, Blacksburg, and Fairfax Retrospectively Viewed." *American Journal of Economics and Sociology* 63 (January): 55–74.

————. 2014. "James M. Buchanan and Me: Reminiscing about a 50-Year Association." George Mason University Department of Economics Working Paper 14-13.

Wicksell, Knut. 1896. *Finanztheoretische Untersuchungen.* Jena: Gustav Fisher.

————. (1896) 1967. "A New Principle of Just Taxation." Translated by J. M. Buchanan. In *Classics in the Theory of Public Finance*, edited by R. Musgrave and A. Peacock, 72–118. New York: St. Martin's Press.

Sorting Charles Tiebout

John D. Singleton

Seminal ideas in the history of economics are frequently identified with eminent economists. Their eminence is attested by peers who credit the author with professional rewards and by successors who connect their work to the original insight. This recognition often imparts parentage to an entire literature, which the originator is eager to foster, and to a research community in which the meaning and significance of the contribution stabilizes. Historical writing reinforces this process even as it aims to document it. For instance, figures around whom the postwar history of public economics is typically framed include Richard Musgrave and James Buchanan, with Paul Samuelson's "Pure Theory of Public Expenditure" (1954) serving as an analytical point of departure. Musgrave's *Theory of Public Finance*, first published in 1959, and Buchanan's *Calculus of*

Correspondence may be addressed to John D. Singleton, Department of Economics, Duke University, P.O. Box 90097, Durham, NC 27708-0097; e-mail: john.singleton@duke.edu. I am grateful for the financial support of the Center for the History of Political Economy and appreciative of the input from colleagues, students, and the family of Charles Tiebout, including William R. Allen, William Beyers, Robert Bish, David Boyce, James Buchanan, W. Lee Hansen, Geoffrey Hewings, Theodore Lane, Douglass North, John Parr, Bruce Tiebout, Robert Warren, and Burton Weisbrod, that made this research possible. Tamara Stasik and the staff of the Lilly Library at the University of Indiana, Bloomington, and the Special Collections staff at the University of Washington deserve numerous thanks. I benefited from comments from H. Spencer Banzhaf, Bruce Caldwell, William Fischel, Craufurd Goodwin, Kevin D. Hoover, Steven G. Medema, Matt Panhans, E. Roy Weintraub, an anonymous referee, and participants at the *HOPE* lunch seminar, the 2014 *HOPE* conference, and the 2014 ASSA meetings.

History of Political Economy 47 (annual suppl.) DOI 10.1215/00182702-3130511

Consent, published in 1962 with Gordon Tullock, represent the research programs in postwar public economics that emerged from an earlier discourse. Richard Sturn (2010) identifies the historical influences that Musgrave drew on in his work, while Maxime Desmarais-Tremblay (2013) evaluates Musgrave's contribution to the modern definition of public goods. Likewise, Samuelson's complex motivations in the 1954 paper are analyzed by Michael Pickhardt (2006), and J. Daniel Hammond (this volume) traces the evolution of Samuelson's thought on public goods through the 1960s. The development of Buchanan's thought and the countervailing public choice research program he built are the subjects of Marciano 2013 and Medema 2000 and 2011. The role of beliefs about the economic role of government in influencing the discourse is highlighted by Marianne Johnson (this volume).

On multiple counts, Charles M. Tiebout and the idea for which he is credited—"voting with your feet"—stands out as a notable exception to this pattern. While teaching at the University of Washington in 1968, Tiebout, known to his friends and colleagues as Charlie or Chas, suffered a sudden heart attack and died at the age of forty-three. Although a well-respected regional economist, colleague, and mentor, the 1956 article for which he is remembered had garnered fewer than fifty citations at the time of his tragic passing.[1] The year after his death, however, Wallace Oates (1969) published his test of the "Tiebout hypothesis," relating local property values to tax rates and public expenditures. This and the multitude of work that followed pursued lines of inquiry in which the Tiebout (1956) mechanism—eventually termed Tiebout sorting—plays a central role. These include studies of its empirical relevance, the theoretical properties, and applications to public, urban, education, and environmental topics via hedonic, sorting, and computational general equilibrium models.[2] Forty-five years on from Tiebout's passing, Tiebout 1956 boasts nearly 11,500 citations, ranking it among the most cited articles in economics. By comparison, there are under 6,000 citations for Samuelson 1954 and about 5,400 and 8,000 citations for Musgrave 1959 and Buchanan and Tullock 1962, respectively.[3] A fitting construct is thus that of a "Sleeping Beauty":

1. Google Scholar search, September 24, 2013. For comparison, twelve years after their publication, Coase 1960 had over 280 citations, while Stigler 1961 had about 180.

2. Recent examples of papers in this literature include Banzhaf and Walsh 2008; Bayer and McMillan 2012; Cellini, Ferreira, and Rothstein 2010; Coate 2013; and Kuminoff 2012. For a compendium of earlier work, see Oates 1998; for a recent review of related work, see Kuminoff, Smith, and Timmins 2013.

3. Google Scholar searches, September 24, 2013.

a "publication that goes unnoticed ('sleeps') for a long time and then, almost suddenly, attracts a lot of attention ('is awakened by a prince')" (van Raan 2004, 467). Tiebout's life came before his own time, complicating the metaphor of his parentage: his early death underscores that the way Tiebout 1956 was used, invoked, and interpreted by the community crediting the insight differs from how Tiebout, and those he communicated with during his life, viewed his work.

The goal of the present article is to articulate the dimensions of the latter—a history of the "sleep"—as viewed through Tiebout's academic biography. The intent is to repersonalize the scientific work of a figure whose work has been profoundly anonymized. As Till Düppe and E. Roy Weintraub (2014, xiii) explain, in abstract mathematized modes of expression, economic knowledge is accessed by a "community that needs to know nothing about the authors to appraise the work." In the case of Tiebout and the literature owning his article's heritage, almost literally nothing is known.[4] Reconstruction of the context is approached by reference to setting, influences, relationships, and motivation by way of archival materials, writings, and interviews. Through Tiebout's engagement with key figures in the construction of public economics, the perspective offers a unique vantage on "science in the making." Finer points of emphasis, disagreement, and personality cannot easily be gleaned from academic publications alone. In this way, the account also explores the historical contingencies present in the stabilization of a particular body of economic knowledge.

As a PhD student at the University of Michigan in the early 1950s, Tiebout first raised the idea of preferences revealed for public goods through mobility in Musgrave's graduate seminar on public finance. Regardless, Musgrave did not find the idea especially compelling, regarding it as a "special case." While an instructor at Northwestern, Tiebout penned the now famous paper as a qualification to Samuelson 1954, which appeared in the *Journal of Political Economy* in 1956. In a short published response two years later, Samuelson questioned both the practicality and the desirability of the mechanism, initiating an exchange of correspondence between the two. In the letters, Tiebout attempted to reassure Samuelson that he did not view sorting as a panacea for public goods problems. Tiebout maintained that it was nonetheless valuable from a planner's perspective in simplifying the problem of supplying optimal public expenditure at the

---

4. William Fischel's thoughtful biographical account on the occasion of fifty years since the publication of Tiebout 1956, Fischel 2006 notwithstanding.

local level. On Musgrave's invitation, Tiebout developed this argument and its implications for federalism more fully in a paper for a National Bureau of Economic Research (NBER) conference in 1959 at the University of Virginia hosted by Buchanan. Even though Tiebout and Buchanan shared an interest in local public finance and appeared to agree on many of the core points, Tiebout did not personally participate in the growing public choice program.

Despite largely failing to excite his economist peers with the idea, Tiebout continued to pursue related lines of inquiry. A move to UCLA in 1958 brought him into contact with the political scientist Vincent Ostrom at the Bureau of Governmental Research. Ostrom initially undertook a significant project to study the incorporation of the city of Lakewood, California, which contracted its municipal services from Los Angeles County. This phenomenon presented a number of connections and challenges to Tiebout's earlier work. Their prospective joint monograph sought to place the organization of metropolitan governments in an explicitly economic framework, where municipal services were bought and sold in a "quasi-market." This theorizing, however, drew the ire of other political scientists in the bureau, resulting in Tiebout's and Ostrom's removal from the project and the eventual joint authorship of an article with Robert Warren instead (Ostrom, Tiebout, and Warren 1961). In the wake of the Lakewood project's collapse, Tiebout relocated to the University of Washington in 1962, where he established the interdisciplinary Center for Urban and Regional Studies. Regardless, in the body of economic knowledge concerned with public expenditure and finance that stabilized during his lifetime, Tiebout's work had been marginalized despite his engagement with key figures in its construction. This equilibrium was only ruptured when Oates 1969 awoke the "Sleeping Beauty."

Two important contexts of Tiebout's scientific work are illuminated by the history of his academic career. First, the social context is tracked by Tiebout's own physical and intellectual migrations. Having grown up in Greenwich, Connecticut, and worked in local government before graduate school, Tiebout was keenly aware of the forces driving commuters into the rapidly expanding New York suburbs and of residents' efforts to try and keep them out. In Chicago, he saw the same phenomenon at work in planned developments like Park Forest. Meanwhile, in Los Angeles, the supply of metropolitan public goods, for example, water and public safety, confronted a dynamic complex of local jurisdictions and municipalities of various size and capabilities. These rapid changes in American urban centers in the postwar period presented a cross-disciplinary assemblage of researchers in the social sciences with novel questions. This context informed and motivated Tiebout's work, an enduring commonality with the expansive literature owning his article's heritage.

Second, although the social context fostered the study of such issues, the knowledge community necessary to recognize and reward credit did not yet exist. This research was thereby situated in the vacuum between established disciplinary boundaries, though it still required appeal to recognized outlets. The social and political phenomena that interested researchers like Tiebout strained received theoretical frameworks, from industrial organization to general equilibrium and welfare economics. Tiebout, for example, attempted to situate his famous sorting model as a contribution to spatial location theory in the presence of locally supplied public goods. Similarly, his later joint work with the political scientists Vincent Ostrom and Robert Warren, in part applying the structure-conduct-performance analysis to the system of municipal governments to evaluate efficiency, met resistance. In his role directing the interdisciplinary Center for Urban and Regional Studies at the University of Washington, Tiebout assembled a community to embed this sort of work. His lasting personal legacy resides with his colleagues and students in the field of regional science.

1. Greenwich

Lying in southwestern Connecticut near the New York border, Greenwich is located about thirty miles from Manhattan. Historically, this proximity, along with the town's characteristic charm and beaches, have made Greenwich a desirable and exclusive locale that today registers on lists of the best places to live and wealth per capita. Even before World War II and the boom that followed, Greenwich, like similarly situated communities in Nassau and Westchester Counties, was ground zero for housing expansion and parkway construction, as well-to-do commuters relocated to the affluent New York suburbs. At the war's end, when the newly formed United Nations considered places to build its headquarters, Greenwich's attractiveness placed Fairfield County, Connecticut, on the top of its short list. This intention, however, elicited a harsh and immediate opposition from Greenwich residents, who worried that the UN complex would congest their idyllic town. As soon as the news leaked, newspaper editorials and cartoons rallied with the concerned citizens who packed local schools to organize.

A town meeting at Greenwich High School, moderated by longtime resident Prescott Bush, resolved to draft an official referendum protesting the
site selection (Mires 2013). This organized opposition helped steer the UN
committee away from the northern suburbs of New York entirely.

One Greenwich resident opposed to the move was a twenty-two-year-
old Navy serviceman who voiced his objection in a letter to the *Chicago
Tribune*. He reflected:

> Greenwich, Conn., is my home town and I am very proud of it. It is what
> you might call a middle of the road town; not industrial and not rural. In
> it people have built homes of which they may be justly proud. Now the
> UNO comes along and says they are going to take it away from us.

Couching the harm to residents in economic terms, he added:

> Our town will be like the parking lot for a world's fair. Our people will
> have to pay higher taxes to offset the loss of property. The UNO says
> they plan to use our beaches in the summer. I promise they won't use
> the town of Greenwich if the veterans have their say.

The letter was signed "Disgusted GI." Its author was Charles M. Tiebout.[5]

In the final year of a three-year stint in the navy and newly married,
Charles Tiebout would return to his studies at Wesleyan University in
Middletown, Connecticut, in the fall of 1946. His father, Harry Sr., a psy-
chiatrist at the Blythewood Sanitarium in Greenwich, is still remembered
for his writings on alcoholism and in the Alcoholics Anonymous community for his treatment of Bill Wilson. Tiebout's older brother by three
years, Harry Jr., had graduated from Wesleyan the year prior and began
his graduate study in philosophy at Columbia that same fall. Tiebout, in
contrast, had dropped out after failing his first semester and enlisted.
After returning to Wesleyan, he undertook a degree in economics and
pursued opportunities in government outside his studies. The summer
before his final semester, Tiebout took a research position with the Middletown Chamber of Commerce and applied for graduate study after completing his degree requirements in the fall of 1949. He then spent the
spring of 1950 in Hartford, employed by the Governor's Committee of
Full Employment, with the title of assistant to the director, Lyle C. Fitch.
Fitch, a professor at Wesleyan, studied local and municipal government.[6]

5. Transcript provided by Bruce Tiebout.

6. It seems probable that Fitch taught one of Tiebout's courses at Wesleyan. Fitch's "Metropolitan Financial Problems" (1957) was the first to cite Tiebout 1956. Fitch eventually became
city administrator of New York City in 1960.

For the committee, Tiebout (1950) produced a study of the summer vacation business's effect on employment in the Connecticut resort communities and shore towns that was published by the Connecticut Labor Department. Although short, the paper acknowledged a dual-sided nature of vacation travel: Tiebout framed the analysis by asking the reader to place "himself in the role of the potential vacationer" and then traced the channels leading to employment effects of alternative decisions (1). Tiebout then observed that "communities of the state are seeking to develop greater employment opportunities and broader tax bases," an impulse that had led many of them to do "a splendid job in building up their vacation business" (11). Though far from developed, in this description of communities' objectives and personification of vacationers like shoppers, it is not difficult to read in an embryonic formulation of the sorting idea for which he was later credited. Equally, the connection between those interactions and larger economic outcomes, in this case employment, provided Tiebout's motivation. Tiebout brought these interests and background in government to the University of Michigan, where he began his PhD in 1950.

2. Ann Arbor

At Michigan, Tiebout made connections with two faculty members influential to the development of his thinking about local communities and public goods, though neither served on his committee. After his first year of coursework, Tiebout worked as a research assistant for Wolfgang Stolper, who had arrived at Michigan in 1949. At the time, Stolper was translating from the German *The Economics of Location* by August Lösch (1954).[7] In his foundational contribution to location theory, Lösch analyzed the general equilibrium arrangement and size of private firms in a circumscribed spatial plane where filling demand incurred transportation costs (Meardon 2000). In the model, firms located in nonoverlapping areas shaped like hexagons, which were each serviced by a single firm. Attempting to connect this sort of spatial general equilibrium to regional balance of payments accounting, Stolper and Tiebout (1978) jointly authored an input-output analysis of the Ann Arbor economy for 1952.

Richard Musgrave was also a recent arrival to the Michigan faculty, having joined in 1948. By the time that Tiebout attended Musgrave's graduate seminar in public economics in either 1951 or 1952, the latter had already begun work on the manuscript of *The Theory of Public Finance*,

---

7. Tiebout also had some fluency in German.

eventually published in 1959. An extension of his thesis work at Harvard, which produced "The Voluntary Exchange Theory of Political Economy" (1939), Musgrave sought to combine the earlier theoretical contributions of Knut Wicksell, Erik Lindahl, and Emil Sax with the more normative German tradition in public finance. These influences are analyzed in depth by Sturn (2010). As Marianne Johnson (this volume) explains, Musgrave (1939, 214) dismantled the voluntary exchange theory—which explained "the revenue-expenditure process as a phenomenon of economic value and price, determined by fundamentally the same 'laws' that govern market price in a private economy"—as a descriptive failure. This material would have not only formed the substance of the course that Tiebout took but also provided Paul Samuelson's understanding of the background material. A fellow Harvard product a few years Musgrave's junior, Samuelson (1954, 387) opened "The Pure Theory of Public Expenditure" with the justification that apart from "Sax, Wicksell, Lindahl, Musgrave, and Bowen," economists had neglected the theory of optimal expenditure. Further, in commenting on the paper's result, Samuelson attested that he had "learned from the published and unpublished writings of Richard Musgrave that their essential logic is contained in the 'voluntary-exchange' theories of public finance of the Sax-Wicksell-Lindahl-Musgrave type" and Bowen's work (388). Samuelson professed his indebtedness in this regard to Musgrave throughout his life.[8]

Samuelson 1954, while a seminal contribution to public good theory, was intended to demonstrate the value of mathematics in economics.[9] Pickhardt (2006) brings this and other motives to light. Samuelson's terseness in the paper, however, precipitated responses (Margolis 1955; Colm 1956) and elaborations from Samuelson in a follow-up article (1955) and at the winter 1955 meetings of the American Economic Association and the Econometric Society. Samuelson's paper also prompted an extended correspondence with James Buchanan (Marciano 2013). The basic analysis of the 1954 article is familiar and remains significant in two respects: first, for establishing a formal definition of public goods as those consumed collectively; second, for the famous condition that optimal public

8. After Musgrave's passing, Samuelson (2008, 167) reflected, "I look back with considerable embarrassment that my 1954 *Review of Economics and Statistics* paper on 'public goods' received so many citations. Certainly *all* that *I* knew of the historic 'public goods' literature came from oral Musgrave words and perusal of his 1939 dissertation."

9. Samuelson moderated the *Review of Economics and Statistics* debate launched by David Novick (1954), which included responses from Lawrence Klein, Tjalling Koopmans, Robert Solow, Jan Tinbergen, and others.

expenditure requires summation over individual marginal rates of substitution. Taken together, the conclusion, in Samuelson's (1954, 389) phrasing, is the "impossibility of [a] decentralized spontaneous solution" because "any one person can hope to snatch some selfish benefit in a way not possible under the self-policing competitive pricing of private goods." The underlying problem of public goods is thus the person's lack of incentive to reveal his or her preferences. While not couched in the terminology by Samuelson, public goods engendered a "market failure."

As Musgrave later recalled the story, he explained this "essential logic" to his University of Michigan seminar. To this, Tiebout responded with the insight with which his name is now associated: if by moving, consumers are able to shop among communities that supply public goods, then consumers' preferences are able to be revealed. In a characterization fitting Tiebout's personality, Musgrave also described the suggestion as offered jokingly.[10]

3. Evanston

While still completing his dissertation work, Tiebout took a position as a lecturer at Northwestern University in 1954. Although he had expressed the original "voting with your feet" idea in Musgrave's course at Michigan, Tiebout had not sought to publish it, pursuing his thesis research on regional input-output analysis and income multipliers under the supervision of Daniel Suits instead. According to Charles Leven, a Northwestern graduate student at the time whose committee Tiebout sat on, it was a lunchtime disagreement with a fellow Northwestern professor and University of Chicago graduate Meyer Burstein that spurred Tiebout to develop the insight. The discussion revolved around Burstein's frustration with paying high taxes for Evanston schools when he had no children. Tiebout pointed out that Burstein should just move to the nearby Rogers Park community then. In Leven's (2003, 236) words,

> What was interesting was the discussion I had with Charlie as we walked back to the office. "You know Chas," Charlie said, "I was absolutely right. People do have a choice over their local public goods and a way of showing their revealed preference simply by moving. In fact, that's a damn good idea. I should stick to my guns and write it up!" And he did.

10. This story is recounted in Fischel 2006. Elsewhere, Musgrave (1983, 101) claimed it was a "concept born in my Michigan seminar of the 1950s."

According to Leven's retelling, Tiebout produced a draft in a matter of days that, after circulating to a few people, he sent off to the *Journal of Political Economy*.[11] That it appeared there was an inside joke—"which he shared with a few trusted liberal friends" (Leven 2003, 236)—on the Chicago "Philistines," since the article, Leven later emphasized, demonstrated that government could be efficient.[12]

3.1. Voting with Your Feet

Tiebout was strategic in situating the ten-page paper, which he titled "A Pure Theory of Local Expenditure." Moreover, his presentation was formal:

> This discussion will show that the Musgrave-Samuelson analysis, which is valid for federal expenditures, need not apply to local expenditures. The plan of the discussion is first to restate the assumptions made by Musgrave and Samuelson and the central problems with which they deal. After looking at a key difference between the federal versus local cases, I shall present a simple model. This model yields a solution for the level of expenditures for local public goods which reflects the preferences of the population more adequately than they can be reflected at the national level. (Tiebout 1956, 416)

In a thought experiment harking back both to the discussion with Burstein and to his own background, Tiebout asked the reader to "consider for a moment the case of a city resident about to move to the suburbs. What variables will influence his choice of municipality?" (418). An important factor was those governmental services for which local municipalities expend money—local public goods: "If he has children, a high level of expenditures on schools may be important. Another person may prefer a community with a municipal golf course" (418). Formalizing the intuition, Tiebout assumed full knowledge, mobility, and no external economies. Although Tiebout considered "pure" public goods in

---

11. Given the framing of Tiebout 1956 as a qualification, the publication of Samuelson 1954 in the intervening period may also have spurred him. As a direct response, though, the natural outlet would seem to have been the *Review of Economics and Statistics*.

12. Though they maintained a long correspondence and Tiebout liked to poke fun at Chicago-trained economists ("members of 'the flock'"), Leven's (2003, 237) account is surely sensationalized. For example, he writes that "the JPE article was the only thing that Charlie ever wrote on local public finance, in fact any kind of public finance."

the sense of Samuelson's assumption, a fixed factor, like limited land and zoning laws, induced convexity in the costs of supplying the good. Two additional key assumptions of the model were an optimal community size and that communities above or below this level sought to attract or jettison residents to lower costs. As examples of the empirical plausibility of the latter, Tiebout cited two prototypical postwar suburban planned developments he was familiar with—Park Forest in South Chicago and Levittown, part of Nassau County. Both communities were postwar entrepreneurial responses to demand for affordable middle-class housing that offered prospective residents—frequently GIs—public amenities like libraries, along with open space, quiet, and safety.

The central mechanism in the paper arose from residents moving to communities that fit their preferences best, which "replaces the usual market test of willingness to buy a good and reveals the consumer-voter's demand for public goods" (420). Tiebout also supposed that the city managers would bid for services in a national market, with the limiting result being that the supply of public goods met the Samuelson 1954 condition for optimal supply of those goods. Consequently, "spatial mobility provides the local public-goods counterpart to the private market's shopping trip" (Tiebout 1956, 422). Rather than a mathematical proof, as Wallace Oates (2006) notes, the crux of the argument relied on establishing assumptions under which the local public sector would approximate a competitive market, with communities behaving like firms and voters like consumers. With respect to mobility costs, Tiebout (1956, 422) cited a Koopmans paper presented at the winter 1954 Econometric Society meetings, summarizing that "in a space economy with transport costs there is *no* general equilibrium solution as set by market forces." Mobility, like shopping, is just the consumer-voter "pay[ing] a cost to register his demand," so the model ostensibly inherited the welfare and existence properties of spatial equilibria (422). Tiebout pointed to the evaluation of municipal integration efforts on grounds of economic welfare as a policy implication.

To situate his contribution, Tiebout returned to Samuelson 1954 in his conclusion. Samuelson (1954, 389) had suggested that the remaining problem of public good provision was how to find the optimal levels. Tiebout (1956, 424) declared:

> It is the contention of this article that, for a substantial portion of the collective or public goods, this problem *does have* a conceptual solution. . . . While the solution may not be perfect because of institutional

rigidities, this does not invalidate its importance. The solution, like a general equilibrium solution for a private spatial economy, is the best that can be obtained given preferences and resource endowments.

Tiebout then drew a distinction between the model and its "reality" in his closing comments. Tiebout suggested, ambiguously, that "those who are tempted to compare this model with the competitive private model may be disappointed" (424). By "competitive private model," it is likely he had in mind the kind of general equilibrium economies whose existence Kenneth Arrow, Gérard Debreu, and Lionel McKenzie had only recently established. On the other hand, Tiebout continued:

> Those who compare the reality described by this model with the reality of the competitive model—given the degree of monopoly, friction, and so forth—*may* find that local government represents a sector where the allocation of public goods need not take a back seat to the private sector. (424)

Rather than as an instance of "market failure," local public goods might be viewed as a "government success"—the punch line. The subtext is clear that he placed himself in this second group. Tiebout mailed a reprint to Samuelson, with the following note: "Since your works are frequently mentioned in this article, I thought you might be interested."[13]

3.2. The First Samuelson Exchange

Although he did not reply directly to Tiebout's letter, Samuelson worked on a follow-up to his original paper, "Aspects of Public Expenditure Theories." While the main text of the paper summarized the conclusions that Samuelson drew from the debate that had ensued from "The Pure Theory of Public Expenditure," it also included an appendix titled "Strotz and Tiebout Discussions." A smaller first section dealt with Robert Strotz's "Two Propositions Related to Public Goods," published in the same issue, but the majority of Samuelson's appendix fell under the subheading "Local Finance and the Mathematics of Marriage" and addressed Tiebout 1956 specifically.

---

13. Tiebout to Samuelson, November 9, 1956, Gen. Corr.: T Box 72, Samuelson Papers, David M. Rubenstein Manuscript and Rare Book Library. Samuelson replied with a thanks on November 19.

Samuelson (1958, 337) summarized Tiebout's contention as "the public expenditure theory simplifies itself at the local level—as people spontaneously join in forming homogenous communities which will legislate what each (and all) want in the way of collective goods." He added that this "attempted solution fits in under one or another of the 'symmetry' principles" (337)—a reference to a parenthetical comment made in the original paper about "utopian voting and signaling schemes" that could be "imagined" (389). Such mechanisms, which Samuelson had extended to include questionnaires or other devices "like a 'parametric decentralized bureaucrat' who *reveals* his preferences" (389), he had stressed, did not contradict the central theorem. In that light, despite a concession that Tiebout (1956) "goes some way toward solving the problem," Samuelson (1958, 337) regarded it as impractical at best. As evidence, he pointed to heterogeneous preferences for school expenditure within "a supposedly homogenous suburb" and argued that people like heterogeneity: "The old don't want to live in homogenous ghettos with their own kind" (337). Samuelson also questioned the ethical implications of allowing groups "to 'run out' on their social responsibilities and go off by themselves" (337). Finally, he provided an illustration of the theoretical problems as he saw it through the example of marriage.

With the remark that "Bob Strotz gave me a copy of your forthcoming paper," Tiebout wrote to Samuelson in May 1958.[14] Strotz, then the managing editor of *Econometrica* and a visiting professor at MIT the following year, was also a senior colleague of Tiebout's at Northwestern. Ignoring Samuelson's main critique given in the appendix, Tiebout commented:

> I'm inclined to agree with your notion that mobility provides no formal solution. In the *Federal Expenditure Policy* . . . I used such terms as "less of a problem," "some choice," and "to some extent through mobility."[15]

Tiebout was referring to a paper he had submitted as a panelist before the Subcommittee on Fiscal Policy of the Joint Economic Committee of Congress. The subcommittee, which included Paul H. Douglas, had solicited expert opinions from a number of leading economists, Musgrave and Buchanan among them, on a report titled "Federal Expenditure Policy for Economic Growth and Stability." While the majority of Tiebout's

---

14. Tiebout to Samuelson, May 27, 1958, Gen. Corr.: T Box 72, Samuelson Papers.
15. Tiebout to Samuelson, May 27, 1958.

statement to the committee had dealt with regional income and growth, the final section argued that the problem for a planner of determining the optimal levels of public expenditure is eased at the state and local level by choice over communities. Tiebout was nonetheless quick to grant qualifications about the mechanism's practicality, such as whether consumer-voters were informed and how much choice was actually available. In addition, mobility only ameliorated the problem for those goods not supplied at the federal level, a decision Tiebout left up to the political process. In his response to Samuelson, Tiebout hoped that pointing to those qualifiers would help place his paper in the proper context. As his concluding statements in Tiebout 1956 had suggested, he did not view mobility as a panacea for public expenditure problems: "Even Charlie knew that he had no real solution to what public services would be provided in equilibrium" (Leven 2003, 235). In a sarcastic remark characteristic of his humor, Tiebout added in his letter to Samuelson:

> By the time of publication I shall not be, "also of Northwestern University." I shall be at UCLA. .The reason is obvious. The level and pattern of public goods provided in Santa Monica is preferable to those in Evanston.[16]

4. Los Angeles

Tiebout arrived at UCLA as an assistant professor in the fall of 1958, along with another new hire for the department the same year, W. Lee Hansen. The UCLA economics department at the time was becoming increasingly centered intellectually around Armen Alchian, bolstered by the eventual arrival of Harold Demsetz in 1960.[17] In William Allen's (2010) account, it was the advent of the department's golden age. Tiebout, meanwhile, enjoyed a laugh that, thanks to his 1956 paper, he had joined the "Chicago farm team" (Leven 2003, 237).

4.1. The Second Samuelson Exchange

After Samuelson's critique appeared in the November 1958 issue of the *Review of Economics and Statistics*, Tiebout reinitiated their exchange

16. Tiebout to Samuelson, May 27, 1958. Samuelson replied on June 3 that "I am reassured to learn there is no basic disagreement between us."

17. Leven claimed Tiebout was important in recruiting Demsetz, whom Tiebout knew from Northwestern, as Demsetz was initially resisted by some faculty members because of his Jewish heritage (Leven 2003).

from earlier that year. In particular, Tiebout now took exception with the example used to implicate the theoretical shortcomings of his mechanism. Samuelson (1958, 337) had posed the hypothetical question that given "a group of men and women who have each a preference rating for members of the opposite sex, who will end up marrying whom?" Samuelson worked with the case of two men and two women. Their possible preference configurations yielded four separate marriage outcomes that he argued only one of which "fits Tiebout's attempt best" (Samuelson 1958, 338). This indisputably Pareto-optimal case was the first woman preferring one of the men and the second woman preferring the other man and the men reciprocating. For all other cases, Samuelson argued that a Pareto improvement might be possible "given a social welfare function" and that the configuration arrived at would not be unique (338).

Tiebout's December 1958 letter to Samuelson bluntly confessed, "I don't see what the mathematics of marriage has to do with local public goods."[18] He offered three points, each implying that the two-sided matching problem Samuelson had posed was inapt. Using his humor to be indirect and remain deferential, the objections Tiebout offered were nevertheless substantive:

1) In terms of a conceptual model—not real world except as a matter of degree—boys A and B have an infinite number of girls to choose from. To be sure, this makes for a rather trivial assignment problem.

2) Disregard this. Do girls (communities) really have any preferences? Like private firms, all they want are customers (husbands).

3) I suppose there might still be a problem if A, with a slight preference for girl 1, got there before B who is wild with passion about 1. Yet, I wonder if this applies to public goods. Aren't they polygamous?

These are some things which bother me.[19]

In his reply to Tiebout, Samuelson conceded the imprecision of the analogy. Still, he maintained its basic relevance, stating, "I don't believe communities as having a sole or a separate existence from the individuals making them up. I think the problem of where people will live is a problem of what associations different individuals voluntarily make."[20]

Despite this exchange, Samuelson's assessment of Tiebout's contribution did not improve with time. He continued to insist that Tiebout had

18. Tiebout to Samuelson, December 17, 1958, Gen. Corr.: T Box 72, Samuelson Papers.
19. Tiebout to Samuelson, December 17, 1958.
20. Samuelson to Tiebout, December 23, 1958, Gen. Corr.: T Box 72, Samuelson Papers.

aimed and failed in disproving the 1954 result. In 1964, he drafted a paper, never published, titled "Public Good Theory: Optimal, Feasible Pricing of Rail, Bridge, and Road." Samuelson described a subset of reactions to his 1954 "impossibility theorem" as "pain and disappointment" because the analysis "proved that there existed no Invisible Hand of decentralized pricing that could provide an efficacious algorithm to lead to the optimum."[21] Among those resistant to this finding he named (in order) Stephen Enke, Buchanan, Tiebout, Ronald Coase, and Milton Friedman, adding the comment that "not one of the writers named, nor anyone else to my knowledge, has been able to refute the theorem."[22] This aside, as Hammond (this volume) describes, Samuelson's attitude regarding the possibility of "solving" the problem developed into nihilism. As a result, beyond the disappointment of failing to convince an eminent peer, Samuelson's reaction was also perhaps a surprising one from Tiebout's vantage: Tiebout had conceivably expected to count Samuelson with himself in the second group of "those who compare the realities" instead of the models. In fact, Samuelson was not a party to the "inside joke."

4.2. The NBER Conference

In 1959, James Buchanan hosted an NBER conference, "Public Finances: Needs, Sources and Utilization," at the University of Virginia in Charlottesville. Musgrave, a co-organizer of the event, invited Tiebout to participate.[23] In a session on state and local governments, Tiebout and Musgrave each presented papers, with Buchanan serving as a discussant. If Buchanan was unfamiliar with Tiebout's 1956 article, he may have recalled Tiebout's contribution to the Joint Economic Committee's report in 1957, to which he also contributed. The paper that Tiebout prepared for the conference, "An Economic Theory of Decentralization," developed lines in the Joint Economic Committee paper in greater detail. Tiebout posited the problem facing a social planner as consisting of two decisions: a choice of the level of

21. "Public Good Theory: Optimal, Feasible Pricing of Rail, Bridge, and Road," February 7, 1964, Box 143, Samuelson Papers.

22. "Public Good Theory." Samuelson also later intimated in a 1988 letter to Musgrave that "in 1954 I was nihilistic on the free-rider problem—too nihilistic, in the sense that Grove and Ledyard and Vickrey (and Tullock, and someone named Clarke in a Chicago thesis that Stigler almost blackballed) have proposed various (almost) cheat-proof algorithms devised to motivate people to reveal their true taste for the public goods" (Samuelson to Musgrave, August 23, 1988, box 54, Samuelson Papers).

23. Buchanan, interview by author, November 5, 2012.

public expenditure to be provided and a method of allocating it. As the baseline case, Tiebout noted that absent public goods, private good production would realize a "Lösch spatial patterning" of nonintersecting areas of provision, referencing the concept from *The Economics of Location*. Except for extreme cases, the planners' problem that Tiebout (1961, 80) posed contained a spatial dimension in which decentralized distribution through "branch" governments was efficient because the "benefits from public services may not accrue equally to all residents of a region."

Tiebout worked with police protection as an illustration, starting from the assumptions of uniform tastes and incomes. Although a pure public good within a precinct, police protection of an entire city required determining the optimal number of precincts to provide uniform protection (82). With costs a function of precinct size and some curvature assumed on the costs and output, an optimal precinct size could be obtained for any given level of output. In principle, taxpayers would be willing "to join with their neighbors" to realize this minimum cost (86). The example highlighted the importance of the spatial dimension, in which fiscal federalism was efficient, for a simplified case: determining the location of many public goods was as important as determining their level. Tiebout then proceeded to discuss some generalizations, such as when the benefits are diminishing in distance from the "site of production," as with fire protection, hospitals, or parks. To determine the boundaries in such cases, he initially supposed a procedure in which a "city planner interviews various residents" (88). By assumption, residents would reveal their true willingness to pay in the thought experiment. Describing the resulting "fiscal patterning" of this model, Tiebout concluded: "When all agencies and branch governments are operating, the spatial patterning will be similar to that for the private sector. . . . The public sector, in other words, will develop along a Lösch pattern" (91). In other words, the branch governments simply replaced firms in Lösch's analysis.

While the hypothetical assumed away the overriding problem of preference revelation and heterogeneity, it was in relaxing these last two restrictions that mobility was beneficial: with differences in tastes, "instead of taking the people as given and trying to fit the nonnational public goods pattern to them, offer a varied pattern of public goods and make it possible for the people to move to suit their tastes" (Tiebout 1961, 92). He continued: "To the extent that demands differ, a partial solution [to the problem of determining taxpayer preferences] at the nonnational level is offered through the mobility of people to communities where the pattern of services provided suits their tastes" (96). In this presentation, therefore, Tiebout framed mobility as useful from the planner's view and as a contribution to spatial general equilibrium theory with local public goods.

The connection to Lösch, as Tiebout viewed it, is all the more clear from an examination of a paper Tiebout gave to the Regional Science Association in 1957. There, Tiebout (1957a, 79) directly quoted Lösch's declaration that for general spatial equilibrium, "there is no scientific and unequivocal solution for the location of the individual firm, but only a practical one: the test of trial and error." Tiebout cited Koopmans and Beckman 1957 in this regard as a formal demonstration. He elaborated:

> This situation may be contrasted with that of finding the optimal short-run output for the firm. Here the conditions and the path, via the step-by-step movement along the quantity axis, may be stated.
>
> The situation with location theory, on the other hand, is analogous to that of a pure theory of public expenditures. As Samuelson shows, the conditions of a public expenditures optimum may be stated, but there is no market mechanism by which this optimum may be reached. (Tiebout 1957a, 79)

By extension, Tiebout's (1956) sorting mechanism becomes the analogue of Lösch's "trial and error."

In his comments as discussant on Tiebout's paper, Buchanan recognized the insight behind Tiebout's mechanism. Putting the externality arising from public goods in terms of an impossibility to "trade" and equalize marginal rates of substitution, Buchanan (1961, 127) noted that "individuals can, in effect, 'trade' public goods by shifting from one locality to the other." This would, when efficacious, be economically efficient.[24] This agreement aside, Buchanan also voiced a reservation with Tiebout's analysis that arose from income inequality: "There would still remain major fiscal advantages to locating in a community with a relatively larger number of high-income receivers" for the marginal taxpayer (Buchanan 1961, 124). Further, with goods of a "partial" sort where marginal benefits are not constant (such as with congestion), "prohibitions on

---

24. While Fischel (2006) points out Tiebout's observation in the conference paper that high rents often accompany good schools, a clearer statement of the "Tiebout hypothesis" is actually made in Buchanan's (1961, 125) comments: "In small communities, such as the residential suburbs of metropolitan regions, the fiscal advantages and disadvantages may, at least for a considerable time period, be almost fully capitalized."

entry become economically rational, provincially considered" (128). Buchanan observed that "zoning restrictions and other like devices can be considered a means through which 'early settlers' attempt to create a structure of property rights in 'taxpayers' surplus" (129). This point anticipates the theory of club goods that Buchanan (1965) later developed, whose complementarity and similarity with Tiebout sorting subsequently provoked questions of a genetic link between the two ideas.[25] For Buchanan, Tiebout had overlooked that the inequitable outcome of the concentration of high-income beneficiaries would then produce fiscal differentials that required redress through revenue transfers. In concluding, Buchanan (1961, 129) nonetheless confessed that "despite Samuelson's interesting recent note on the economics of marriage" in response to Tiebout 1956, "I must somewhat reluctantly conclude that my position in support of substantial interarea transfers has been modified under the influence of . . . the interesting local government models of Stigler and Tiebout."[26] While Tiebout, the Musgrave student through and through, and Buchanan, the "champion" of voluntary exchange (Johnson, this volume), appeared to be on similar intellectual wavelengths at the same time, their personal interaction began and ended in Charlottesville.

For Musgrave's part, his "epic"—as Tiebout later referred to it—*The Theory of Public Finance* finally appeared in print in 1959. In it, Musgrave offered a page-length discussion of the implications of Tiebout 1956 for the efficient supply of public goods. Musgrave (1959, 133) noted the simplifications, but concluded, consonant with Tiebout's framing in the conference paper, that "the possibility of moving to other communities establishes something equivalent to a market mechanism in local finance" such that "the task of finding a satisfactory solution is simplified." While, in contrast with Samuelson, Musgrave's qualifications hinted at questions about both the properties of sorting under relaxed assumptions and its empirical importance, local public finance remained the "special case." This designation bears the influences of its time and context. Although state and local public expenditure accounted for approximately half of all

25. Scotchmer 1994 is a thoughtful analysis of the theoretical relationship. See also Oates 2006. Buchanan 1965, which generalized Samuelson's (1954) taxonomy, does not cite Tiebout 1956. Buchanan did not link this later contribution in his own mind with Tiebout's (interview by author).

26. The Stigler paper Buchanan referenced was the former's statement submitted to the Joint Economic Committee in 1957.

public expenditure, as William Fischel (2006, 7) notes, it was planning, growth, macroeconomic stabilization, and the Cold War that tended to occupy concerns: "The 1940s and 1950s were pretty much the nadir of regard for local government." In successive decades, the shift of attention to local issues, such as public education, would complicate this earlier hierarchy.

4.3. The Lakewood Project

The same year that Tiebout arrived at UCLA, 1958, Vincent Ostrom also accepted an offer to return, having earned his PhD in political science eight years prior from UCLA. The offer included a part-time appointment in the Bureau of Governmental Research, a research center at the university directed by Winston Crouch and partially funded by the Haynes Foundation. Ostrom brought a prior history with both back to UCLA. Crouch had been the vice chairman of his thesis committee, while Ostrom's dissertation, "A Study of Water Policies and Administration in the Development of Los Angeles," had been published by Haynes. Ostrom had spent 1955–56 at the Center for Advanced Study at Stanford. His research plan there included a "community study of policy formation in which theoretical inquiry and research design have been my special concern."[27] He elaborated:

> A more serious part of efforts will be to extend this work in the direction of a systematic approach to the study of the political system of a local community with particular implications for the comparative study of political behavior.[28]

Specifically, Ostrom was already interested by the implications of the 1954 incorporation of the city of Lakewood, California—a postwar planned development like Levittown and Part Forest—which, in an unprecedented political bargain, would contract out the majority of its municipal services with Los Angeles County. The "Lakewood Plan," as it came to be called, quickly became the model for succeeding contract cities in Los Angeles and nationwide.

At the Bureau of Governmental Research, Ostrom acted as director of the "Lakewood Project" in the temporary absence of John Bollens, a senior professor and scholar of urban government. With money from the

27. Plan of Study at the Center for Advanced Study, Palo Alto, Calif., 1955–56.
28. Plan of Study.

Haynes Foundation, Ostrom organized the project around a seminar the bureau hosted for local administrators, like the mayor of Lakewood, and for graduate student presentations. Robert Warren, a graduate student in political science, supervised the research team, which included fellow graduate student Elinor Ostrom née Awan. Tiebout began attending the seminars, where he connected with Vincent Ostrom. Interested in developing the theoretical framework, Tiebout joined the project. The minutes of a 1959 seminar of the bureau outlined their intents:

> The Lakewood Project—the study of the contract system in Los Angeles—will be approached in light of the model furnished by economics. Rather than as a limited examination of relations between political units, this study will evaluate the performance of the county government as a seller of goods and services, and of particular local units as the buyers of these services, as unions organized to meet the demand of consumers (the citizens).[29]

Economic theory would be invaluable for escaping political scientists' "compulsion to want to superimpose a structure in such political situation[s]."[30] As the research plan explained, in contrast with the political scientist:

> The economist might apply a model of industrial organization and treat the interaction within the area as the operation of the market system, recognizing the existence of imperfect competition in an oligopolistic setting.[31]

The document adopted the framework of structure-conduct-performance analysis. The rough draft of the monograph's first chapter further emphasized the methodological point: just as firms made up the "basic entities" of an industry, the study would conceive "of government in a metropolitan area as involving a variety of political jurisdictions with independent decision makers or as a poli-centric political structure."[32] In this regard, Tiebout's earlier work on local public goods pointed a way forward.

For Tiebout, the project likely held a few promises. First, the question of metropolitan government integration was a direct application of the

---

29. "An Approach to Metropolitan Areas," Research Seminar Minutes, September 23, 1959, Bureau of Governmental Research.

30. "An Approach to Metropolitan Areas."

31. "An Approach to Metropolitan Areas."

32. "Chapter 1: The Problem of Metropolitan Government," n.d., p. 2.

policy implication he suggested in Tiebout 1956. Second, the project echoed an assumption invoked in his model that had remained undeveloped: that community managers purchase municipal services upstream in a competitive manner. Exemplified by the Lakewood Plan, the outline of the monograph described this as a "quasi-market" whose efficiency and performance in providing public goods were of special interest.[33] Finally, in relating the project to Tiebout 1956, their collaborative draft argued that the model, another "quasi-market," faced limitations when applied to "undifferentiable public goods such as public parks, [and] air pollution abatement which are not easily confined to the boundaries of a given political jurisdiction."[34] The theoretical work thus also aimed to extend the analysis to these cases.

While the importance that Ostrom placed on theorizing enabled (or even necessitated) the cross-disciplinary collaboration with Tiebout, it also situated their inquiry on the margins of prevailing boundaries in political science. Their overt adoption of economic theorizing did not sit well with everyone at the bureau, and tensions eventually came to a head. After a March 1960 meeting with Crouch and Bollens, Ostrom wrote a letter to Crouch, a copy of which he sent to Tiebout, conveying his belief that the situation created at the bureau was "intolerable so far as my interests are concerned."[35] The letter described the nature of their objections. Crouch and Bollens were "anxious about the theoretical context in which the Lakewood study was being developed."[36] The description of communities as "competitors," a municipal services "market," and of residents and city managers as "shoppers" would have been anathema. They had suggested that the draft of the first chapter, written with Tiebout, be adapted as a journal article instead and removed from the project altogether. In his letter, Ostrom emphasized: "My interests in this study are explicitly of a theoretical nature. I do not care to associate myself with another survey of some municipal problem."[37]

Ostrom was incensed. He suggested turning over the project report to Bollens entirely, effectively removing himself and Tiebout from the study,

---

33. "Chapter 1: The Problem of Metropolitan Government," 39–40.

34. "Chapter 1: The Problem of Metropolitan Government," 28.

35. Ostrom to Crouch, March 21, 1960, Vincent Ostrom Papers, Lilly Library Manuscript Collections, University of Indiana Bloomington.

36. Ostrom to Crouch, March 21, 1960.

37. Ostrom to Crouch, March 21, 1960. Ostrom was also upset about the "strange ethic of non-controversy and non-criticism" that he felt destroyed the research seminar at the bureau. He relayed his belief in the importance of a research seminar in response to an inquiry about his availability from Arizona shortly thereafter (Ostrom to Currin, December 7, 1960).

and acquiesced to pursuing the theoretical development through other outlets. The eventual product published by the bureau did not bear his, Warren's, or Tiebout's names. The episode and the disappointment it caused Ostrom led him to entertain outside offers to leave UCLA.[38] As for the theoretical work, Ostrom, Tiebout, and Warren (1961, 831) resolved to rework the chapter into a paper that they sent to the *American Political Science Review* analyzing polycentric political systems, defined as the "multiplicity of federal and state agencies, counties, cities, and special districts that govern within a metropolitan region." To Ostrom's frustration, the reviewers wanted the theoretical content scaled back considerably, causing an aggravating back and forth.[39] Still, Ostrom wanted to adapt the Lakewood project research into a book, titled "A New Approach to the Study of Metropolitan Government," that would expand on the contents of the article.[40] Ostrom pitched the book collaboration under his and Tiebout's names to potential publishers, though it never materialized.[41] Instead, Ostrom, Tiebout, and Warren's erstwhile collaboration, a prehistory of sorts to the Bloomington school (Aligica and Boettke 2009; Bish 2014), came to a premature end. Upon completion of his PhD under Ostrom, Warren joined the political science department at the University of Washington in 1960, while Ostrom, along with his new wife, Elinor, moved to the University of Indiana in 1964. Tiebout likewise decamped from UCLA to the University of Washington, where he was granted tenure and associate status on a joint appointment with the business school and the economics department.

5. Seattle

Although spatially separated, Tiebout's, Ostrom's, and Warren's subsequent work was influenced by their Lakewood project collaboration. In her Nobel Prize lecture, Elinor Ostrom (2010) pointed to the Vincent-Tiebout collaboration at UCLA as the origin of a general framework for analyzing and evaluating institutional arrangements. Warren's dissertation work, "A Municipal Services Market Model of Metropolitan Organization" (1964), furthered the theoretical analysis of the "quasi-market" of city council and administrators-cum-shoppers. Tiebout discussed the

---

38. Ostrom to Hinderaker, December 6, 1960; Ostrom to Shields, December 7, 1960.
39. Ostrom to Warren, November 21, 1960.
40. Ostrom to Hogen, November 21, 1960; Ostrom to Warren, November 21, 1960.
41. Grimes (Dorsey Press) to Ostrom, December 1, 1960; Ostrom to Ierardi (Wiley and Sons); Ostrom to Warren, November 21, 1960.

paper at the 1962 annual meeting of the American Political Science Association. Warren (1966) also published the Lakewood project findings and his analysis as a monograph. Tiebout's own limited later work in local economics took the "chaos" of metropolitan finance arising from "balkanization" as the relevant context. David Houston and Tiebout (1962) proposed a framework to understand the implications of economies of scale in the production of "social" goods by local governments, and Benjamin Chinitz and Tiebout (1965) evaluated the prospects of cost-benefit analysis for determining local public expenditure.

A reason Tiebout had been enticed by the University of Washington offer was the opportunity to found and codirect with Edward Ullman, a geographer, the Center for Urban and Regional Studies. Warren joined the interdisciplinary collection of researchers affiliated with the center, which also included professors in civil engineering, history, law, public affairs, sociology, and urban planning. From the economics department, Douglass North was an affiliate. The center distributed work, such as Ullman's presidential address to the Regional Science Association, "The Nature of Cities Reconsidered," and hosted conferences in urban planning and municipal organization. Outside speakers included authorities in regional economics such as Walter Isard, Leon Moses, and Andreas Predöhl. The intellectual environment at the center provided Tiebout a home where cross-disciplinary investigations to problems were cultivated and where his twin interests in regional development and local governance could both reside. Moreover, for the first time, it provided with Tiebout with students, pulled from and bounced between the various affiliated departments. Tiebout and Warren failed to recruit Ostrom, then still at UCLA, to the University of Washington in 1964, while Tiebout spurned an offer from Bloomington in 1966.[42] By then, Tiebout was occupied with activities connected with the center and with travel for consulting and policy work.

6. Conclusion

Warren wrote to Ostrom on January 16, 1968:

> Perhaps you will have heard by the time this reaches you, but I thought it important to write that Charlie Tiebout has died. He was working in

---

42. Tiebout to Martin, January 12, 1966. Also, in a letter dated October 30, 1963, to Ostrom, Tiebout remarked: "Needless to say, I am pleased about the Indiana possibilities, not that it enhances our attractiveness, but because it gives evidence of the recognition that some fatheads failed to give."

his office early this morning and had a heart attack. I have none of the details but apparently it was impossible to revive him.

It is a strange and disquieting task to write this letter. Yes, I saw Charlie yesterday. No, no one expected it. Yes, there are many things to say but "a friend is dead" covers them all. (Warren to Ostrom, January 16, 1968).

At the time of his passing, Charles Tiebout was not regarded as an eminent economist. Nor was he remembered as the originator of a seminal idea in public economics. Rather, Tiebout was best known for irreverent humor, for generosity with colleagues and students, and for his notable work in regional economic analysis. The latter included his collaboration with W. Lee Hansen (1963) on an input-output model of the California economy, a model of the Washington state economy, and analyses of the impact of defense and space expenditures on local economies (Peterson and Tiebout 1964; Houston and Tiebout 1964). On these matters, his expertise was frequently sought by industry and policymakers. Regardless, in the body of economic knowledge concerned with public expenditure and finance that stabilized during his lifetime, Tiebout's work had been marginalized despite his engagement with the key figures in its construction. The year after his tragic death, this equilibrium was ruptured, however: Wallace Oates's (1969) test of the "Tiebout hypothesis" awoke the "Sleeping Beauty."

References

Aligica, Paul Dragos, and Peter J. Boettke. 2009. *Challenging Institutional Analysis and Development: The Bloomington School*. New York: Routledge.

Allen, William R. 2010. "A Life among the Econ, Particularly at UCLA." *Econ Journal Watch* 7 (3): 205–34.

Banzhaf, H. Spencer, and Randall P. Walsh. 2008. "Do People Vote with Their Feet? An Empirical Test of Tiebout's Mechanism." *American Economic Review* 98 (3): 843–63.

Bayer, Patrick, and Robert McMillan. 2012. "Tiebout Sorting and Neighborhood Stratification." *Journal of Public Economics* 96:1129–43.

Bish, Robert. 2014. "Vincent Ostrom on Local Government: The Evolution of an Inquiry." Paper presented at the Public Choice Society meetings, March 6.

Buchanan, James. 1961. "Comments." In *Public Finances: Needs, Sources, and Utilization*, edited by James Buchanan, 122–29. Princeton, N.J.: Princeton University Press.

———. 1965. "An Economic Theory of Clubs." *Economica* 32 (125): 1–14.

Buchanan, James, and Gordon Tullock. 1962. *The Calculus of Consent: Logical Foundation of Constitutional Democracy*. Ann Arbor: University of Michigan Press.

Cellini, Stephanie Riegg, Fernando Ferreira, and Jesse Rothstein. 2010. "The Value of School Facility Investments: Evidence from a Dynamic Regression Discontinuity Design." *Quarterly Journal of Economics* 125 (1): 215–61.

Chinitz, Benjamin, and Charles M. Tiebout. 1965. "The Role of Cost-Benefit Analysis in the Public Sector of Metropolitan Areas." In *The Public Economy of Urban Communities*, edited by Julius Margolis. Washington, D.C.: Resources for the Future.

Coase, Ronald. 1960. "The Problem of Social Cost." *Journal of Law and Economics* 3:1–44.

Coate, Stephen. 2013. "Evaluating Durable Public Good Provision Using Housing Prices." National Bureau of Economic Research Working Paper 18767.

Colm, Gerhard. 1956. "Comments on Samuelson's Theory of Public Finance." *Review of Economics and Statistics* 38 (4): 408–12.

Desmarais-Tremblay, Maxime. 2013. "On the Definition of Public Goods: Assessing Richard A. Musgrave's Contribution." CES Working Paper 2014.04.

Düppe, Till, and E. Roy Weintraub. 2014. *Finding Equilibrium: Arrow, Debreu, McKenzie, and the Problem of Scientific Credit.* Princeton, N.J.: Princeton University Press.

Fischel, William A. 2006. "Footloose at Fifty: An Introduction to the Tiebout Anniversary Essays." In *The Tiebout Model at Fifty: Essays in Public Economics in Honor of Wallace Oates.* Cambridge, Mass.: Lincoln Institute of Land Policy.

Fitch, Lyle C. 1957. "Metropolitan Financial Problems." *Annals of the American Academy of Political and Social Science* 314 (1): 66–73.

Hansen, W. Lee, and Charles M. Tiebout. 1963. "An Intersectoral Flows Model of the California Economy." *Review of Economics and Statistics* 45:409–18.

Houston, David B., and Charles M. Tiebout. 1962. "Metropolitan Finance Reconsidered: Budget Functions and Multi-level Governments." *Review of Economics and Statistics* 44 (4): 412–17.

———. 1964. "Defense-Space Expenditures and Western Economic Growth: The Non-manufacturing Impact." Paper presented at the Regional Science Association meeting, Tempe, Ariz.

Koopmans, Tjalling, and Martin Beckmann. 1957. "Assignment Problems and the Location of Economic Activities." *Econometrica* 25 (1): 53–76.

Kuminoff, Nicolai. 2012. "Partial Identification of Preferences in a Dual-Market Sorting Equilibrium." Working paper.

Kuminoff, Nicolai, V. Kerry Smith, and Christopher Timmins. 2013. "The New Economics of Equilibrium Sorting and Policy Evaluation Using Housing Markets." *Journal of Economic Literature* 51 (4): 1007–62.

Leven, Charles. 2003. "Discovering 'Voting with Your Feet.'" *Annals of Regional Science* 37:235–38.

Lösch, August, 1954. *The Economics of Location.* Translated by W. H. Woglom and Wolfgang F. Stolper. New Haven, Conn.: Yale University Press.

Marciano, Alain. 2013. "Why Market Failures Are Not a Problem: James Buchanan on Market Imperfections, Voluntary Cooperation, and Externalities." *History of Political Economy* 45 (2): 223–54.

Margolis, Julius. 1955. "On Samuelson and the Pure Theory of Public Expenditure." *Review of Economics and Statistics* 37, no. 4: 347–49.

Meardon, Stephen J. 2000. "Eclecticism, Inconsistency, and Innovation in the History of Geographical Economics." In *Toward a History of Applied Economics*, edited by Roger E. Backhouse and Jeff Biddle. *History of Political Economy* 32 (supplement): 325–59.

Medema, Steven G. 2000. "'Related Disciplines': The Professionalization of Public Choice Analysis." In *Toward a History of Applied Economics*, edited by Roger E. Backhouse and Jeff Biddle. *History of Political Economy* 32 (supplement): 289–324.

———. 2011. "Public Choice and the Notion of Creative Communities." *History of Political Economy* 43 (1): 225–46.

Mires, Charlene. 2013. *Capital of the World: The Race to Host the United Nations.* New York: New York University Press.

Musgrave, Richard. 1939. "The Voluntary Exchange Theory of Political Economy." *Quarterly Journal of Economics* 53 (2): 213–37.

———. 1959. *The Theory of Public Finance.* New York: McGraw-Hill.

———. 1983. "Public Finance, Now and Then." In *Public Finance in a Democratic Society*, 1:89–101. New York: New York University Press.

Novick, David. 1954. "Mathematics: Logic, Quantity, and Method." *Review of Economics and Statistics* 36 (4): 357–86.

Oates, Wallace E. 1969. "The Effect of Property Taxes and Local Public Spending on Property Values: An Empirical Study of Tax Capitalization and the Tiebout Hypothesis." *Journal of Political Economy* 77 (6): 957–71.

———. 1998. *The Economics of Fiscal Federalism and Local Finance.* Northampton, Mass.: Edward Elgar.

———. 2006. "The Many Faces of the Tiebout Model." In *The Tiebout Model at Fifty: Essays in Public Economics in Honor of Wallace Oates.* Cambridge, Mass.: Lincoln Institute of Land Policy.

Ostrom, Elinor. 2010. "Beyond Markets and States: Polycentric Governance of Complex Economic Systems." *American Economic Review* 100 (3): 641–72.

Ostrom, Vincent, Charles Tiebout, and Robert Warren. 1961. "The Organization of Government in Metropolitan Areas: A Theoretical Inquiry." *American Political Science Review* 55, no. (4): 831–42.

Peterson, Richard, and Charles M. Tiebout. 1964. "Measuring the Impact of Regional Defense-Space Expenditures." *Review of Economics and Statistics* 46:421–29.

Pickhardt, Michael. 2006. "Fifty Years after Samuelson's 'The Pure Theory of Public Expenditure': What Are We Left With?" *Journal of the History of Economic Thought* 28 (4): 439–60.

Samuelson, Paul. 1954. "The Pure Theory of Public Expenditure." *Review of Economics and Statistics* 36, no. 4: 387–89.

———. 1955. "Diagrammatic Exposition of a Theory of Public Expenditure." *Review of Economics and Statistics* 37 (4): 350–56.

———. 1958. "Aspects of Public Expenditure Theories." *Review of Economics and Statistics* 40 (4): 332–38.

———. 2008. "Affectionate Reminiscences of Richard Musgrave." *FinanzArchiv / Public Finance Analysis* 64 (2): 166–68.

Scotchmer, Suzanne. 1994. "Public Goods and the Invisible Hand." In *Modern Public Finance*, edited by John M. Quigley and Eugene Smolensky, 93–119. Cambridge, Mass.: Harvard University Press.

Stigler, George J. 1961. "The Economics of Information." *Journal of Political Economy* 69 (3): 213–25.

Stolper, Wolfgang F., and Charles M. Tiebout. 1978. "The Balance of Payments of a Small Area as an Analytical Tool." *The Analysis of Regional Structure: Essays in Honour of August Lösch, Karlsruhe Papers in Regional Science* 2:92–109.

Sturn, Richard, 2010. "'Public Goods' before Samuelson: Interwar Finanzwissenschaft and Musgrave's Synthesis." *European Journal of the History of Economic Thought* 17 (2): 279–312.

Tiebout, Charles. 1950. "Employment in the Summer Vacation Business in Connecticut." *Connecticut Labor Department Monthly Bulletin*, July, 1, 11.

———. 1956. "A Pure Theory of Local Expenditures." *Journal of Political Economy* 64 (5): 416–24.

———. 1957a. "Location Theory, Empirical Evidence, and Economic Evolution." *Regional Science Association Papers and Proceedings* 3:74–86.

———. 1957b. "A Regional Framework for Government Expenditures." In *Federal Expenditure Policy for Economic Growth and Stability*, 818–24. Hearings before the Subcommittee on Fiscal Policy of the Joint Economic Committee. Washington, D.C.: US Government Printing Office.

———. 1961. "An Economic Theory of Fiscal Decentralization." In *Public Finances: Needs, Sources, and Utilization*, edited by James Buchanan, 79–96. Princeton, N.J.: Princeton University Press.

van Raan, Anthony F. J. 2004. "Sleeping Beauties in Science." *Scientometrics* 59 (3): 467–72.

Warren, Robert. 1964. "A Municipal Services Market Model of Metropolitan Organization." *Journal of the American Institute of Planners* 30 (3): 193–204.

———. 1966. *Government in Metropolitan Regions: A Reappraisal of Fractionated Political Organization*. Davis, Calif.: Institute of Government Affairs.

K. William Kapp's *Social* Theory of Social Costs

Sebastian Berger

This article deals with the theory of social costs by K. William Kapp, namely, the origin, gestation, and further development of *The Social Costs of Private Enterprise* (1950). This article analyzes archival material to show that Kapp viewed *Social Costs* as a continuation of his contribution to the socialist calculation debate (Kapp 1936), in which he defended the socialist position on the possibility of rational planning, including the need to prevent social costs *ex ante*. In this defense he proposed a "countervailing impossibility thesis," according to which social costs are proof that the market calculus disregards social needs, which cannot be rational from the perspective of society. Kapp understood his position in the debate as defending Max Weber's notion of the substantive rationality of planning against Ludwig von Mises's "impossibility thesis." During his career Kapp refined his defense of the substantive rationality of planning. The result of this refinement is a foundation for social economics, which Kapp viewed as synonymous with the intellectual project of American institutional economics. This foundation consists of a framework for social-democratic planning based on theories of social costs and benefits, social needs, social value, social minima, socio-ecological indicators, and social

Correspondence may be addressed to Sebastian Berger, Bristol Business School, University of the West of England, Coldharbour Lane, Bristol BS16 1QY, UK; e-mail: Sebastian.Berger@ uwe.ac.uk. I would like to thank Guy Oakes for his help in translating Kapp's quotations of Menger, and the referees, conference organizers, and editors for their valuable comments.

History of Political Economy 47 (annual suppl.)   DOI 10.1215/00182702-3130523

knowledge. While the socialist calculation debate is the origin of Kapp's defense of planning, he continuously developed it to take account of instances where public administration in Soviet Russia and India fell short of being substantively rational. Kapp never adopted the polarization of capitalism versus socialism. Instead he envisioned a social-democratic framework that effectively ties market, state, and civil society actors to a substantive rationality, that is, social minima. This approach is also dubbed "new rational humanism" because it aims to guarantee social minima that are rooted in existential human needs. The latter are analyzed in a new science of integrated social knowledge on the existential biological and cultural structure of the human being in society. Thus, Kapp's social economics provides a crucial link to ecological economics, environmental sociology, and philosophical anthropology. Hence, Kapp developed a genuinely *social* theory of social costs, which originated as an explicit defense of the substantive rationality of planning to prevent social costs and guarantee social minima, which became the foundation of a comprehensive theoretical framework of social economics.

The Birth of "Social Costs" out of the Spirit of the Socialist Calculation Debate

The trajectory of the social costs discourse in the twentieth century is crucially shaped by the reaction of the Chicago school to American institutionalism, including Kapp's institutional theory of social costs (Berger 2012, 2013; Franzini 2006). What has not been sufficiently registered is that this ideological conflict is an extension of the socialist calculation debate of the 1920s and 1930s, which was the cradle of Kapp's theory of social costs. In this debate, his dissertational treatise "Planwirtschaft und Aussenhandel" ("The Planned Economy and International Trade") (Kapp 1936) sided with the socialists. This work has never been translated into English, and thus the present analysis sheds new light on the genesis of Kapp's theory of social costs.

The thesis of the present article, namely, that Kapp's dissertation contains the nucleus of the theory of social costs, is confirmed by the introduction to *The Social Costs of Private Enterprise* (Kapp 1950b, xxvii–xxviii):

> The basic idea of the present study was first advanced in a highly tentative manner in the author's attempt to deal with the problem of economic calculation in connection with his analysis of the economic relations between a foreign trade monopoly and private exporters and importers.

Kapp argued in his dissertation that Mises's (1920) thesis about the impossibility of a rational economy under socialism needs to be countered with an impossibility thesis regarding the market economy. This thesis should be that the economic calculus based on market prices does not meet the requirement of the economic principle from the perspective of society. Kapp sought to defend the possibility and necessity of rational planning by pointing out the one-sidedness and the resulting blind-spots in the Mises argument about the superior rationality of markets. In an unpublished interview (Kapp n.d.a), Kapp explained that he understood the emergence of his argument on social costs to be the result of various factors, including the "great debate initiated by Ludwig v. Mises and Max Weber," the economic calculation controversy, his background of dealing with problems of economic planning, and his critical attitude toward a "free enterprise economy." Kapp's own explicit understanding of the nucleus of his argument as a case of "Weber vs. Mises" on the rationality of the price system is also confirmed in "Social Costs and Social Benefits: A Contribution to Normative Economics" (Kapp 1963b). Arguing that markets are only formally rational but not from the perspective of society, Kapp adopted Weber's analytical framework of the conflictual relationship between formal and substantive rationality. In Kapp's "countervailing thesis," social damages serve as proof of the impossibility of markets to rationally allocate goods and services from the perspective of society. Thus, in this light they reflect the market's purely *formal* rationality, which from the perspective of society appears limited, biased, and even arbitrary.

The Fatal Flaws in the Market's Calculus

The dissertation presents three distinct arguments why a calculus based on market prices only formally meets the requirements of the economic principle while failing to do so from a societal perspective. First, it attends to the issue that insolvent needs are disregarded in a "free exchange-economy" by quoting the second edition of Carl Menger's (1923, 49) *Grundsätze der Volkswirtschaftslehre* (*Principles of Economics*). Menger maintains that in business, even the most compelling and urgent needs of the destitute have no weight at all, even among financially comfortable people who are the most sympathetic. The business world disregards the genuine human needs of the population while eagerly pursuing the needs of those who are able and willing to pay. Second, Kapp notes that the market calculus is a source of error and irrationality in the formation of individual valuation, quoting again Menger (1923, 3) on illusionary, undeveloped, and pathological needs. Psychological manipulation of consumers through advertisement means, according to Kapp, that the economic principle is only fulfilled *formally* because less important needs are satisfied at the cost of more important ones.

Third, Kapp argues—partly with reference to A. C. Pigou (1929, 186, 197)—that the disregard for numerous damages under an economic calculus of market prices means that this calculus is uneconomic from the standpoint of society while being completely consistent with the economic principle that secures the profitability of the private business. The numerous social damages mentioned are the disruption of national health; increases in crime, accidents, and employment-related illnesses and accidents; inadequate protection of motherhood; excessive smoke concentrations; noise pollution; unhealthy construction work; retardation of scientific progress because of patents; advertisement; and premature resource depletion. In a footnote to this closing section on social costs, Kapp (1936, 42) anticipates his future research agenda, which was to materialize in *Social Costs*:

> It would be an interesting task for statistics to develop correct methods for the capturing of disadvantages and damages which accrue to society in a free market economy due to the activity of independent entrepreneurs that is solely based on the principle of highest profitability.

The above limitations of an economic calculus based on market prices necessitates, in Kapp's view, economic planning for social benefits. That the valuation of goods according to market prices frequently disregards societal needs and interests reflects a basic incapacity of markets to incorporate these needs in its calculus. In this perspective, economic viability from a societal perspective cannot be achieved by markets alone. As evidence for this conclusion, Kapp refers to social policies in capitalist economies, which compensate retroactively for social damages via laws, and charitable measures. Kapp further concludes that the planned economy can calculate potential damages beforehand and take them into consideration in economic decisions. This conclusion is the origin of Kapp's later fully developed argument about the necessity to prevent social costs *ex ante* and thus to guarantee the fulfillment of social needs. As examples of social needs, Kapp initially considers foremost the defense against dangers that threaten the existence of society, such as epidemics, illnesses, enemy attacks, but also agencies that improve the general welfare, public health, and the cultural level of society. The important task for the planned economy is, according to Kapp, to establish principles for the valuation of goods based on the needs and goals of society. Just like in the case of social costs above, it is a footnote that indicates the future course of study on social valuation:

> Because this question would exceed the frame of this work a systematic treatment of the system of economic calculation on the basis of "social value" should be reserved for a later treatment. (Kapp 1936, 46)

Kapp traces the problem of social valuation to Albert Schäffle's *Bau und Leben des Sozialen Körpers* (*The Structure and Life of the Social Body*) (1881), and Friedrich Wieser's (1924, 116) "Theorie der Gesellschaftlichen Wirtschaft" ("The Theory of the Social Economy"). In conclusion, Kapp's argument on social costs can be traced back to the socialist calculation debate, in which it was forged as a critique of the formal rationality of the market calculus and a justification for economic planning that guarantees the fulfillment of social needs.

The Graduate Institute of International Studies and the Institute for Social Research

Kapp's early work was supported by the Institut universitaire des haute études internationales (IUHED, Graduate Institute of International Studies) in Geneva. Archival research indicates that Kapp had attempted to enroll at the University of Frankfurt to work on his doctorate in 1933. The university's enrollment form, however, asked for evidence of Aryan descent, and perhaps the rise of Nazism is the principal reason that Kapp emigrated together with his future wife, Lili Lore Masur, who was Jewish, to pursue doctoral studies at IUHED. The latter also provided a haven for "concerned liberals" in the 1930s, some of whom became leading protagonists in building the neoliberal flagship organization, the Mont Pèlerin Society (Mirowski and Plehwe 2009). The preface to his dissertation expresses Kapp's gratitude to Mises for his continuous suggestions and stimulations, and both Mises and Eugene Stanley of the University of Chicago for the friendly interest they took in his work. The fact that Kapp's argument on social costs emerged at this particular institute buttresses my thesis about its origin. As an economist with socialist leanings,[1] Kapp used the phenomenon of social costs to defend the socialist position on planning against Mises's antisocialist thesis.

---

1. Kapp's secondary school teacher, the notable German novelist and poet Ernst Wiechert, writes in his post–World War II autobiography that Kapp played a leading role in the school's socialist youth organization.

Kapp also relied for support on the so-called neo-Marxist Frankfurt school, with which he was acquainted in its Geneva exile between 1933 and 1936. Reconstituted as the Institute for Social Research at Columbia University, it supported Kapp's work on social costs financially and was most likely decisive in providing Kapp with a teaching position at Columbia. The principal reason for this affiliation is that Kapp's framing of social costs as a problem of rationality is in line with what Michel Foucault ([1979] 2008, 106) dubbed the "post-Weberian" project of the Frankfurt school, to investigate the irrational rationality of markets. Previous archival research shows that Kapp was a close friend of Friedrich Pollock, the economist of the Frankfurt school (Berger and Forstater 2007), and his dissertation cites the latter's research on the increased capabilities of planning that result from improved statistical methods and technologies (Kapp 1936, 25). Pollock also influenced *Social Costs*:

> I also wish to acknowledge gratefully a grant-in-aid which I received from the Institute of Social Research at Columbia University from November 1943 to May 1944. In this connection I wish to record my gratitude to Dr. F. Pollock, Associate Director of the Institute of Social Research, who read the entire manuscript and made many valuable suggestions related to specific phases of the study. (Kapp 1950b, xxx)

It was also Pollock who invited Kapp to participate in a leading role in the formation of the newly founded Institute for Social Research in Frankfurt in the 1950s.[2] Furthermore, *Social Costs* references leading authors of the Frankfurt school, such as Erich Fromm and Max Horkheimer. The position of *Social Costs* within the intellectual project of the Frankfurt school's post-Weberianism turns it into an important link between sociology and economics. In conclusion, the institutional context reflects the origin and core of his argument on social costs. The doctoral candidate Kapp used the latter to launch a post-Weberian attack à la Frankfurt school on Mises's liberalism in order to defend the necessity for economic planning.

The Early International and Environmental Focus

The close affiliation of IUHED with the League of Nations and ILO also proved decisive for the early international and environmental orientation

---

2. Research in the Kapp Archive has shown no evidence that Kapp accepted the invitation. The present author's inquiries with the institute on this matter have not been answered.

of Kapp's research on social costs. On the one hand, it provided Kapp with an early learning experience on how to insert his economics within the context of international organizations of outstanding importance. See, for example, his membership on the expert committee that prepared the United Nations conference on the human environment in Stockholm, and his membership on the Standing Committee of the Social Science Council of UNESCO. Combined with his dissertation's discussion of pollution and resource depletion, his early international orientation led to Kapp's work on the League of Nation's discussions on natural resources. As a research assistant of John B. Whitton (Princeton University) between January and September 1937, Kapp prepared the "Memorandum on the Efforts Made by the League of Nations towards a Solution of the Problems of Raw Materials" (1937) and submitted it to the 1937 International Studies Conference held in Paris under the auspices of the International Institute for Intellectual Cooperation. Following an invitation from the International Industrial Relations Institute in The Hague, Kapp delivered a report on the work of the League of Nations Committee for the study of the problem of raw materials at the institute's conference in 1937. Later Kapp also published *The League of Nations and Raw Materials, 1919–1939* (1941). His relatively early involvement with issues of environmental disruption and natural resources as economic themes continued after his immigration to the United States, where he initially concentrated on social damages in agriculture, which lead him to also see the interrelatedness with water and air pollution (see Kapp n.d.a). This explains *Social Costs'* environmental focus, that is, its five chapters on issues such as air and water pollution, renewable and nonrenewable resources, and resource utilization. This special attentiveness to nature and the environment earned him the recognition as one of the earliest economists to comprehensively analyze environmental problems and even as augur of the environmental crisis.[3]

However, this early interest in the environment may be only partly related to the influence of Pigou's work and the research opportunities at IUHED. Rather, it is documented that Kapp's susceptibility to the theme of industrial society's relationship with nature antedates the 1930s. The profound and lasting ethical influence of his teacher, the famous German novelist Ernst Wiechert, is acknowledged in a series of articles and also documented in their extensive post–World War II correspondence (Berger,

---

3. See also Marc Tool's and Wilfred Beckerman's special recognition of Kapp as augur of the environmental crisis (Berger 2012).

forthcoming). Kapp highlights Wiechert's lessons on the great importance of nature as refuge, inspiration, and mental and physical restora-
tion, but also the ethics of "love for all suffering creatures."[4] The focus on
nature is, thus, deeply rooted in Kapp's biography since his formative
years in the 1920s.

"Social Costs and Social Returns:
A Critical Analysis of the Social Performance
of the Unplanned Market Economy"

Archival material shows that in the 1940s Kapp continued to develop
his defense of the socialist position in the socialist calculation debate by
elaborating the social cost argument as a critique of the market calculus
and a rationale for economic planning. Two unpublished drafts of the
introduction to *Social Costs* state that the intention is to provide a critique of the unplanned market economy, equilibrium economics, and
capitalism:

> As an analysis of the social inefficiency of the unplanned market econ-
> omy the study was bound to assume the character of a critique not only
> of capitalism but also of traditional equilibrium economics. (Kapp
> n.d.b)

The unpublished project outline "Social Costs and Social Returns: A Critical Analysis of the Social Performance of the Unplanned Market Economy" restates this aim with reference to the liberalism of Mises and
Friedrich Hayek:

> Social Costs and Social Returns: A Critical Analysis of the Social Per-
> formance of the Unplanned Market Economy—In harmony with the
> faith of 19th century liberalism traditional equilibrium economics
> states that the unregulated forces of supply and demand in an unplanned
> market economy tend to lead to an optimal allocation of scarce
> resources among competing ends and objectives. This doctrine contin-
> ues to be regarded by many as an apparently scientific foundation for
> all arguments against positive intervention with the economic process
> in the capitalist economy; its strength is attested by the current success

4. For a brief comparison between Kapp's economics and the early land ethic of Aldo Leopold, see Swaney 2006. For a more detailed account of Leopold's early ecological economics,
which exhibit striking similarities to Kapp's approach, see Goodwin 2008.

of the books by Hayek and Mises. . . . This study offers a critique of the basic premises of 19th century economic liberalism by examining the social performance of the unplanned market economy in the light of several facts which are usually omitted and neglected in economic theory. . . . In the first place it attempts to indicate the limitations of all economic calculations in terms of private costs and private returns. To allocate economic resources merely in accordance with private costs and private returns defeats any endeavour to find a rational solution to the economic problem. (Kapp n.d.c)

These materials clearly show that Kapp continued his defense of the socialist position from the socialist calculation debate by developing the argument on social costs as a critique of liberalism while adding the targets "capitalism," the "unplanned market economy," and "equilibrium economics." This is also confirmed in a letter to John M. Clark, which laments the strength of the liberal tradition reflected in the considerable response enjoyed by the recent works—presumably Hayek's *Road to Serfdom* (1944) and Mises's *Bureaucracy* (1944)—of these "intransigent economic liberals [Hayek, Mises, and Robbins]" (Kapp to Clark, December 12, 1945, quoted in Berger 2013).

The above unpublished outline also pitches the project against the "prophets of gloom [Hayek and Tocqueville]" who believe that economic planning would imply an inevitable road to serfdom. However, chapter 2 of the final version of *Social Costs* states that the important questions raised by the "current debate on the 'road to serfdom'" were only indirectly related to the problems under discussion in *Social Costs* and are thus not addressed in more detail in the book (Kapp 1950b, 24). This makes sense when we take into consideration that Kapp separated the initial project, publishing *Social Costs*, while leaving unpublished the sections on social benefits. Only the latter would have been directly related to Hayek's critique of planning in *The Road to Serfdom*. The unpublished second part was described in the initial project outline as

the re-orientation of economics; . . . [exploration of] the possibilities for the setting up of valid criteria for economic planning and the formulation for economic policy, and perhaps to prepare the way for the elaboration of a positive theory of social value are the chief ultimate purposes of this inquiry. (Kapp n.d.b)

Kapp aimed at developing a theory of social benefits

derived from the gratification of collective needs; from international economic policies designed to achieve a balanced economy . . . and from the improvement of transportation facilities . . . scientific research, multiple purpose projects (such as TVA), and the maintenance of a social minimum with respect to essential foodstuffs, medical care, housing, and education. (Kapp n.d.b)

The decision not to publish the part on planning for social benefits raises questions as to the reasons for excluding this important material. After all, economic planning for social benefits was the larger goal, for which the argument on social costs had merely been intended as a rationale with respect to Mises's thesis. Likewise, in the Kapp-Clark correspondence *Social Costs* was deemed only a first step for the development of a social economics based on theories of social benefits and social valuation (Berger 2013).

What happened to the important social benefits part of the initial project? Previous archival research (Berger 2013) evidences the critical nature of John M. Clark's comments on Kapp's draft manuscript. In a nutshell, Clark considered Kapp to have failed in providing any detailed formulation and evaluation of the potentials and limitations of a "collectivist alternative." Clark urged him to consider that every system, including alternative collectivist ones, would have imperfections and that the desired comprehensive social accountancy might not come about in such a system and that the dispute would be shifted from the "machinery of the markets" to the "political machinery." The unpublished project outline provides further reasons for delaying the work on social benefits. It states that providing solutions via social benefits for each instance of social costs would have unduly enlarged the manuscript, destroyed the continuity of the text, and raised the important issue of liberty, which needs a separate treatment (Kapp n.d.c).

The absence of a discussion of freedom in *Social Costs* was also a point of critique made by Frank Knight, who noted, however, that this issue had been dealt with in a separate article published in the same year, that is, "Economic Planning and Freedom" (Kapp 1950a; Knight 1951). Presumably, the decision to publish *Social Costs* without a discussion of social benefits of planning made a treatment of the issue of freedom in the planned economy unnecessary. This also explains Kapp's above comment that the issues raised by Hayek's *Road to Serfdom* are not directly related to *Social Costs*, which is solely a critique of the unplanned market economy and capitalism. In a later interview Kapp (n.d.a) mentioned as further reasons for the separation of the initially intertwined projects that completing the entire argument on social benefits would have taken too long at the time and that he had completed only three chapters. He also explained that he viewed his work on development planning in India in the late 1950s and early 1960s as a continuation of this work. This view is confirmed by the chapter "Social Costs and Social Benefits: Their Relevance for Public Policy and Economic Planning" published in his book on economic planning in India (Kapp 1963c).

"Private," "Free," or "Business" Enterprise

The Social Costs of Private Enterprise is Kapp's most significant publication in terms of scholarly impact. The work was reviewed widely, most notably by Frank Knight (1951) and John M. Clark (1950), and it attracted responses from economists such as James Buchanan (1962), Guido Calabresi (1961), and Wilfred Beckerman (1972) (for a discourse analysis, see Berger 2012). Google Scholar lists around 630 citations, while the second enlarged and revised edition, which was titled *The Social Costs of Business Enterprise* (Kapp 1963a), shows upward of 220 citations.

Social Costs exerted a significant influence on the community of scholars forming under the banner of ecological economics (Ropke 2004), especially those working on the environmentalism of the poor (see, e.g., Martinez-Alier 2002), and the integration of social-ecological economics (Spash 2011), but also environmental sociologists (Foster 2010). Even leading environmental economists like Allen Kneese relied on *Social Costs* in his critique of Pigou's and Coase's theories of externalities: "A perspective more like that of the present paper is found in Kapp" (Ayres and Kneese 1969, 282n1, 295). The group of scholars who awarded most recognition to Kapp's work on social costs is found in the American institutionalist movement, reflected most notably in the works of James Swaney (2006) and Marc Tool (1978, 1):

> Dr. K. William Kapp and his forty-year career as a front rank institutional economist . . . [established] the relevance of the holistic, institutional mode of thinking to the complex and urgent problems of environmental deterioration and economic development. Indeed, Kapp was among the first to explore the interdependent significance of these two problems.

This appreciation was also reflected in Kapp's contribution to the formation of the Association for Evolutionary Economics and his collaboration with Gunnar Myrdal on the (unsuccessful) formation of an international association of institutional economists (see Berger and Steppacher 2011 for details). Upon arrival in the United States in 1937, Kapp endeavored to connect his arguments on social costs and benefits with the conceptual frameworks of the American institutionalists. In fact, he even developed the book project *The Foundations of Institutional Economics* with the initial working title "The Foundations of Social Economics." This clearly demonstrates Kapp's recognition of the identity of the American institutional movement and his project of social economics (see Berger and Steppacher 2011). Kapp explicitly placed *Social Costs* in the tradition of social and institutional economics, notably Thorstein Veblen's theory of business enterprise, in the preface to the second enlarged and revised edition, which was titled *The Social Costs of Business Enterprise* (1963a, xxvii):

> The change of the title to *Social Costs of Business Enterprise* is intended to express more explicitly the affinity of our analysis to the intellectual tradition of . . . institutional economic theory. . . . [It was] Veblen who, as early as 1921, called for an investigation by economists in consultation with the technical expert, "of the various kinds and lines of waste that are necessarily involved in the present businesslike control of industry."

Kapp viewed Veblen's theory of social waste as consistent with his own views since the socialist calculation debate. Namely, social waste and damages are viewed as evidence of a systemic problem that needs to be remedied via systemic social controls. This is consistent with the finding that the theory of social waste is a "source theme" of American institutionalism (Rutherford 2011, 36; this volume), which expresses the view of the Progressive Era's experts that there are inherent market flaws and not just market failures (Leonard, this volume). But also the significant influence of John M. Clark's social economics is acknowledged by Kapp (1950b, xxvii):

> His [Kapp's] interest in the problem of social costs was further stimulated by J. M. Clark's contributions to "Social Economics" as well as by the results of the unique and still largely neglected research carried out under the auspices of the National Resources Planning Board. Profes-

sors J. M. Clark and Robert Lynd read an earlier draft of the introductory and concluding chapters and have offered critical comments, which are gratefully acknowledged.

Unfortunately, Kapp decided to publish this second enlarged and revised edition of *Social Costs* in India with Asia Publishing House, which explains the relatively low level of attention it received in the United States, especially when compared with the first edition, which was published by Harvard University Press. This decision must be seen in the light of the Fulbright appointments at the Gokhale Institute of Politics and Economics and the University of Rajasthan during which he conducted research on economic planning for social benefits in India (Kapp 1963c). It may be surmised that he viewed the revised *Social Costs* not only as complementary to the latter but also as important support for the case for economic planning in India.

Further archival evidence suggests that the terms *private enterprise* and *free enterprise* (used in Kapp n.d.d) were eventually discarded because they were perceived to be "too ambiguous" in an economy characterized by large-scale government involvement (Kapp n.d.a). One might wonder why Kapp did not use a more radical title, such as "The Social Costs of Capitalism," since his initial project outline aimed at a critique of capitalism. The early preference for the Weberian framework since his dissertation and his insistence on the need for detailed institutional analysis are significant here, as they suggest a preference for the approach of the younger German historical school (Weber) and the American institutionalists (Veblen, Clark) over the conceptual framework and terminology of Marxism. However, this distinction may not be that decisive, since even the so-called neo-Marxist Frankfurt school was associated with a post-Weberian intellectual project (see above). Additionally, references to Marx abound in *Social Costs*, and Kapp published three of his major books on economic planning in countries with socialist or communist governments, that is, Soviet Russia (1936), India (1963c), and China (1974). The latter is favorable to Maoist economic planning, especially the recycling and zero-waste schemes, and relies on Marx's theory of social use value as a theoretical framework. Most likely, the decision to avoid the more radical title "The Social Costs of Capitalism" in the United States of the 1940s was partly related to the "red scare era" characterized by severe repression of economists of socialist or communist orientation (Lee 2009).

"Shifting," "Externalizing," or "Socializing" Costs?

The search for the appropriate terminology in the 1940s also continued with regard to social damages, as Kapp tried to position his work within the US institutionalist movement. While Kapp and Clark agreed on the concept of cost shifting as a rationale for social economics and social controls, they disagreed on what to call the shifted portion of the total costs of production:

> [Your definition of] "social" values and costs differs from mine in applying to non-market quantities only, where mine [Clark's] included also the quantities the market "measures." (Clark to Kapp, December 4, 1945; quoted in Berger 2013)

In the literature, this important difference between Kapp's and Clark's definition of the concept of social costs has unfortunately been conflated by describing Clark's "shifted costs" as "social costs" (see, e.g., Prasch 2005). Distinguishing, as Kapp did, private costs from social costs (social losses, damages, inefficiencies) emphasizes that the logic of maximizing private returns is a built-in incentive for businesses to *socialize* as many costs as possible. According to Kapp, adding social to private costs results in total costs. This is an important terminology turn from the original notion of "shifted costs":

> The term [*social costs*] covers all direct and indirect losses suffered by third persons or the general public as a result of private economic activities. (Kapp 1950b, 13)

This difference in defining social costs is significant, since Clark's definition of social costs as nonmarket plus market costs is in the neoclassical tradition of Pigou. This neoclassical conceptualization of social costs is deemed incompatible with the project of social economics by Kapp and the principal reason for its rejection. Commentators noted early on that Kapp's definition is inconsistent with Pigou's (Pearce and Sturmey 1966, 152n1). While Kapp noted that Pigou had radicalized his political-economic conclusions ("bankruptcy of capitalism" and "extending public ownership") (Pigou, quoted in Kapp 1963a, 38), he viewed Pigou's conceptual framework as imbued with the limitations of the neoclassical theories of price and value, and closed system and equilibrium preconceptions. The latter preclude an adequate understanding of the circular cumulative causation of social costs, that is, complex causal relationships that determine the magnitudes and qualities of the damages. The term *external costs* is seen as a consequence of neoclassical preconceptions that suggest that the issue at hand is a relatively minor and temporary aberration from a functioning mechanism, remediable with ad hoc measures within the existing system. Kapp criticized the reform proposals for environmental control that emerge from the "polluter pays principle" that underlies all market-based (taxes, bargaining) and even tort law–based approaches to social costs. The main point of critique was that these solutions address the problem of social costs *ex post* without emphasis on prevention. While he acknowledged that taxation of polluters is better than nothing, he viewed this approach as ineffective, piecemeal, and too conservative (Kapp 1971, n.d.e). Conversely, Kapp's understanding of social costs was more akin to the American institutionalists' conception of social costs as large-scale and systemic problems caused by the institution of business enterprise, which require far-reaching changes at the system level. In reassessing twenty years of discussions on *Social Costs*, Kapp maintained the fundamental point of dispute in the preface to the 1971 edition:

> *The Social Costs of Private Enterprise* undertakes to diagnose the causes that tend to give rise to the disruption of our physical and social environment. . . . a system of decision-making operating in accordance with the principle of investment for profit cannot be expected to proceed in any way other than by trying to reduce its costs whenever possible and by ignoring those losses that can be shifted to third persons or to society at large. Predictably, this critical view, which runs counter to the presuppositions and biases of conventional economic analysis, has not *met* with general approval. Thus, various alternative explanations for *the* occurrence of social costs have been advanced. These have one thing in common: to exonerate the principle of investment for profits from any causal connection with environmental disruption. (xiii–xiv)

Stating the fundamental point of dispute as the principle of investment for profits mirrors Veblen's terminology and reiterates the view from the socialist calculation debate that social costs are evidence of a systemic flaw in the rationality of markets. This is also interpreted as a fundamental conflict between individual and social interests (Kapp 1963b), which has not only the power to shape history:

> The political history of the last 150 years can be fully understood only as a revolt of large masses of people (including business) against the

shifting of part of the social costs of production to third persons or to society. (Kapp 1950b, 16)

It also means that the relative power positions of companies and industries reflect their ability to socialize costs. The extent to which the victims can leverage countervailing power determines the extent of social costs (Kapp 1963b). Thus, Kapp's theory is a social conflict theory of social costs.

The Substantive Rationality of Planning: Social Minima, Social Benefits, and Social Knowledge

His theory of social costs led Kapp to far-reaching conclusions presented in the final chapter of *Social Costs*, "Toward a New Science of Political Economy." Principal among them is the demand to "return to philosophy," referring to the words of Max Horkheimer: "Economic science must overcome 'the horizon of contemporary society'" (Kapp 1950b, 246–47). This demand is specified in the chapter in "The Broadening of the Scope of Economic Investigations," "The Reformulation and Enlargement of Basic Concepts," and "Social Choices, Social Evaluation, Social Value." The task of this new science included the objectification and quantification of social costs. The principal way to achieve this goal was to investigate social costs as deficiencies in the satisfaction of scientifically derived and socially determined minima of adequate living conditions (Kapp 1963b, [1975] 2011). Social minima reflecting social needs can be scientifically derived:

> In the field of air and water pollution it is possible to work out minimum standards of public health in the form of maximum permissible levels of concentration of pollutants. Social costs and social objectives can be identified in terms of existing deficiencies by comparing the actual state of pollution with the maximum permissible concentration of pollutants. Similarly, it is possible to work out safe social minima or maximum rates of depletion of renewable resources (e.g. wildlife and fisheries) as well as water and soil by the definition of a *critical zone* beyond which any increase of depletion would give rise to an irreversible process of destruction of the resource. Minimum standards of requirements can be defined also in such fields as public health, medical care, education, housing, civilian defense, transportation and recreation. (Kapp 1963b, 195)

Thus, social minima and indicators are the main policy tools for the planning of social benefits. The initial unfinished manuscript of social benefits from the mid-1940s had already included a chapter on social minima such as the extent of unsatisfied social needs, the obsolescence of residential urban dwellings, inadequate medical care, and deficiencies in the field of public health (Kapp n.d.f). Kapp defined four main characteristics of the social benefits of planning for social minima that result from the existence of social needs and make them a necessary object of government action because private enterprise will not provide them: they are highly defused, cannot be withheld, accrue to all members of society, and are indivisible (Kapp 1963b). This approach to social benefits is explicitly rooted in Weber's concept of substantive rationality:

> Substantive rationality . . . measures the extent to which a given group of persons is or could be adequately provided with goods by means of an economically oriented course of social action. (Kapp 1963b, 190)[5]

Thus, substantive rationality meant for Kapp an approach to economic planning that guarantees social minima. In contrast to Weber, Kapp argued that substantive rationality can be objectified via a scientific inquiry into need satisfaction, such that Weber's caveat about the infinite possible value standards under a regime of substantive rationality is unwarranted. Kapp's effort to objectify and quantify social costs and benefits in a substantive and scientific manner was also directed against Mises's argument about the alleged lack of rationality in economic planning. Kapp (1963b) maintained that the price system's quantitative character is only seemingly objective and rational because in actual fact it is highly arbitrary (manipulation of consumers and disregard for the poor, social damages, and needs). In other words, Kapp continued the defense of the socialist position since his dissertation against Mises's impossibility thesis. Yet the quest to scientifically objectify and quantify social costs and benefits also aimed at providing an alternative to the purely monetary appraisal of social costs in neoclassical economics. Social minima, according to Kapp, objectify and quantify social costs and benefits by removing them from the realm of pure ideology into the realm of science and the pragmatic test.

Kapp acknowledged that the problem of social costs and benefits would always remain partly political in nature because of the necessity of social

---

5. For Kapp's substantive economics, see Berger 2008.

evaluation of essential and less essential human needs. Here, Kapp (1963b) referred to the need for a democratic theory of consumption based on majority votes and referendums.[6] Based on Weber and Otto von Neurath, Kapp adopted the position that substantive rationality can be based on an economic calculation in real terms that compares real physical units of available resources. Yet the potential inefficiencies of substantive rationality are also acknowledged in terms of delays, coercion, and vested interests in the political system. This realistic view of the issues faced by economic planning is characteristic of Kapp's work since the 1960s when he conducted empirical research on economic planning and public administration in India (Kapp 1963c).

Thus, in conclusion, the argument on social costs maintained the central target of the dissertation. Relying on Weber's critique of formal rationality and Veblen's critique of pecuniary principles, Kapp (1963b) continued to attack Mises's purely formal defense of the rationality of the price system. Adopting Neurath's proposal for planning in real terms, Kapp solidly tied himself to the very socialist position that had been the reason for Mises's initiation of the socialist calculation debate. Kapp epitomized in important respects the Progressive Era expert who has a "faith in the scientific state," sees himself as a "forward-looking modernist," and believes himself to be an "ethical economist," a "guide to the social good" with the "public interest at heart" (Leonard, this volume).

Kapp's ([1975] 2011) plea for a "new science of political economy" and "return to philosophy" materialized in the above-mentioned unfinished book project "Foundations of a Social Economics" but also *Towards a Science of Man in Society: A Positive Approach to the Integration of Social Knowledge* (1961). In fact, this concern was so important to Kapp that it later became the main mission statement of the Kapp Foundation for the Integration and Humanization of the Social Sciences. Joining the issues of economic planning and a positivist approach to a unified social science had previously been a project associated with Neurath, but Kapp did not acknowledge this source of inspiration in *Science of Man* (for a discussion of this link, see Spash 2012). Instead, the final chapter closes with references to "realtypical" and Gestalt analysis (Weber, Spiethoff) and substantive economics (Polanyi 1957). Thus, Kapp's approach to social knowledge is best understood as part of a means-ends instrumentalism (Kapp 1963b, [1975] 2011; Berger and Forstater 2007). His own

6. Kapp's social minima approach can also be viewed as a science-based social-democratic alternative to Hayek's nondisgressionary rules argument (Burczak 2011).

recognition of the kinship with instrumental analysis, that is, the theory of economic knowledge for controlled economic systems, is decisive here (Kapp 1976; Lowe 1965). In this, social knowledge about the dynamic structure of human needs in society is part of the process of scientifically deriving means, while social minima are part of the process of socially determining normative ends. Kapp's democratic approach to social control is strongly influenced by John Dewey and thus differs from the notion of politically unaccountable expert control enacted by many Progressive Era economists (Leonard, this volume). Throughout his works Kapp (2011, 88n9) explicitly targeted Mises's instrumentalism, that is, his "purely positivist [read: value-free], formal and subjectivist procedure [i.e., praxeology]," revealing once more the continuity of his main intellectual thrust since the socialist calculation debate but also *Social Costs*. The latter doubts that Mises would be prepared to apply his definition of economics as a science of human action (means-ends) to social choices and evaluations, that is, "decisions of government in matters of economic policy" (see Kapp 1950b, 252). Kapp's integrated and social conceptualization of knowledge is a contribution to the "economics of scientific knowledge" (Mirowski and Sent 2002) that provides an alternative to purely individualist conceptualizations of knowledge, such as personal knowledge (Polanyi 1958) and commodified knowledge (Hayek 1945).

The Life of Kapp's Ideas in the Material World: Environment and Development, Science and Technology, Law and Economics

The major impact of Kapp's ideas emerged during the 1970s and 1980s, which is mainly attributable to their ability to attract organizational and financial support.[7] Most notable are Kapp's influential membership on the expert panel for environment and development, which helped prepare the 1972 UN conference on the human environment, and his chairmanship of the German ministerial commission on green technologies. His vision is credited as inspiring the conception of at least four major organizations still operating today, that is, the Socialist Environment and Resource Association (SERA), the Centre for Environment and Development in Paris, the European Association for Evolutionary and Political Economy (EAEPE), and the German Association for Ecological Economics (VÖÖ).

7. For the social epistemology adopted here, see Mirowski and Nik-Khah 2008 and Mirowski 2013.

Significant also was the fact that Kapp's work on social costs attracted financial support from the Institute for Social Research and the Fulbright Foundation. Additionally, since the early 1980s the K. William and Lore L. Kapp Foundation for the Humanization and Integration of the Social Sciences continued to support research and to be involved in the awarding of the Kapp Prizes of EAEPE and VÖÖ. Additionally, collected volumes on Kapp's economics flourish in the heterodox economics community (Gerber and Steppacher 2012; Ramazzotti, Frigato, and Elsner 2012).

Richard Gaskins (2010) has recently pointed out that a major source of support for Kapp's "whole-society" perspective of social costs and precautionary *ex ante* approach of social controls of technologies exists within public health studies of injury and disease. This seems correct, as Kapp explicitly referred to the kinds of technological controls effective in the industries of food, pharmaceutics, and nuclear power as ways to reduce social costs and guarantee social minima:

> In this context the burden of proof that a new technology, a new product, a new process, and a particular input (and output) pattern are safe would have to rest in principle upon the producer and not upon the damaged person or society. Institutionalized agencies would have the function and responsibility to anticipate, appraise, and judge beforehand the hazards and benefits of alternative technologies, techniques, and locations. On the basis of such an assessment it would be possible to direct investments with respect to both permissible choice of factor inputs and the location of specific industries, in accordance with criteria that take account of the full range of the costs and consequences of new techniques for the individual and society as well as the world community. (Kapp 1971, xxi)

Kapp concluded that this approach would imply radically new forms of decision making and planning by institutions responsible to society and more responsive to human needs. The individual allocation and investment decision, the private choice of technology, and the selection of the site of production would be replaced. A detailed framework for technological controls was elaborated during Kapp's chairmanship of the German ministerial commission Governmental Furtherance of Environmentally Friendly Technologies (Kapp [1975] 2011): (1) goal formulation, which involved (a) dealing with goal conflicts, (b) societal assessment of alternative technologies as a prerequisite of selecting an objective, and (c) choice of goal and participation in research policy decisions; (2) problems in coordinating research, which involved (a) coordination of research on the national level and (b) international cooperation; (3) financing the research and promoting the diffusion of environmentally sound technologies, entailing (a) possibilities of financing research, (b) state profit sharing, (c) state support of research projects with great risk and relatively small prospects of commercial utilization, (d) state research institutes, (e) measures of promoting the dissemination of environmentally sound technologies, methods, and products, (e1) legal and institutional bases, (e2) dissemination of information about environmentally sound technologies, (e3) new patent and license regulation, and (e4) financial aids to promote the dissemination of environmentally sound technologies; and (4) from the causation principle to the objective principle: technology as a dependent variable.

Another application of Kapp's theory pointed out by Richard Gaskins (2007) occurred within the field of law and economics (for references to Kapp in legal scholarship, see Kimball 1959, 934; Koplin 1955, 840). Kapp (1950b, 63) had clearly exposed the problems with legal solutions to social costs in the case of work injuries, such as the inability of victims to receive their rewards because of insolvent employers or private insurance companies. Citing the 1939 report of the National Resource Committee, Kapp also noted that court action failed to resolve problems such as water and air pollution because of the problems of large numbers of affected parties, prohibitively expensive legal fees, and the burdensome if not impossible proof of specific damages, their amounts, and the possibility of abatement (80–81). The "liability law solution," Mises's preferred solution (Dawson 2013; Cordato 2004), is criticized just like the "bilateral market approach," which is the preferred solution of Coase and Stigler (Coase 1960; Medema 2011) as an instance of the ideology of individual decision making underlying the "polluter pays principle" (see above for Kapp's rejection of this principle) (Kapp n.d.e).

Partly because of the influence of J. M. Clark, legal realists adopted a perspective on social costs akin to that of Kapp (Gaskins 2007). They recognized the complexity of social cost cases and supported the idea of a "community responsibility" for social costs in the form of a social insurance scheme. The latter was viewed a public law alternative to tort law, which would introduce the responsibility to prevent social costs *ex ante*, resorting to, for example, "criminal penalties, industrial health and safety laws, and a comprehensive prevention strategy aimed at reducing injuries and environmentally caused diseases" (Gaskins 2007, 4). This kind of community responsibility proposed by legal realists for the account of social costs of a community is today recognized by New Zealand's Accident Compensation Corporation (ACC), based on three remediation strategies, that is, "prevention, rehabilitation and compensation, stressing that order of priority" (Gaskins 2010, 39). Trying to prove the defendants' fault or negligence, or even establishing causality according to tort law in complex economy-environment interactions with time lags and cumulative circular interactions, is viewed as erratic, inconsistent, time consuming, and administratively expensive. The chances of becoming a victim is viewed as a statistical inevitability because of the injury-generating practices of complex industrial societies and a risk of social progress, and is not due to individual fault. The simplistic, individualistic, and linear view of causation and compensation of the nineteenth-century fault principle is deemed inappropriate to deal with the complexity underlying social costs because the attempt to disentangle the multiplicity of causations behind individual social cost cases is either very inefficient or even ineffective because of being impossible or too time consuming. Additionally, the unnecessarily expensive administration of legal solutions to cases of social cost makes it cost inefficient. An inconsistency of legal rulings across similar cases is likewise problematic. That is, tort law is perceived as unsuitable for dealing with social costs because it leaves a large part of the social costs unpaid for, that is, a social costs deficit. ACC aims to make it impossible that social costs stay with the victim and are not compensated for unless the victim's claim can pass the court's fault test. Insidious avoidance strategies of defendants with deep pockets are likewise unnecessary. While the ACC's prevention strategy remains underdeveloped because of conflicts over the distribution of costs of preventing social costs, it maintains Kapp's idea that the most efficient and just solution to social costs is prevention via effective health and safety regulation (Gaskins 2010, 39–45).

Conclusion

The article has demonstrated that K. William Kapp provided a genuinely *social* theory of social costs. This genuinely social character is the result of a consistent effort to defend the socialist position from the socialist calculation debate, that is, the possibility of substantively rational planning to prevent social costs. The core argument is that social costs reflect the violation of social needs by the market's calculus. Substantive rationality in planning is needed to guarantee the fulfillment of social needs.

Social needs are scientifically objectified and quantified via the elaboration of social minima, that is, minimum adequate living conditions. The latter are rooted in the structure of existential human needs, which are investigated in a science of integrated social knowledge. Social costs, according to Kapp's view, are a genuinely social, that is, complex macro-phenomenon, resulting from circular cumulative causation between the open economic system and its social and natural environment. Consequently, Kapp's theory of social costs is not based on the "polluter pays principle" underlying individualist and *ex post* solutions to social costs, such as neoclassical taxation or bargaining, or Mises's tort law solution. Instead, Kapp proposed and developed a framework for systemic social legislation that prevents social costs *ex ante* via safety limits, social minima, and technological controls. Today, the continued presence of his approach in economic discourse and its application to policymaking are a testament to the power of Kapp's ideas.

References

Ayres, Robert, and Allen Kneese. 1969. "Production, Consumption, and Externalities." *American Economic Review* 59 (3): 282–97.

Beckerman, W. 1972. "Environmental Policy and the Challenge to Economic Theory." In *Political Economy of the Environment: Problems of Method*. Paris: Ecole pratique des hautes etudes and Mouton.

Berger, Sebastian. 2008. "Karl Polanyi's and Karl William Kapp's Substantive Economics: Important Insights from the Kapp-Polanyi Correspondence." *Review of Social Economy* 66 (3): 381–96.

———. 2012. "The Discourse on Social Costs: Kapp's Impossibility Thesis vs. Neoliberalism." In *Social Costs Today: Institutional Analyses of the Present Crisis*, edited by Wolfram Elsner, Pietro Frigato, and Paolo Ramazzotti. London: Routledge.

———. 2013. "The Making of the Institutional Theory of Social Costs: Discovering the K. W. Kapp and J. M. Clark Correspondence." *American Journal of Economics and Sociology* 72 (5): 1106–30.

———. Forthcoming. "Culture and Economics: How the Poet Ernst Wiechert inspired Kapp's Humanist Economics." *Journal of Economic Issues*.

Berger, Sebastian, and Mathew Forstater. 2007. "Towards a Political Institutionalist Economics: Kapp's Social Costs, Lowe's Instrumental Analysis, and the European Institutionalist Approach to Environmental Policy." *Journal of Economic Issues* 41 (2): 539–46.

Berger, Sebastian, and Rolf Steppacher. 2011. Introduction to *The Foundations of Institutional Economics*, by K. William Kapp, 1–13. Edited by Sebastian Berger and Rolf Steppacher. Abingdon: Routledge.

Buchanan, James M. 1962. "Politics, Policy, and the Pigovian Margins." *Economica* 29 (113): 17–28.

Burczak, Theodor. 2011. "A Socialist Spontaneous Order." In *Hayek, Mill, and the Liberal Tradition*, edited by Andrew Farrant, 130–47. London: Routledge.

Calabresi, Guido. 1961. "Some Thoughts on Risk Distribution and the Law of Torts." *Yale Law Journal* 70 (4): 499–553.

Clark, John M. 1950. "The New Economic Community." *Yale Review* 40 (1): 171–74.

Coase, Ronald. 1960. "The Problem of Social Costs." *Journal of Law and Economics* 3 (October): 1–44.

Cordato, Roy. 2004. "Towards an Austrian Theory of Environmental Economics." *Quarterly Journal of Austrian Economics* 7 (1): 3–16.

Dawson, Graham. 2013. "Austrian Economics and Climate Change." *Review of Austrian Economics* 26 (2): 183–206.

Foster, John Bellamy. 2010. *The Ecological Rift: Capitalism's War on Earth*. New York: Monthly Review Press.

Foucault, Michel. (1979) 2008. *The Birth of Biopolitics*. Basingstoke: Palgrave Macmillan.

Franzini, Maurizio. 2006. "Social Costs, Social Rights, and the Limits of Free Market Capitalism: A Re-reading of Kapp." In *Social Costs and Public Action in Modern Capitalism: Essays Inspired by Karl William Kapp's Theory of Social Costs*, edited by Wolfram Elsner, Pietro Frigato, and Paolo Ramazzotti, 56–71. London: Routledge.

Gaskins, Richard. 2007. "Social Insurance and Unpaid Costs of Personal Injury: A Second Look at K. William Kapp." Paper presented at the 2007 conference of the European Society for Ecological Economics, Leipzig.

———. 2010. "Accounting for Accidents: Social Costs of Personal Injury." *Victoria University of Wellington Law Review* 41:37–50.

Gerber, Julien-François, and Rolf Steppacher, eds. 2012. *Towards an Integrated Paradigm in Heterodox Economics: Alternative Approaches to the Current Eco-Social Crises*. Basingstoke: Palgrave.

Goodwin, Craufurd. 2008. "Ecologist Meets Economist: Aldo Leopold, 1887–1948." *Journal of the History of Economic Thought* 30 (4): 429–52.

Hayek, Friedrich. 1944. *The Road to Serfdom*. Chicago: University of Chicago Press.

———. 1945. "The Use of Knowledge in Society." *American Economic Review* 35 (4): 519–30.

Kapp, K. William. n.d.a. "Interview by The Economist."

———. n.d.b. "Draft Introduction." Unpublished manuscript.

———. n.d.c. "Project Outline." Unpublished manuscript.

———. n.d.d. "The Social Costs of Free Enterprise." Unpublished manuscript.

———. n.d.e. "Environmental Control and the Market Mechanism." Unpublished manuscript.

———. n.d.f. "Social Returns." Unpublished manuscript.

———. 1936. *Planwirtschaft und Aussenhandel*. Geneva: Georg & Cie.

———. 1937. *Memorandum on the Efforts Made by the League of Nations towards a Solution of the Problems of Raw Materials. Submitted to the Tenth Session of the International Studies Conference of the International Institute of Intellectual Cooperation*. Geneva: Geneva Research Center.

————. 1941. *The League of Nations and Raw Materials, 1919–1939.* Geneva Studies vol. 12, no. 3. Geneva: Geneva Research Center.

————. 1950a. "Economic Planning and Freedom." *Weltwirtschaftliches Archiv* 64:29–54.

————. 1950b. *The Social Costs of Private Enterprise.* Cambridge, Mass.: Harvard University Press.

————. 1961. *Toward a Science of Man in Society: A Positive Approach to the Integration of Social Knowledge.* The Hague: Martinus Nijhoff.

————. 1963a. *The Social Costs of Business Enterprise.* London: Asia Publishing House.

————. 1963b. "Social Costs and Social Benefits: A Contribution to Normative Economics." In *Probleme der normativen Ökonomik und der wirtschaftspolitischen Beratung,* edited by E. v. Beckerath and H. Giersch, 183–210. Berlin: Duncker & Humblot.

————. 1963c. *Hindu Culture, Economic Development, and Economic Planning in India.* Bombay: Asia Publishing House.

————. 1971. Introduction to the 1971 edition of *The Social Costs of Private Enterprise.* New York: Schocken Books.

————. 1974. *Environmental Policies and Development Planning in Contemporary China and Other Essays.* Paris: Mouton.

————. (1975) 2011. "Science and Technology in the Light of Institutional Analysis." In Berger and Steppacher 2011, 203–44.

————. 1976. "The Open System Character of the Economy and Its Implications." In *Economics in the Future,* edited by Kurt Dopfer, 90–105. London: Macmillan.

————. 2011. *The Foundations of Institutional Economics.* Edited by Sebastian Berger and Rolf Steppacher. Abingdon: Routledge.

Kimball, Spencer L. 1959. "Traffic Victims: Tort Law and Insurance by Leon Green." *Michigan Law Review* 57 (6): 933–37.

Knight, Frank. 1951. Review of *The Social Costs of Private Enterprise,* by K. William Kapp. *Annals of the American Academy of Political and Social Science* 273:233–34.

Koplin, H. T. 1955. "Conservation and Regulation: The Natural Gas Allocation Policy of the Federal Power Commission." *Yale Law Journal* 64 (6): 840–62.

Lee, Frederic S. 2009. *A History of Heterodox Economics: Challenging the Mainstream in the 20th Century.* London: Routledge.

Lowe, Adolph. 1965. *On Economic Knowledge: Towards a Science of Political Economics.* New York: Harper and Row.

Martinez-Alier, Joan. 2002. *Environmentalism of the Poor: A Study of Ecological Conflicts and Valuation.* Cheltenham: Edward Elgar.

Medema, Steven G. 2011. "A Case of Mistaken Identity: George Stigler, 'The Problem of Social Costs,' and the Coase Theorem." *European Journal of Law and Economics* 31 (1): 11–38.

Menger, Carl. 1923. *Grundsätze der Volkswirtschaftslehre.* 2nd ed. Vienna: Holder-Pichler-Tempsky.

Mirowski, Philip. 2013. *Never Let a Serious Crisis Go to Waste*. London: Verso.

Mirowski, Philip, and Edward Nik-Khah. 2008. "Command Performance: Exploring What STS Thinks It Takes to Build a Market." In *Living in the Material World*, edited by Trevor Pinch and Richard Swedberg, 89–130. Cambridge, Mass.: MIT Press.

Mirowski, Philip, and Dieter Plehwe, eds. 2009. *The Road from Mont Pèlerin: The Making of the Neoliberal Thought Collective*. Cambridge, Mass.: Harvard University Press.

Mirowski, Philip, and Esther-Mirjam Sent, eds. 2002. *Science Bought and Sold: Essays in the Economics of Science*. Chicago: University of Chicago Press.

Mises, Ludwig von. 1920. "Die Wirtschaftsrechnung im Sozialistischen Gemeinwesen." *Archiv für Sozialwissenschaften* 47 (1): 86–121.

———. 1944. *Bureaucracy*. New Haven, Conn.: Yale University Press.

Pearce, D. W., and S. G. Sturmey. 1966. "Private and Social Costs and Benefits: A Note on Terminology." *Economic Journal* 76 (301): 152–58.

Pigou, Arthur Cecil. 1929. *The Economics of Welfare*. 3rd ed. London: Macmillan.

Polanyi, Karl. 1957. *Trade and Markets in the Early Empires*. Glencoe, Ill.: Free Press.

Polanyi, Michael. 1958. *Personal Knowledge: Towards a Post-critical Philosophy*. Chicago: University of Chicago Press.

Prasch, Robert. 2005. "The Social Costs of Labor." *Journal of Economic Issues* 39 (2): 439–45.

Ramazzotti, Paolo, Pietro Frigato, Wolfram Elsner, eds. 2012. *Social Costs Today: Institutional Analyses of the Present Crisis*. London: Routledge.

Ropke, Inge. 2004. "The Early History of Modern Ecological Economics." *Journal of Ecological Economics* 50 (3): 293–314.

Rutherford, Malcolm. 2011. *The Institutionalist Movement in American Economics, 1918–1947*. Cambridge: Cambridge University Press.

Schäffle, Albert. 1881. *Bau und Leben des Sozialen Körpers*. Vol. 3. Tübingen.

Spash, Clive. 2011. "Social Ecological Economics: Understanding the Past to See the Future." *American Journal of Economics and Sociology* 70 (2): 340–75.

———. 2012. "Towards the Integration of Social, Economic, and Ecological Knowledge." In *Towards an Integrated Paradigm in Heterodox Economics: Alternative Approaches to the Current Eco-Social Crises*, edited by Julie-Francois Gerber and Rolf Steppacher, 26–46. Basingstoke: Palgrave Macmillan.

Swaney, James A. 2006. "Policy for Social Costs: Kapp vs. Neo-classical Economics." In *Social Costs and Public Action in Modern Capitalism: Essays Inspired by Karl William Kapp's Theory of Social Costs*, edited by Wolfram Elsner, Pietro Frigato, and Paolo Ramazzotti, 106–25. London: Routledge.

Tool, Marc. 1978. Review of *Economics in Institutional Perspective: Memorial Essays in Honor of K. William Kapp*. *Journal of Economic Issues* 12 (4): 891–901.

Wieser, Friedrich. 1924. "Theorie der Gesellschaftlichen Wirtschaft." In vol. 1, pt. 2, of *Grundriss der Sozialökonomik*. Tübingen.

Framing the Economic Policy Debate

David Colander

Economists' current policy frame, which is organized around the concept of market failure, provides a powerful lens through which to view the world and organize one's thoughts about policy. It is not the only, or most natural, frame through which to view policy. It is a product of history, and it coevolved with the analytic technology of the time. That analytic technology is changing, and as it changes, other policy frames become slightly more likely to be adopted. This article discusses that historical evolution and how changing analytic technology is opening up the possibility for movement away from the market failure policy frame.[1]

Let me be clear from the beginning: my argument is about policy frames, not about current economic theory or mainstream understanding. I am not making an argument that the current theory is wrong or that most economists do not understand or are unfamiliar with the limitations of the current market failure policy frame. One can find many insightful discussions throughout the literature exploring the nuances, caveats, and limitations of the current model. But the discussions seldom make it down to the layperson summaries of economic policy. So the issue is not knowledge or insight of the economics profession. The issue is what might be called the

Correspondence may be addressed to David Colander, 215 Munroe, Interdepartmental Studies, Middlebury College, Middlebury, VT 05753; e-mail: colander@middlebury.edu.

1. This article summarizes and further develops arguments made in Colander and Kupers 2014.

History of Political Economy 47 (annual suppl.) DOI 10.1215/00182702-3130535

simplification process—what gets chosen as a standard textbook policy model, which structures laypeople's thinking about what economics has to say about economic and social policy.

Why can we arrive at a policy frame that is limiting even though the underlying economic understanding is not limiting? Because policy frames are not chosen through explicit choice. In current academic institutional structures there is little incentive for economists to reflect on policy frames.[2] Thus the policy frame tends to be selected by historical, institutional, and marketing factors that reflect the needs of economic researchers, teachers, and publishers, not top economists' judgments as to what would be an ideal policy frame from a social perspective. For example, the chosen frame reflects what authors believe the textbook market wants, not their consideration of what they believe students need to learn or of how best to convey deep economic understanding to laypeople.[3]

The article is organized as follows. First, I summarize the current "market failure" policy frame as it is generally presented to policymakers and students. Second, I discuss how that policy frame evolved from a much looser and more inclusive classical policy frame. I conclude with a brief discussion of how recent advancements in analytic and computational technology are increasing the chances for the policy frame to change.

2. I do not discuss the evolution of policy frames here; I have discussed it elsewhere, and my argument is that institutional incentives lead economists to convey a policy frame to laypeople that is nonoptimal. One could argue that a frame is just a frame, and that with appropriate nuances and caveats that one can find in the existing literature, the existing frame, or any well-specified policy frame, can be consistent with the same policies I am advocating be explored. So frames are not necessarily limiting. People familiar with the technical literature surrounding any policy frame should be able to go beyond any specific policy frame and recognize its assumptions and limitations. Thus policy frames are generally considered a pedagogical issue, not a limiting issue for policy. I disagree with that way of seeing policy frames. I see frames as highly limiting. Most laypeople, and many economists, do not have the time and have not explored the technical literature, noting nuances and assumptions of the frame they are using. For that reason, the nuances and caveats necessary to move from the existing policy frame to the one I am advocating, while they were part of the development of ideas, tend to be lost and have not become part of most laypeople's and policymakers' policy frames.

3. An example of this process can be seen in the reviewer pool for economic principles books. This pool is drawn from potential adopters who generally are not cutting-edge economists, deep theorists, or specialists in the area being taught. This group of economists seldom teaches principles and thus, unless one of them decides to write a book, has little to do with the principles course. Those who do write a text quickly learn that the focus groups guiding the edition are not specialists in areas but nonspecialist teachers who are more interested in pedagogy than in nuanced content. They want a better, more teachable, presentation of the existing frame rather than a consideration of broader issues that are not part of the existing frame.

Economists' Current "Market Failure" Policy Frames

The current economic policy frame has two variations—one an activist policy frame, the other a "free market" policy frame. The variant presented in most textbooks is the activist "market failure" policy frame. In this frame, an individual's tastes are given, and the invisible hand of the market is assumed to guide the economy to desirable results. But that guidance is not perfect; for example, externalities and other market failures may exist that the market does not account for. Government policy is needed to correct for these market failures in which private costs do not equate to social costs.[4] The goal of government policy in this policy frame is to make private costs equal to social costs in individual decisions.

The groundwork for the "market failure" frame occurred in the 1930s when multivariate calculus was introduced into economic theory. Multivariate calculus allowed economists to study the theory of optimal allocation in a much more precise manner than they could heuristically or with geometric tools. Although multivariate calculus had been around for a long time, before the 1930s and 1940s mathematical economics was seen simply as a small branch of economics, not as the core. That changed in the 1940s as economics shifted from a Marshallian partial equilibrium "one-thing at a time" approach, in which intuition and judgment guided policy discussion, to a Walrasian general equilibrium approach in which policy discussion was closely connected to theory. Structuring the economic problem within a mathematical control theory framework allowed a much clearer understanding of pure allocative rationing processes and how those processes related to markets. John Hicks's *Value and Capital* (1939) and Paul Samuelson's *Foundations* (1947) changed the way that economic theory was thought about, and laid the groundwork for the market failure policy frame.

The pedagogically focused market failure framework was introduced into economics in Abba Lerner's *Economics of Control* (1944).[5] Paul Samuelson (1948) then took that "economics of control" framework and

---

4. This sense of it as an activist frame can be seen in its introduction into economics. It was introduced by economists such as Abba Lerner and Paul Samuelson who favored an active role for government and was opposed by many of the more laissez-faire economists such as Lionel Robbins, Friedrich Hayek, and Frank Knight. For a discussion of how this came about, see Colander and Freedman 2011.

5. I discuss this history in more detail in Colander 2005 and 2011 and Colander and Kupers 2014.

put it at the core of his textbook presentation of microeconomic policy. Other texts followed, and, over the years, the market failure policy framework has become so built into the economist's mind-set that few, other than historians of economic thought and heterodox economists, know that other frameworks exist.[6]

This market failure policy frame is built on a theory of costless market success that can be mathematically specified as a multiperson constrained optimization problem with government as an outside controller. It structures the economic policy problem as a LaGrangian constrained optimization problem and in doing so provides important insights into the problem of allocating scarce resources among alternative ends. This framework assumes an institutional structure within which individuals know what they want and have exogenous tastes. They can trade costlessly at equilibrium prices that are somehow determined by the market. Given these assumptions market success can be costlessly achieved through market transactions by individuals voluntarily trading. There are no transactions costs or problems of strategic interaction. Economists' theoretical general equilibrium model demonstrates that the equilibrium achieved after these trades has certain desirable characteristics. The intuitive essence of the policy model is that if people make a voluntary trade, they do so because the trades make them better off. As individuals become better off, society tends to be better off.

While a costless market success model underlies this policy frame, the policy focus of the frame is on market failures. It directs attention to situations in which voluntary trades will not make society better off even though the trades are costless. Much of the policy discussion centers on the possible existence of externalities that occur when there are third parties not explicitly part of the trade who are positively or negatively affected by the trade. When externalities exist, there is a market failure associated with voluntary trade, since all the costs of the trade are not being taken into account by the voluntary traders. In such cases, assumed costless government intervention can bring private costs and social costs into equilibrium, increasing social welfare.

Government's role in this policy frame is not only to internalize externalities. It is also to adjust the income distribution to maximize social welfare. The reason is that private optimization does not necessarily achieve a social optimum; it simply allows improvements from an initial

6. Malcolm Rutherford (this volume) nicely discusses the institutionalist alternative.

position. Whether a social optimum is achieved depends on the distribution at the initial starting point. The market failure policy frame integrates distributional issues into the analysis through the use of a social welfare function that embodies outside-specified normative judgments into the analysis.[7] The government is assumed to know this social welfare function and to have the desire and ability to undertake the appropriate redistributional policies to achieve the optimal social welfare.[8]

Recognition of Limits of the Standard Policy Frame

As I emphasized at the beginning of the article, my focus is on policy frames, not economists' understanding of the issues. The limitations and problems of the market failure policy frame are well known to economists and specialists in public policy. The literature has an extensive discussion of just about any aspect of the policy frame's limitations, and did from early on. As an example of early developers of the frame recognizing its limitations, in this section I briefly consider some of the qualifications included in early seminal work by Abram Bergson (1938) on social welfare functions and Francis Bator (1958) in developing the market failure policy frame. Let me start with Bergson.

In his seminal 1938 article, Bergson carefully distinguished between a social welfare function, W, and an economic welfare function, E. The difference between the two was a set of variables, $r, s, t \ldots$, which were catch-all variables that included all the other elements that affected social welfare. These were allowed to vary in the social welfare function, but were taken as given in the economic welfare function. By distinguishing a *social* welfare function from an *economic* welfare function, he was making the point that any consideration of economic policy needed to be seen as an input into a broader social consideration of policy before it is applied. It could not be applied directly.

By including $r, s, t \ldots$'s in the analysis, market failure is no longer the only way in which the market can fail. There can also be failures of

---

7. Usually the social welfare function that the government is assumed to use is an equality-preferring social welfare function that weights low-income people's utility higher than high-income people's utility. If costless redistribution is assumed, as it generally is, then by redistributing income appropriately, the government can achieve a social optimum.

8. How government accomplishes its task is unspecified. Government is assumed to be an outside controller, which allows the model underlying the framework to be specified as an optimal control theory model.

market outcomes (Colander 2003). Failures of market outcomes occur when the market is doing everything it is supposed to in terms of the economic welfare function, but the indirect effects of economic actors on social welfare through the $r, s, t \ldots$'s are overwhelming the direct effects. In Bergson's approach, any application of the social welfare version of the market failure policy frame to real-world problems would have to explicitly explore whether these additional elements were important. He writes:

> The symbols r, s, t . . . , denote elements other than the amounts of commodities, the amounts of work of each type, and the amounts of the non-labor factors in each of the production units, affecting the welfare of the community.
>
> Some of the elements r, s, t . . . , may affect welfare, not only directly, but indirectly through their effect on (say) the amounts of X and Y produced with any given amount of resources, e.g., the effects of a change in the weather. On the other hand, it is conceivable that variations in the amounts of commodities, the amounts of work of each type, and the amounts of non-labor factors in each of the production units also will have a direct and indirect effect on welfare; e.g., a sufficient diminution of x_i and y_i may be accompanied by an overturn of the government. But for relatively small changes in these variables, other elements in welfare, I believe, will not be affected. To the degree that this is so a partial analysis is feasible.

The market failure policy frame that economists use today does not distinguish between a social welfare function and an economic welfare function. Hence, it does not direct students and policymakers to think of the limitations of focusing their analysis of welfare on material goods rather than on broader social welfare, as it would have had the distinction between social and economic welfare been emphasized.[9]

A second example of the early work recognizing the limitations in the market failure policy frame can be found in Francis Bator's seminal "Anatomy of Market Failure." Bator (1958, 378–79) writes:

> More important, at this level of discourse—though perhaps it hardly need be said—is that statical market efficiency is neither sufficient nor necessary for market institutions to be the "preferred" mode of social

9. The distinction between social and economic welfare was lost rather quickly, as Samuelson (1947) did not distinguish Bergson's economic welfare function from a social welfare function.

organization. Quite apart from institutional considerations, Pareto efficiency as such may not be necessary for bliss. If, e.g., people are sensitive not only to their own jobs but to other people's as well, or more
generally, if such things as relative status, power, and the like, matter,
the injunction to maximize output, to hug the production-possibility
frontier, can hardly be assumed "neutral," and points on the utility frontier may associate with points inside the production frontier. Furthermore, there is nothing preordained about welfare functions which are
sensitive only to individual consumer's preferences. As a matter of fact,
few people would take such preferences seriously enough to argue
against any and all protection of individuals against their own mistakes
(though no external effects be involved).

All this is true even when maximization is subject only to technological and resource limitations. Once we admit other side relations, which
link input-output variables with "noneconomic" political and organizational values, matters become much more complicated. If markets be
ends as well as means, their nonefficiency is hardly sufficient ground for
rejection. On the other hand, efficient markets may not do, even though
Pareto-efficiency is necessary for bliss. Even with utopian lump-sum
redistribution, efficiency of the "invisible hand" does not preclude preference for other efficient modes of organization, if there be any.

In a footnote he adds:

This is too crude a formulation. It is not necessary that markets as such
be an "ultimate" value. Political and social (non-output) values relating
to the configuration of power, initiative, opportunity, etc., may be so
much better served by some form of nonefficient market institutions
than by possible alternative modes of more efficient organization as to
warrant choice of the former. The analytical point, in all this, is that the
outcome of a maximization process and the significance of "efficiency"
are as sensitive to the choice of side-conditions as to the welfare-func-
tion and that these need be "given" to the economist in the same sense
that a welfare function has to be given. (378n4)

Throughout his article, one can find such nuanced discussion of the
strengths and weaknesses of the market failure policy frame he is developing. Few texts, including graduate texts such as Mas-Colell, Whinston,
and Green 1995, today include such nuanced discussions so that that
nuance found in the early specification of the market failure policy frame
has not become associated with laypeople's, politicians', and students'

conceptions of what economics has to say about policy. Given the lack of discussion of nuance, laypeople are led to see the economic policy frame as *the* policy frame to use when thinking about economic policy, not as a useful, but as a limited, policy frame, which needs to be applied carefully with many addenda, as Bator presented it.

The Stigler-Coase Promarket Policy Frame Variant: The Market Success Policy Frame

While the above market failure policy frame was being explored and built into the textbooks, there was a general concern about its use by many economists who had a promarket orientation. Their concern was that the market failure policy frame seemed to justify government intervention because it downplayed many of the reasons that they opposed government interventions. For example, some opposed government intervention because of ethical considerations; laissez-faire advocates argued that freedom of choice found in markets was desirable in its own right independent of whether it maximized economic welfare or not.

Others such as James Buchanan and Gordon Tullock (1962) argued that the standard market failure policy frame obscured the public choice problems with government intervention. They argued that politics, not altruism, guided government, and so there should be no presumption that the government would maximize social welfare even if it could specify it. Their work led to the development of a concept of government failure that paralleled the concept of market failure. Government failure occurs when government does not act in the way assumed by the model. This idea of government failure has become part of the standard textbook market failure policy frame, and policy is now often presented in a more ideologically neutral setting than previously. It now involves determining the least-worst option: market failure or government failure.

These, and other concerns, were all important, but they are adjustments, not alternative frames. The theoretical promarket alternative frame to the market failure policy frame is not those, but rather what might be called the Stigler-Coase "market success" policy frame. The difference between the standard market failure policy frame and the Stigler-Coase market success policy frame is that the standard "market failure" policy frame assumes externalities are pervasive in the economy; thus it focuses on the need for government policy to deal with them. The Stigler-Coase alternative sees externalities as almost nonexistent because of the private market's ability to internalize externalities on its own.

The reason externalities are nonexistent is to be found in the assumption of the standard model. If there are no transactions and negotiations costs, as there are not in the formal specification of the market failure model, then why should any externalities exist? Individuals affected by any trade can enter into negotiations with anyone affected to see that their interests are protected. Since trades are assumed to take place only after all negotiations are complete, and there are no negotiations costs, the end result of voluntary activity is that all beneficial voluntary trades are undertaken.[10] Any externalities are internalized by private traders. There is no need for government; given the assumptions of costless negotiations and zero transactions costs, the private market comes to the ideal solution.[11]

From a Classical Policy Frame to the Current Policy Frame

As I have discussed in other papers and books (Colander 2005, 2011; Colander and Friedman 2011; Colander and Kupers 2014), the movement to the current market failure policy frames occurred from the 1930s through the 1960s as economics was moving away from a classical economics methodology, which strictly separated economic theory from economic policy, to a Walrasian neoclassical methodology, which did not. Instead, the Walrasian neoclassical methodology, which underlies the market failure policy frame, blended theory and policy in a formal mathematical model, directly drawing policy results from theoretical models.

I specifically do not call the current policy frames "neoclassical," because doing so makes it seem as if all neoclassical economists would accept them. This is definitely not the case. Many early neoclassical economists, such as Alfred Marshall, Lionel Robbins, and J. M. Keynes, did not use a Walrasian methodology or a mathematical model. Instead, they continued to use a classical methodology that blended the market failure frame into the classical policy frame, making it much more ambiguous as to the policy implications of economic theory. In the classical policy frame, in order to decide policy implications, one had to explore the nuances as well as

10. The social welfare addition is much more difficult to add to this model, but advocates of this market success frame usually take the position that government should have no role in redistribution or any other aspect of social welfare that the economic welfare function does not include.

11. An excellent discussion of how this development occurred can be found in Medema 2011. In Colander and Freedman 2011, we explore the development of these ideas and how they related to policy.

the formal theory. Thus Marshall saw economic theory as an engine of analysis; it was only one of the tools to be used by economists in developing policy. Theory had to be combined with judgment and other insights. Those following a Walrasian neoclassical methodology saw economic theory differently; they saw it as providing direct guidance for policy.

This Walrasian market failure frame of government policy is quite different from the "sophisticated Classical policy frame" found in John Stuart Mill (1848) and some early neoclassical non-Walrasians such as Marshall, Robbins, or even A. C. Pigou. While these non-Walrasians might discuss market failure, that discussion was closely tied to the limitations and nuances of the analysis. The sophisticated classical policy frame presents policy as much more complicated than anything that could be presented in a formal model; it involved numerous noneconomic, philosophical, and normative issues, all of which had to be integrated into the analysis before one could move from theoretical conclusions of models to policy conclusions. Classical economists saw this policy integration as belonging in a different branch of economics than pure theoretical scientific economics.[12] Within this classical policy frame, policy was built on the insights of economic science, but was not based directly on economic science.

The classical justification for laissez-faire was not a theoretical justification that the market was efficient. Laissez-faire was supported by classical economists as a precept, not a theorem. A "precept" is a reasoned judgment based on a consideration of all real-world issues—not just problems highlighted by economic theory. Classical economists' support for laissez-faire was not a theoretical support for an abstract market; it was a practical support for dealing with the problems outside the state because, in their judgment, the state generally could not be relied on to arrive at better solutions. In making that judgment, they incorporated problems of government failure and ethical judgments with economic theory.

Laissez-faire was justified not by science or theory but by appeal to Adam Smith's impartial spectator's judgment. It is a policy position that they felt an educated economist whose ethical judgments reflected the general ethical and moral views of existing society would hold.[13] Laissez-faire held that, while highly imperfect, real-world free markets were the

---

12. J. N. Keynes (1890) called the policy branch of economics "the art of economics." Lionel Robbins (1981) called it "political economy."

13. Classical economists' support for laissez-faire had important ethical elements—classical economists favored individuals having as much freedom as possible. Thus freedom was seen as an end in itself. It was also a means to an end. Freedom allowed individuals to try out new ways of doing things, and generated economic growth.

least-worst option in many cases. But not in all cases. The policy frame came to no noncontextual conclusions; and judgments would have to be continually made—there was no blanket proposition that the market was the best option or that government should or should not intervene in the market.

Why the Classical Policy Frame Was Replaced

The explanation for why the profession moved from the classical policy frame to the market failure policy frame is complicated and deeply integrated with the institutional structure of the profession. My short story goes as follows.[14] In the 1930s economists were discovering how useful multivariate calculus was for thinking about multiple market resource allocation problems. As they did, cutting-edge theorists began moving away from the Marshallian generalized partial equilibrium analysis in which the model's limitations were emphasized, replacing it with a Walrasian general equilibrium approach in which the limitations received less emphasis. Because they were trained in a classical methodological tradition, most initial developers such as Hicks, Samuelson, and Bergson used the market failure policy frame in a nuanced manner. But as their students, and their students' students, moved away from that literary tradition, and as economics became more of a mathematical science, the nuance faded. As a shorthand, economists starting thinking about economic policy as closely connected to the Walrasian model and the market failure policy frame. As that happened, the nuanced classical policy frame gave way to the less-nuanced market failure policy frame.

The classical policy frame was replaced not because economists felt that the classical approach to policy was wrong or because they believed that the market failure frame was a better frame. Instead it was replaced because the market failure policy frame fit better with the mathematical specification of theory that they were developing. Given the analytic technology, it was more teachable; it better fit the evolving pedagogical needs of the economics profession at the time. Specifically, the market failure policy frame nicely fit the technological and analytic developments of the time that were focused on analyzing efficient allocation problems rather than other aspects of economic policy. The policy frame provided elegant simple mathematical models through which these ideas about allocative efficiency could be taught.

14. I develop this explanation more in Colander and Rothschild 2010 and Colander 2011.

Changing Analytic Technology and the Future
of the Market Failure Policy Frame

As I have emphasized above, the "market failure" policy frame is closely tied to the Walrasian general equilibrium model. An implication of that close tie-in is that as analytic technology diverges from the analytics association with Walrasian general equilibrium, the market failure policy frame will come more and more into question. There are some indications that that is happening. Specifically, new work in behavioral economics, encouraged by a blossoming empirical experimentation technology, is allowing economics to explore models in which individuals do not exhibit the strong rationality needed for the Walrasian model. As that happens, new policy proposals such as nudges (Thaler and Sunstein 2008) are developing that do not fit the market failure policy frame. With nudges, economists are suggesting policies to guide individuals in a certain way; policies are not designed to internalize an externality.

Similarly, new analytic technologies are allowing economists to explore multiple equilibria models, in which the policy issues involve a consideration of which basin of attraction the economy will gravitate to and how government policy might influence that gravitation. Such equilibrium selection mechanism problems involve a quite separate set of issues and models that go far beyond single equilibrium Walrasian models. An analysis of tipping points becomes the policy focus, not an analysis of externalities or market failures.

Similarly, new computational technology is allowing economists to explore pattern-matching data models, agent-based models, network models, and epistemic game-theoretical models in which multiple social dimensions can be analyzed simultaneously. Culture and norms no longer need to be taken as given; they can become endogenized and part of the policy discussion.[15] As this new work develops, the evolutionary

15. As an example of how the types of issues considered in pure theory go far beyond the Walrasian framework, consider the following abstract of a recent paper (Hedges et al. 2014): "We introduce a new unified framework for modelling both decision problems and finite games based on quantifiers and selection functions. We show that the canonical utility maximisation is one special case of a quantifier and that our more abstract framework provides several additional degrees of freedom in modelling. In particular, incomplete preferences, non-maximising heuristics, and context-dependent motives can be taken into account when describing an agent's goal. We introduce a suitable generalisation of Nash equilibrium for games in terms of quantifiers and selection functions. Moreover, we introduce a refinement of Nash that captures context-dependency of goals. Modelling in our framework is compositional as the parts of the game are modular and can be easily exchanged. We provide an extended example where we illustrate concepts and highlight the benefits of our alternative modelling approach."

story used to support markets becomes a broader evolutionary story in which, in a single equilibrium model, all we can say about efficiency is that "that which is, is efficient." Government and the market coevolve, undermining any "I Pencil" evolutionary justifications of the market (Read 1958).

None of these analytic and computational approaches fit nicely with the "market failure" policy frame; they go beyond it and raise questions that cannot be easily addressed as market failures. Thus, just as changes in analytic and computational technology encouraged the movement from the classical policy frame to the market failure policy frame, today changes in analytic and computational technology are creating pressures for a change in the existing market failure policy frame to a policy frame broad enough to incorporate these new models and insights. That, at least, is my hypothesis.

References

Bator, Francis. 1958. "The Anatomy of Market Failure." *Quarterly Journal of Economics* 72 (3): 351–79.

Bergson, Abram. 1938. "A Reformulation of Certain Aspects of Welfare Economics." *Quarterly Journal of Economics* 52 (2): 310–34.

Buchanan, James, and Gordon Tullock. 1962. *Calculus of Consent: Logical Foundations of Constitutional Democracy.* Ann Arbor: University of Michigan Press.

Colander, David. 2003. "Integrating Sex and Drugs into the Principles Course." *Journal of Economic Education* 34 (1): 82–91.

———. 2005. "From Muddling through to the Economics of Control: Views of Applied Policy from J. N. Keynes to Abba Lerner." In *The Role of Government in the History of Economic Thought*, edited by Steven G. Medema and Peter Boettke. *History of Political Economy* 37 (supplement): 277–91.

———. 2011. "Applied Policy, Welfare Economics, and Mill's Half-Truths." In *The Elgar Companion to Recent Economic Methodology*, edited by John Davis and Wade Hands, 173–86. Cheltenham: Edward Elgar.

Colander, David, and Craig Freedman. 2011. "The Chicago Counter-revolution and the Loss of the Classical Liberal Tradition." Working paper, Middlebury College.

Colander, David, and Roland Kupers. 2014. *Complexity and the Art of Public Policy: Solving Society's Problems from the Bottom Up.* Princeton, N.J.: Princeton University Press.

Colander, David, and Casey Rothschild. 2010. "The Sins of the Sons of Samuelson: Vision, Pedagogy, and the Zig Zag Windings of Complex Dynamics." *Journal of Economic Behavior and Organization* 74 (3): 277–90.

Hedges, Jules, Paulo Oliva, Evguenia Winschel, Viktor Winschel, and Philipp Zahn. 2014. "A Higher-Order Framework for Decision Problems and Games." arxiv.org /abs/1409.7411.

Hicks, John. 1939. *Value and Capital: An Inquiry into Some Fundamental Principles of Economic Theory.* Oxford: Clarendon Press.

Keynes, J. N. 1890. *The Scope and Method of Political Economy.* London: Macmillan.

Lerner, Abba. 1944. *The Economics of Control: Principles of Welfare Economics.* New York: Macmillan.

Mas-Colell, Andreu, Michael Whinston, and Jerry Green. 1995. *Microeconomic Theory.* New York: Oxford University Press.

Medema, Steven. 2011. *The Hesitant Hand: Taming the Self-Interest in the History of Ideas.* Princeton, N.J.: Princeton University Press.

Mill, John Stuart. 1848. *Principles of Political Economy.* London: Longmans, Green.

Read, Leonard. 1958. "I Pencil: My Family Tree as Told to Leonard E. Read." www.econlib.org/library/Essays/rdPncl1.html.

Robbins, Lionel. 1981. "Economics and Political Economy." *American Economic Review* 71 (May): 1–10.

Samuelson, Paul. 1947. *Foundations of Economic Analysis.* Cambridge, Mass.: Harvard University Press.

———. 1948. *Economics.* New York: McGraw-Hill.

Thaler, Richard, and Cass Sunstein. 2008. *Nudge.* New Haven, Conn.: Yale University Press.

Contributors

Nahid Aslanbeigui is professor of economics at Leon Hess Business School, Monmouth University. Her books include *Rethinking Economic Principles: Critical Essays on Introductory Textbooks* (1996, with Michele I. Naples) and *Arthur Cecil Pigou* (forthcoming, with Guy Oakes).

Roger E. Backhouse is professor of the history and philosophy of science at the University of Birmingham. Supported by the Leverhulme Trust, he has been working on an intellectual biography of Paul Samuelson. Recent books include *Transforming Modern Macroeconomics: Exploring Disequilibrium Macroeconomics, 1956–2003* (2013, with Mauro Boianovsky), *The Puzzle of Modern Economics: Science or Ideology?* (2010), and *The Ordinary Business of Life: A History of Economics from the Ancient World to the Twenty-First Century* (2002).

Bradley W. Bateman is the author of *Keynes's Uncertain Revolution* (1996) and coauthor (with Roger E. Backhouse) of *Capitalist Revolutionary: John Maynard Keynes* (2011). He is also coeditor (with Roger E. Backhouse) of the *Cambridge Companion to Keynes* (2006). His work on the religious influences on American economics has appeared in many journals, including the *Journal of Economic Perspectives*, *History of Political Economy*, and the *Journal of the History of Economic Thought*. He is coeditor (with H. Spencer Banzhaf) of *Keeping Faith, Losing Faith: Religious Belief and Political Economy* (2008). Bateman is a professor of economics and president of Randolph College in Lynchburg, Virginia.

Sebastian Berger is senior lecturer of economics at the University of the West of England. His research has focused on the discourse of social costs, the reconstruction

History of Political Economy 47 (annual suppl.) DOI 10.1215/00182702-3130547

of K. William Kapp's economics, and the economics of scientific knowledge. He has worked as a visiting assistant professor of economics at the University of Missouri–Kansas City, has completed a postdoc at the Department of Economics at Harvard University, and serves as a trustee of the Kapp Foundation for the Humanization and Integration of the Social Sciences. His current research interests are the philosophy of economics, in particular, the open-systems-approach to economics.

David Colander is Distinguished College Professor at Middlebury College, Middlebury, Vermont. He has authored, coauthored, or edited over forty books (including a principles and intermediate macro text) and two hundred articles on a wide range of topics. He received his PhD from Columbia University and has taught at Columbia University, Vassar College, the University of Miami, and Princeton University, where he was the Kelly Professor of Distinguished Teaching. In 2010 he was awarded the Henry H. Villard Research Award by the National Association of Economic Educators. He is a former president of both the Eastern Economic Association and the History of Economic Thought Society. His latest book, *Complexity and the Art of Public Policy: Solving Society's Problems from the Bottom Up* (2014, with Roland Kupers), published by Princeton University Press, explores the implications of new developments in complexity theory for policy.

J. Daniel Hammond is Hultquist Family Professor and Chair of the Department of Economics, Wake Forest University. His research is mostly on the history of American economics in the twentieth century. He is a member of the European Society for the History of Economic Thought and the History of Economics Society (HES) and served as president of the HES in 2001–2. Hammond's publications include *Theory and Measurement: Causality Issues in Milton Friedman's Monetary Economics* (1996), "More Fiber Than Thread? Evidence on the Mirowski-Hands Yarn" (2006), and *Chicago Price Theory* (2013, with S. G. Medema and J. D. Singleton).

Marianne Johnson is professor of economics at the University of Wisconsin–Oshkosh. Her research focuses on the use and evolution of theories of public finance as well as the connection between theory and tax policy. Her work has been published in *History of Political Economy, Journal for the History of Economic Thought, Journal of Economic Issues*, and the *History of Economic Ideas*.

Thomas C. Leonard is research scholar in the Council of the Humanities at Princeton University, where he is also affiliated faculty in the Department of Economics. He is a two-time winner of the Richard D. Quandt Prize for outstanding teaching in the Department of Economics. His recent research has focused on American economics and American economic reform in the Gilded Age and the Progressive Era. His book, *Illiberal Reformers: Race, Eugenics, and American Economics in the Progressive Era*, is forthcoming from Princeton University Press.

Alain Marciano is associate professor at the University of Montpellier. His research focuses on the history and methodology of post–World War II economics and, more specifically, on the history of law and economics and public choice. He has published articles in *History of Political Economy*, the *Journal of the History of Economic Thought*, the *European Journal of History of Economic Thought*, the *Journal of Economic Methodology*, the *International Review of Law and Economics*, *Public Choice*, *Constitutional Political Economy*, the *Journal of Economic Behavior and Organization, Law and Contemporary Problems,* and the *Journal of Institutional Economics*. He is a member of the editorial board of many journals, including journals in history of economic thought.

Steven G. Medema is University Distinguished Professor of Economics at the University of Colorado Denver. His research focuses on the history of twentieth-century economics and on theoretical controversies over the economic role of government throughout the history of economic thinking. He is the author of numerous books and articles, including *The Hesitant Hand: Taming Self-Interest in the History of Economic Ideas* (2009), which was awarded the 2010 ESHET (European Society for the History of Economic Thought) Book Prize. He served as president of the History of Economics Society in 2009–10.

Guy Oakes is Jack T. Kvernland Professor of Philosophy and Corporate Social Policy at Monmouth University (USA). His books include *Weber and Rickert: Concept Formation in the Cultural Sciences* (1988) and *Joan Robinson: The Making of a Cambridge Economist* (2009, with Nahid Aslanbeigui).

Malcolm Rutherford is professor of economics at the University of Victoria in British Columbia. He has published widely on the topic of institutional economics in *History of Political Economy*, the *Journal of the History of Economic Thought*, the *European Journal of the History of Economic Thought*, the *Journal of Economic Issues, Labor History*, and the *Journal of Economic Perspectives*. He is the author of *Institutions in Economics: The Old and the New Institutionalism* (1994) and *The Institutionalist Movement in American Economics, 1918–1947: Science and Social Control* (2011). The latter book won the best book award from the European Society for the History of Economics in 2013. In the same year he was given the Veblen-Commons Award by the Association for Evolutionary Economics.

John D. Singleton studies the economics of education, public economics, industrial organization, and the history of economics for his doctoral work in economics at Duke University. His research has been published in *History of Political Economy* and presented at the Center for the History of Political Economy's annual conference and the History of Economics Society's meetings. He is coeditor of *Chicago Price Theory* (2013, with J. Daniel Hammond and Steven G. Medema) and received his prior education at Calvin College and the University of Colorado Denver.

Index

AALL. *See* American Association for Labor Legislation

Ability-to-pay taxation, 175–76, 185

Absolutism, 191

ACC (Accident Compensation Corporation), 248

Accidents, industrial, 175–76, 185

Adams, H. C., 77, 87

Addams, Jane, 57

Administered prices, 112–13, 116

Advertising, 81–82, 230

AEA (American Economic Association), 51, 54, 71, 106–7, 169

Agriculture, 32–33, 37–38, 129, 130n6

Akerlof, George, 15

Alchian, Armen, 212

Allen, William, 212

Allocations, 4–5, 11

Altman, Oscar, 116–17, 119, 121, 122

Altruism, 155

American Association for Labor Legislation (AALL), 54, 59, 67, 71

American Economic Association (AEA), 51, 54, 71, 106–7, 169

American Economic Association and the Econometric Society, 206

American institutionalist movement, 237–38

American Keynesianism, 101, 120–21

American Tobacco, 60–61

America's Capacity to Produce (Nourse et al.), 108–9

Amery, Leo, writing as "Tariff Reformer," 34

"Anatomy of Market Failure" (Bator), 3–4, 258–60

Ann Arbor, Michigan, Tiebout and, 205–7

Antimonopolism, 60

Antitrust regulations, 60–61, 107, 112

History of Political Economy 47 (annual suppl.) DOI 10.1215/00182702-3138771
Copyright 2015 by Duke University Press